NAKED INSTINCT

NAKED INSTINCT

The Unauthorized
Biography of
Sharon Stone

FRANK SANELLO

A BIRCH LANE PRESS BOOK
Published by Carol Publishing Group

A Birch Lane Press Book
Published by Carol Publishing Group
Birch Lane Press is a registered trademark of Carol Communications, Inc.

Editorial, sales and distribution, rights and permissions inquiries should be
addressed to Carol Publishing Group, 120 Enterprise Avenue, Secaucus, N.J.
07094

In Canada: Canadian Manda Group, One Atlantic Avenue, Suite 105, Toronto,
Ontario, M6K 3E7

Carol Publishing Group books may be purchased in bulk at special discounts
for sales promotion, fund-raising, or educational purposes. Special editions
can be created to specifications. For details, contact Special Sales Department,
Carol Publishing Group, 120 Enterprise Avenue, Secaucus, N.J. 07094.

Manufactured in the United States of America

10 9 8 7 6 5 4 3 2 1

Library of Congress Cataloging-in-Publication Data
Sanello, Frank.
    Naked instinct : the unauthorized biography of Sharon Stone /
Frank Sanello.
        p. cm.
    "A Birch Lane Press book."
    ISBN 1–55972–402–1
    1. Stone, Sharon.   2. Motion picture actors and actresses—United
States—Biography.   I. Title.
PN2287.S755S26   1997
791.43'028'092—dc21
    [B]   97–1013
                                                           CIP

For my terrific circle of friends,
who deserve a booth at the Algonquin

The moral flabbiness born of the exclusive worship of the *bitch-goddess* success...is our national disease.

—WILLIAM JAMES,
Harvard psychologist and
philosopher, 1906

Woman is the *bitch goddess* of the universe....Sharon Stone's performance [in *Basic Instinct*] was one of the great performances by a woman in screen history."

—CAMILLE PAGLIA,
Yale lecturer and revisionist
feminist, 1993

She has created a brand-new old-fashioned screen siren: a goddamn goddess for the postfeminist era.

—*Vanity Fair* cover story,
1993

She can be so goddamned mean.

—PAUL VERHOEVEN, director
Basic Instinct, 1992

She's the Antichrist.

—HART BOCHNER, former beau
and costar

CONTENTS

What Makes Sharon Run?

SHARON STONE DOES SEEM to be a hybrid of William James and Camille Paglia's kind of gal.

If they ever finally get around to a screen adaptation of Budd Schulberg's classic 1941 Hollywood novel, *What Makes Sammy Run?* they should change the lead's sex and cast Sharon Stone as the careerist studio chief. Stone has been playing the movie-star equivalent of Sammy Glick for years.

Some people adore her: The most powerful woman in Hollywood, Sherry Lansing, chairwoman of Paramount, and Mark Rydell, director of Stone's 1994 film *Intersection,* are charter members of the Sharon Stone fan club.

Others are plain scared of the beautiful actress with the genius IQ.

Just how terrifying is Sharon? Lansing, who oversees an annual production budget of half a billion dollars and a cast of thousands for the studio, first called Sharon's publicist at PMK, Jennifer Allen, to ask Allen's permission before she granted me an interview that amounted to a verbal massage on Stone's all-encompassing wonderfulness. Listening to Lansing, I was reminded of the subtitle of a fanzine bio about *Melrose Place*'s Queen Lear:

"A Celebration of All Things Heather." (You can be sure it was a sexist *male* studio executive and not Lansing who famously called the actress "Sharon *Stones* because she has the biggest balls in Hollywood." Stone good-naturedly agreed when the quote was repeated to her.)

Lansing is not only the most powerful woman in the movie industry, she's also one of the nicest. Lansing was so charming on the phone, if I had an Oscar in my hands, I might feel compelled to put it down and type: "I liked her. I really liked her!" Instead, I'll just repeat what she said to me from her office at Paramount. "I met Sharon before *Basic Instinct* came out. Our mutual friend Michael Douglas suggested we'd like each other. She came into my office. She wasn't a big star yet, but I just liked her. I thought she was extraordinarily direct. Extra honest. Just like a great person. She seemed to have no bullshit about her. We formed a really nice friendship from that moment on. As I watch her fame and talent both grow, I continue to think she's one of the neatest people I know. Her talent is extraordinary."

Lansing's boosterism is understandable. Their collaboration on *Sliver* was a box-office dud in the States ($38 million domestic), but it grossed $116 million worldwide. Video sales were equally muscular.

Perhaps that's why the chairwoman approached me with kid gloves, although oven mitts are more like it. Lansing can say no to Martin Scorsese and producer Jerry Bruckheimer with equanimity, but she wouldn't say yes to me until Stone's flack greenlighted the phone interview. (Not for nothing has the beautiful former fashion model and high school math teacher been called the Will Rogers of studio chiefs. Lansing never met a superstar she didn't like.)

Mark Rydell flat out refused to talk to me, even though I assured his assistant, Debbie Leonard, via fax and phone, that Lansing had already praised Sharon almost orgiastically and that I was desperate to get the same heavy breathing from Rydell so that my book would have at least a semblance of balance. Rydell's assistant said his refusal was "a matter of loyalty to Sharon," as though praising Stone would be an act of betrayal. The assistant implied that Rydell felt as though I were Benedict Arnold selling West Point real estate to Rupert Murdoch. Prior to researching her life, I did not plan or particularly care to spend some 300-odd pages dumping on a superstar. I had just finished a hagiographic, 100,000-word manuscript on the life and times of Jimmy Stewart, the kindest man who ever walked the planet known as Hollywood. It was appropriately titled *Saint Jim,* although I expect the publisher's marketeers to somehow work "unauthorized" into the subtitle. Poison-pen biographies may sell better, but as a writer, I personally prefer to send valentines to the homes of the Hollywood stars.

Unlike Lansing and Rydell (the latter praised Stone in *Vanity Fair* but wouldn't even return my phone calls), many other colleagues don't have Sharon Stone fan-club membership cards in their wallet. And unlike the gracious Lansing and the loyal Rydell, these coworkers have gone on the record in countless interviews.

Stone once asked her two-time co-star James Woods (*Casino, The Specialist*) why he never made a pass at her. Woods explained, "We've had a running gag for eight years. She says, 'You never asked me out—how come?' And I say, 'Look, Sharon, maybe everyone can't wait to get in there, but once they get it in, the big problem is getting it out again,'" Woods told *Vanity Fair*. "'You're a Cuisinart with legs and a million-dollar face.' She thinks that's very funny."

A reporter who has been covering Stone for years—from a safe distance—described her alternating acts of kindness and cruelty. "She seems to have a Dr. Jekyll/Ms. Hyde personality." Perhaps fearing an appearance of Ms. Hyde, the hard-boiled reporter asked to remain anonymous.

Director Paul Verhoeven agrees with this description of her duality: A reporter for *Rolling Stone* once asked the director of *Basic Instinct* if he felt his leading lady could be diabolical. "I surely do." Verhoeven said. "She's very seducing. She does a lot of flirting. One of the most threatening things about her is she can change in a split second so that in her eyes there's either a loving person or the Devil. I have hated her with all my heart, and I have loved her too....She can be very clever with words and hit you with them right in front of the whole crew. And if you're not careful, she can be the victor."

Who is Sharon Stone, and why is she behaving this way?

Chris Harris, a longtime Hollywood press agent who has worked with her in the past and seems to be suffering from post-traumatic stress disorder because of it, believes Stone is basically a decent human being with the unfortunate knack of surrounding herself with goons and a support group of handlers from hell. Call it the Tom Cruise syndrome. The superstar is a genuinely nice, even heroic, guy who rescues entire families from burning yachts in the Mediterranean and rushes hit-and-run victims to UCLA's emergency room. Unfortunately, like so many other celebrities whom everyone seems to want a piece of, Cruise keeps a kennel of human pit bulls, ranging from the "Pope of Scientology," David Miscavige, to flack fatale Pat Kingsley. (Kingsley is the "K" in PMK, the publicity firm that represents both Cruise and Stone. PMK, which has been nicknamed PMS by journalists who felt its wrath, has hard-boiled reporters terrified lest they offend her and get blacklisted from covering her stable of stars, which rivals that of M-G-M's heyday. The *New York Times* once said that PMK's star clients are treated with the "deference usually accorded North Korean heads of state" by writers who fear a blacklist more destructive than that of the House Un-American Activities Committee.)

Harris offers an alternate hypothesis: that Stone's behavior is motivated by the fear that the career heap she has clawed her way to the top of will suddenly supernova: "I think she is afraid that her star might begin to fizzle out, so it's like: 'I have to be this distant bitch who's got a whip in one hand and maybe a surprise in the other....' Living with her would be like living with Norma Desmond."

Stone seems to have embraced William James and Camille Paglia's high concept, worshiping at the altar of her inner deity, the B-goddess herself. She told the *Los Angeles Times* in 1994 on the set of *The Quick and the Dead* that "having the reputation as a bitch makes people stay back a little bit, which gives me room to breathe. I don't mind it that much."

Stone will go to extremes for that extra air. Her sister, Kelly, once retained the services of a publicist, who warned me as I delved deeper into the enigma wrapped inside a mystery that is Stone, "Sharon hires goons when people piss her off."

Sheepishly, but deferring to Henry Kissinger's observation that even paranoid people have enemies, I stashed copies of inflammatory tapes, floppy disks, and transcripts with friends, among them a corporate attorney, a low-budget film director, and a firefighter who works in beautiful downtown Burbank.

My sheepishness about paranoia vanished on September 4, 1996, when news stations across the country aired footage of her hired handlers beating up Stuttering John, Howard Stern's verbally challenged reporter-at-large, during a press conference at MTV's Video Music Awards show.

His offense? Stuttering John's inquiring mind wanted to know if Ms. S-s-stone planned any more, uh, beaver shots in her films. His punishment: a night in the ER. At last report, John, who specializes in grunge reportage, is still pondering legal action.

Sharon, in case I've made your greatest-hits list, take note. The horse has already eaten the children, and it's too late to close the barn doors.

INTRODUCTION

Date Rape at the Beverly Hills Hotel

MRS. LEW ROTHENBURG IS THE KIND of source journalism students dream about. Impeccable, unimpeachable, an upstanding citizen of the community, a pillar, in fact. A wealthy socialite, philanthropist, and wife of a publishing tycoon. A grandmother of three. In a courtroom she would be called a star witness. For my purposes she would have the same effect on my reportage and career as Deep Throat had on the then unknown Woodward and Bernstein's. Only instead of red-eye rendezvous late at night in underground parking structures with a chatty turncoat deep inside the Nixon White House, I didn't have to go any further than Beverly Hills's directory assistance and my home phone to talk to Mrs. Rothenburg on hers.

The wealthy socialite didn't ask for money for her story, and Mrs. Rothenburg is not her real name. That was the only condition for spilling her guts. (Other minor identifying traits have also been changed to protect the outspoken.) Our phone interview on August 24, 1996, was either off the record or not for attribution, but definitely not "deep background," distinctions which, frankly, I have never understood and are perhaps best left to journalism-school assistant professors in pursuit of that other elusive bitch goddess—tenure.

My star witness was also a fly on the wall.

The wall happened to be in the ladies' rest room of the Beverly Hills Hotel, the most lavish hostel in Southern California's poshest hamlet, owned by the richest man in the world, the sultan of Brunei. How Grandma Rothenburg stumbled upon Sharon

Stone *in flagrante delicto* is a tale of bad timing and good luck. (Guess whose?)

A journalist who writes an etiquette column had this to say when the incident was repeated to her: "I don't care if Sharon Stone makes it with a llama in the privacy of her own palace. I don't know about you, but I don't want *my* eighty-year-old grandmother stumbling on people of either sex doing it in a public toilet. My grandma would have a coronary."

When I asked a studio executive if Stone's alleged behavior that evening jibed with his knowledge of her, he answered, slightly downscaling her modest girlhood home, "You can take the girl out of the trailer park, but you can't take the trailer park out of the girl."

Mrs. Rothenburg was less epigrammatic and more frank. The fifty-seven-year-old socialite called Stone's behavior "a lot of crap....I wasn't morally offended. There's nothing objectionable to [being a] lesbian."

The bathroom incident Mrs. Rothenburg witnessed was the climax to a *Twilight Zone* kind of night. Planet Hope, a charity for homeless children founded by Sharon's sister Kelly, held a fundraiser on December 4, 1995, in the Crystal Ballroom of the Beverly Hills Hotel. Mrs. Rothenburg was a major benefactress of Planet Hope as well as dozens of other charities and attended the banquet.

The first curious event of the evening was finding herself seated next to a nurse, Jane Payne (her real name), who had worked for Lew Rothenburg's doctor. Formerly of Las Vegas, the nurse had given Stone injections of vitamin B_{12} during location shooting of *Casino*. By way of a thank-you, Stone had given the nurse two free tickets to the inaugural ball.

Early in the evening, the nurse told Mrs. Rothenburg that Stone was interested in starring in a film based on the nurse's adventures as a paramedic for Lifeflights, airborne missions of mercy to downed jets and disaster areas. It would make a rip-roaring action adventure, and Stone could do a Streep stretch *à la The River Wild,* only hopefully with better box office.

"They seated us at a table with this nurse from Las Vegas. She proceeded to tell me [Stone] had bought an option to her life story. The girl was not familiar with Hollywood. She was truly starry-eyed that night. She was impressed to be there. She wore a borrowed gown," said Mrs. Rothenburg, who that evening happened to be coutured to the hilt.

Halfway through dinner, the nurse's new benefactress, the bitch goddess incarnate, materialized at their table and, according to Mrs. R, said to the nurse, "Come back here, because I can't talk to you." Fans and paparazzi were apparently pestering Stone, and the star and the subject of her upcoming biopic left the room.

They never came back.

Mrs. Rothenburg's story jibes with an item in a gossip column called the "Yellow Pages" in the reputable *Los Angeles* magazine. The January 1996 issue commented on Stone suddenly pulling a Howard Hughes at the ball: "In a foul mood [Stone] fled the VIP reception and went to an adjoining room, leaving co-honoree Lee Iacocca to accept the award by himself."

The magazine also mentioned that Stone refused to meet another honoree that evening, a ten-year-old former homeless girl named Lupe Tapia. Lupe was crushed that her idol refused to let her worship. Her mother, Connie, told *Los Angeles,* "Lupe was so disappointed she didn't get to honor Ms. Stone."

Stone wasn't being a snob by stiffing the homeless child. That night, she also snubbed one of the richest men in the world, Kirk Kerkorian, a megadonor to her sister's charity, as well as Iacocca. She did shoot Kerkorian an "icy stare" before walking away without meeting him, according to *Los Angeles*.

Meanwhile, it was already dessert time and the nurse hadn't returned to the banquet room. The nurse's male escort had left the group several times in fruitless searches. He finally concluded that the only other place his date could possibly be was the ladies' rest room, the one place he couldn't check out. He asked Mrs. Rothenburg to do so.

The philanthropic Mrs. Rothenburg for once regretted her volunteerism. When she entered the bathroom, it turned out that the nurse's date was right. There was Sharon Stone with the nurse and "several other ladies."

At that point, the evening really began to turn into an episode of the *Twilight Zone*; that is, if Paul Verhoeven directed episodic television. In fact, the incident eerily echoed the famous bathroom scene in Verhoeven's *Basic Instinct,* but instead of Michael Douglas crashing the men's room at a disco and finding Stone making out with her blond *doppelgänger,* it was the luckless grandmother of three.

"So I went to the ladies' room, and sure enough, they were there with several other ladies. They were all quite friendly," Mrs. Rothenburg says with no irony. "Sharon was smoking one of those little brown cigars, what do you call them?"

Cigarillos.

"I said to the nurse, who used to work for my husband's doctor, 'Your escort is concerned. You've missed the entire dinner.'

"She wasn't the least bit interested in going back to dinner. Sharon was saying what a terrific body the nurse had. A lot of crap. Fondling her, touching her, holding her, patting her.

"It upset me."

The other "ladies" weren't participating, Mrs. Rothenburg assured me, but they weren't calling hotel security, either. In the words of the advertising copy for Stone's *Sliver,* perhaps they, too, "like to watch."

Helpful Mrs. Rothenburg still felt compelled to act as the nurse's social secretary. "I said, 'I'm going to tell [her date] you're, uh, engaged right now and will be back shortly."

Mrs. R was overly optimistic. After dessert, when the Rothenburgs were ready to leave, the nurse still hadn't returned to the table. Her date once again asked Mrs. Rothenburg to play bounty hunter.

"So I went back to the bathroom," the intrepid socialite told me. The actress did not appreciate this second intrusion. "Sharon said [to the nurse], 'Let's go over here in the stall. I want to talk to you in private.'

"They disappeared into the stall. I went back and told [the escort], 'I don't know how much longer she's going to be....'"

The Rothenburgs left the dateless date alone.

It is a truly bizarre feeling to talk to a grandmother, a near sexagenarian, about sex in public places, but public sex is exactly what Mrs. Rothenburg presumed was going on in the ladies' room at the Beverly Hills Hotel. "I think she was making a pass at her in the stall. She certainly was making a pass at her *outside* the stall. It just got more serious. I think the girl—actually she was a woman who looked like she was in her early thirties—was too naive, didn't get the picture. Or maybe she didn't care.

Mrs. Rothenburg was also surprised that the nurse was so drab looking, mousy and flat-chested. "She was literally a plain Jane," she said.

Stone's unusual spin on "going to the ladies' room" is particularly surprising. She successfully spiked all rumors of bisexuality when she told *Esquire,* "It don't mean a thing if it ain't got that *schwing,*" punning on Wayne and Garth's corruption of the Yiddish *schlong.*

Rumors were further quashed by a well-publicized incident at a basketball game in Miami. Stone and her costar James Woods were separated from another blond superstar, Madonna, by the full width of the court. That didn't stop the Material Omnivore from sending a note to Woods. She wanted him to play John Alden to her tongue-tied Miles Standoffish. (As we shall see, not too tongue-tied.) The note requested a "big wet kiss" from Woods's date. Still seething at the request years later, Stone told *People* magazine her response to the mash note: "Not in this lifetime! Christ, why? Because I'm the only one left she hasn't done it to? Like, excuse me, Madonna, could you please take that salami out of my face! Hell, it's just unfathomable to me."

On another occasion, though, Stone conversely seemed to encourage speculation about her sexual I.D. when she told Irish author Rosemary Mahoney, "I think it's important to have a certain degree of [sexual] compulsion, that euphoria, in romantic love—and even in your friendships. There are things about my best friend that make me *in* love with her."

Mrs. Rothenburg doesn't care which way Stone *schwings*. The socialite insists she's not a homophobe. She just doesn't like to witness what she suspects may have amounted to date rape, since the nurse struck her as being heterosexual.

"I wasn't morally offended. If she's gay, fine. I just don't think this girl was gay and simply didn't know how to handle the situation. I felt Sharon was taking advantage. [The nurse] was impressed that Sharon was taking all this time to spend with her. She did have Sharon's full attention."

As the putative producer and star of a movie based on the nurse's life, Stone had transferred a hoary Hollywood institution, the casting couch, to a public toilet. The incident thoroughly disillusioned the philanthropic Mrs. Rothenburg. "I'm burned out on Hollywood. I got very jaded."

She told the event's publicist, Chris Harris, that Planet Hope was a terrific charity, but "it's a shame it turned out this way. You just need to get somebody who's going to do something for it rather than hang out in the bathroom." Mrs. Rothenburg herself has donated a small fortune and, she estimates, thirty hours of her time to the nonprofit organization.

The publicist was shocked to learn about Stone's location after her disappearing act. When the flustered press agent asked for Stone's return ETA (estimated time of arrival), Mrs. Rothenburg was not encouraging. "I told Chris, 'She's in the ladies' lounge and not in any hurry to come out.'"

When a chauvinist friend, a stand-up comic and wingback psychologist, heard of Stone's potentially career breaking behavior, he began working on material for his new act: "Not since Charlie the Tuna has a fish had such a death wish...."

Stone takes the fascination with her love life in stride and claims that most of it is exaggerated, although Mrs. Rothenburg's matter-of-fact revelations don't seem like exaggerations. Stone once told Carrie Fisher, "I've often thought that if I could get a 900 number and charge all the people who say they've had sex with me—or say they know someone who's had sex with me— two dollars a call, I'd never have to work again."

Stone may want to charge her own law firm considerably more than $2. According to a partner in the Beverly Hills firm of

Rosenfeld, Meyer, Susman, the actress is just as forthright when a *man* tickles her libido. Stone is represented by Marvin Meyer, a name partner. Although I had identified myself as Stone's biographer, one of Meyer's partners, William Skryzniarz, told me after two bottles of merlot on New Year's Eve 1996, "When Sharon wants someone, she rents a hotel room and tells him exactly when and where to show up. She makes it clear it's a one-time opportunity, take it or leave it. She's made the move on some major names." Skryzniarz became circumspect when I asked him to name names.

Hotel reservations are discreet; making out in a public john is insane. More clinically, Beverly Hills psychologist Dr. Brian Miller labels such risky business "self-sabotage." Stone could easily have had Heidi Fleiss send over a $2,000 beauty *dressed* as a nurse rather than feeling up the real thing in the most elegant hotel in L.A. Why would a supersuccessful person risk a $20-million-per-year paycheck for something easily and more safely obtainable elsewhere?

Dr. Miller calls self-sabotage "getting in your own way, ruining your own self-stated goals." The doctor nicknamed it "Hugh Grant Syndrome." Self-sabotage can come from thrill seeking. Stone may also be fighting a good-girl image which she has said began in childhood. "It's an incomplete self, a phony self, because no one can be that good. One extreme promotes the other extreme in order to achieve psychological balance," Dr. Miller says. Self-sabotage in such cases is unintentional, a consequence of the need to do a balancing act between a good image and "bad" desires.

Self-loathing can also cause self-sabotage. *I don't deserve success. I've risen too high too fast. I haven't paid my dues.* This feeling of unworthiness may have led Dick Morris, savvy adviser to Clinton, to step out on to a public balcony in a bathrobe with a hooker on his arm. Similarly, Jimmy Swaggart, a video icon to millions of fundamentalists, cruised a red light district in the middle of the Bible Belt. Dr. Miller explains, "People feel undeserving of success. They feel they have to restore a sense of justice to a life that is undeserved."

How and why Stone ended up on top and in the ladies' room is a tale of determination and psychodynamics. Our biodyssey begins thirty very odd years ago and three quarters of a continent away in northwestern Pennsylvania, geographically and psychosocially light-years away from the john of the pleasure dome that Brunei's Kublai Khan decreed (and put $400 million into).

NAKED INSTINCT

1

Mudville

SHARON STONE was born in Meadville, Pennsylvania, on March 10, 1958. To call Meadville (pop: 15,000) a two stoplight town, as *Playboy* did, is to overstate its cosmopolitan flavor.

In search of friends and family, I asked local directory assistance the name of the nearest big city. The operator said, "There are no big cities near Meadville." Worse, the operator didn't know her geography or her neighboring state. The Paris of the Prairies, Cleveland, is only eighty-eight miles away but light-years distant in sophistication and culture.

The number-one occupation in Meadville's Crawford County is milking cows. The town has even counted its most prolific "residents" (24,101 at last milk). There's even a social organization, either for the cows or their owners, called the Holstein Club. We don't even dare to imagine the membership of another civic group, the Northwest Pennsylvania Colored Breeds Association. Sheep and wool growers, as well as beekeepers, also have their own fraternal organizations. The Meadville Chamber of Commerce hands out a list of twenty places in the county where you can have all your fertilizer needs satisfied. Climatically, Crawford

County, Pennsylvania is no Ixtapa. The average temperature in January is literally freezing, 32.1 degrees Fahrenheit. July averages a sweaty, humid 80.9.

It's rainy or buried under snow (annual rainfall, 43.19 inches, annual snowfall, 112.2 inches)! Optimistically, the chamber includes this come-on in its brochure: "There is a 90 percent probability that there will be at least a 126-day frost-free period." Let's start building the luxury resort now.

There are only thirteen libraries for a population of 86,000, which means almost 1,400 people have to crowd into each repository of knowledge, whose books, like the cows, have been individually counted. Total: 750,000.

Meadville, however, is a good place to find God. Although there are only thirteen libraries in the entire county, Meadville's fifteen thousand lucky worshipers have ninety churches from which to choose. There is only one synagogue, but Mennonites rate three meeting places.

Meadville's brochure ends with a cheery list called "Focal Point (sic) for Fun" of these putative "points of interest." They include Drake's Well and the Erie Amtrak Station, although the brochure does warn of a forty-five-minute drive from Meadville to these glam destinations.

In homage, perhaps, to their most famous citizen's past beauty-pageant success, the cover of the chamber of commerce brochure features a young woman wearing a tiara identified as "Feather Thomas, 1996 Pennsylvania Fair Queen." Her parents were perhaps fans of TV's fall girl Heather but got their consonants confused.

The preceding stats aren't meant to be cruel. They represent the roots Stone rejected, the small-town life she fled for big-town glamour. Some people love the boondocks, are born, grow old, and die there happily.

The congenitally ambitious Stone was not one of them. Never a big civic booster, at sixteen she was already calling the northwestern Pennsylvania site "a dumpy little town." When the city fathers decided to honor its most famous native daughter and proclaimed Sharon Stone Day in 1995 as part of the celebration of

Crawford County Fair's fiftieth anniversary, the actress RSVP'd for the homecoming festivities but didn't show. She sent an 8-by-10 glossy as stand-in. Literally.

It was a kinder, gentler, and considerably less famous Stone who, in 1989, deigned to return to nearby Saegertown to deliver the commencement address at her high school. Saegertown must have been desperate for a celebrity speaker, because Stone's biggest and most recent credit was 1988's *Action Jackson*.

Unlike the superstar who stiffed Sharon Stone Day, Stone in 1989 not only showed up, she daylighted as Florence Nightingale. Fans were kept waiting while she consoled Richard Baker, whose son had committed suicide two years earlier. Baker said, "I was deeply moved that she took time from the public. She was truly a good listener and was trying to help me."

The second of four children, Stone is the daughter of Joe and Dorothy. Her parents worked at or owned a mom-and-pop tool-die shop, depending on which official press bio you read. Dorothy supplemented the family's income by moonlighting as a book-keeper. Dad dropped out of school after the sixth grade; Mom only made it to her sophomore year in high school. They were grade-school sweethearts before marrying at eighteen. Mr. and Mrs. Stone are still together in Meadville and still in love, their daughter says.

The Stones were not dirt-poor, but they weren't the Car-ringtons, and they didn't own a second home in Southfork. Today the chatelaine of an eleven-thousand-square-foot Mediterranean palazzo in Beverly Hills, Stone has never tried to hide her roots or inflate her pedigree. "I come from blue collar," she has said. On another occasion, she described her ancestors as "dirt-poor Irish potato farmers."

These days, her collar is more likely to be attached to a $35,000 ensemble by Lagerfeld. The down-home gal prefers home in the hills of Beverly. She is a Clampett with a 90210 Zip code. "I'm happy in luxury," she said in 1992 after moving out of a twelve-hundred-square-foot pied-à-terre in the Hollywood Hills in the wake of *Basic Instinct*'s windfall and the terrifying attention of a stalker who camped out in her backyard. "I'm decadent in my own way. I can't be happy in a one-room apartment with a dirt floor."

After she collected $7 million for a single film, Stone said, "A hundred dollars was a lot of money in our family."

Her parents made up with love what they lacked in material riches. She remains close to both and showers her family with major game show–quality gifts: homes, cars, and large infusions of cash.

Her father was and is a rarity, a blue-collar feminist. Joe's own father had died when he was four, and he was raised the only male amid an adoring matriarchy. The goddess's father unknowingly grew up to be a feminist. "I've been raised by women all my life," Joe has said. "I like to see women get a fair shot in life. I think they haven't for a long time."

Dad's liberated mind-set wasn't all love and kisses, however. As he did with his male children, Joe pushed his daughter hard, perhaps harder than the boys, because he knew her stunning intelligence was capable of meeting his demands. Years later, Stone would express mixed feelings about his carrot-and-stick approach, although the imagery she used sounds more like lion taming than child rearing. "My father was very rigid when we were young," the actress said. "Since I had the ability to do things that other kids didn't, he drove me toward perfection with a whip and a chair. That's very overwhelming. He's not like that now. Now he's the sweetest guy. We've all grown."

She's made peace with her hard-driving dad, but the memory hasn't completely left her consciousness. As late as 1996, a female reporter from *Mirabella* magazine asked the actress to read her interviewer's face. Stone revealed more about herself than the journalist and engaged in a bit of classic projection when she described what she saw in the woman's face: "Tough, like someone was tough with you growing up, probably your dad. Like, drove you tough." The reporter said Stone was half right. She had picked the wrong parent.

Her mother also never programmed her ambitious daughter to settle for a housewife's lot. "You have to be strong," she lectured her daughter, "or men discount everything you say." The executive who nicknamed her Sharon *Stones* probably felt she paid too much attention to that particular lecture. Stone herself never objected to that sexist pun on her surname and seemed to embrace it when she said, "I've got the biggest balls in Hollywood. It's good that they're scared of me. The longer they stay scared, the longer I keep my job."

Her father reinforced his wife's protofeminism. Stone recalls: "My dad never raised me to believe that being a woman inhibited any of my choices or my possibilities to succeed. To be a feminist like Dad in that blue-collar, middle-class world is a big stand."

The Stones were anything but a dysfunctional family, although some of their children would fail miserably at adult life. In 1996, Sharon would offer, unasked, a bit of family biography in an interview for *Mirabella* magazine: Her brother Michael did time in Attica for cocaine possession. "I don't think I'm telling tales out of school, because he's done interviews about this even in the newspaper," she added.

Despite parental support and affection, her childhood was a miserable one. She was cursed with a genius IQ of 154. While others might find brilliance a blessing, Stone said her intelligence made her feel like "an alien girl-child, a brainy geekoid with only one close friend and regular visits to the principal's office."

The visits ended abruptly at fifteen when Stone's 154 IQ forced her involuntary transfer to a place that doesn't have a principal, the local college. At fifteen, she was already a senior, because the brainy alien had entered school a year early, then skipped a grade. Stone is probably the smartest actress in Hollywood, although she's in close competition with another brilliant beauty, Geena Davis (IQ: 153).

Stone didn't know her IQ until Larry King did a typical ego-boosting ambush interview on his call-in TV show. Before the interview, King did his homework and called Stone's alma mater, Saegertown High, where he learned something Stone didn't know, her intelligence quotient.

When he surprised her live on the air, Stone was not pleased with the flattering revelation. "It's like someone gives you a turd sandwich and you have to sit there for half an hour," she said afterward. Someone with perhaps more self-esteem would have been delighted to learn in front of 30 million viewers that she was a genius. Her response also reflects a fondness for lunch metaphors. The most famous quote attributed to her had the actress refer to an ex-boyfriend as a "dirt sandwich."

Stone couldn't have known that it was her IQ that made her feel like a fish out of water in school. Her childhood resembles that of so many other youthful misfits who overcompensate by becoming superachievers in whatever field they decide to conquer. (Tom Cruise, Steven Spielberg, and Sylvester Stallone were all misfits. And, like Stone, who was also bored with school, they tended to be C students—or worse. Stallone flunked out of a Swiss prep school. One blushes to use a tabloid as a source, but the usually unreliable *National Enquirer* claimed that the sweetheart of Saegertown High ranked 52 out of 115 classmates. The story probably ran right next to the one about the two-headed bisexual pig abducted by aliens from a Kansas wheat field.)

A more reliable source, London's *Observer,* quoted Stone describing herself as a "weird bookish child whose high IQ made it hard to relate to her slower contemporaries." Her mother, even though she adores her famous and generous daughter, suggests that Stone is embroidering the self-consciousness she felt as a child. Dorothy, who generously services the press worldwide, told the same British magazine, "Sharon has been posing from the day she arrived. She *came out* posing."

Stone politely disagreed with her mother, telling *Parade* magazine:"I was a nerdy, ugly duckling who sat in the back of the closet with a flashlight and read. I was never a kid. I walked and talked at 10 months. I started school in the second grade when I was five, a real weird, academically driven kid, not at all interested in being social. Recess was a drag until I realized I didn't have to play, that I could lean up against a wall and read."

The actress lampooned her self-pity when she joked, "I was a poor black child."

By the fourth grade, anticipating her reluctant transfer to college at fifteen, Sharon spent half days at a Mensa experimental program for children with high IQs, further reinforcing her alienation and fish-out-of-water miasma.

Stone felt that the advanced classes were bogus experiments at best, child abuse at worse. One fast-track course left her permanently mired in the land of the subliterate. The school didn't believe in teaching phonics, and "the result is that now I can't spell at all, because I learned in a different way."

Stone was gifted at math and science. In fact, after a half day at community college, she would return to high school and tutor the slow learners in the mysteries of quadratic equations and other obscure rites of algebra. Despite her spelling handicap, she also tutored ninth-graders in English lit when she was a senior.

Stone remains bitter to this day about all the messing with her mind by the Crawford County school system in the name of higher education. "My education was totally fucked up by these ridiculous experiments," she said twenty years after the trauma. The curricula "made me unable to adapt socially, because I was never consistently involved with kids my own age. I come from this small town where kids drove tractors to school and nobody ever traveled anywhere, and now I'm an international star!"

Comments like that didn't endear her to classmates. At Saegertown High, Rhonda Darling agreed that Stone's precociousness was off-putting, but it had more to do with game-playing than intelligence. A local freelance journalist, Chris Rodell, generously shared this quote from Darling: "Most of the kids couldn't stand her. People thought she was standoffish because she just didn't care what other people thought. All the other kids her age were playing kids' games, and she was impatient to start playing the games adults play."

It didn't help when she announced on the playground with no self-irony, "I *am* the new Marilyn Monroe." Even the goddess's acolyte Sherry Lansing wouldn't go that far.

Another Saegertown alum, Patrick Ernig, believes that her ambition and not her brains created the resentment of her peers. "She let everybody know she was going to make something of herself, and people around her resented her for that. They all thought she was too good for them. I think it made her mad that people didn't believe in her. Well, she believed in herself, and that's all she needed. If she hadn't gotten into acting, she would have been a ruthless executive, using her looks, her brains, and her ambition to drive her company to the very top. The people here made her more determined than ever that she was going to make it big. And you could tell she was impatient to get out of Crawford County."

Classmates weren't the only ones who found Stone's self-possession a turn-off. Her relationship with her only sister, Kelly, remained difficult well into adulthood, although these days it thrives. Sharon said, "She used to really annoy the living shit out of me. Just her voice on my answering machine was like nails on a chalkboard, and now I think of her as one of my friends."

In researching this book, I found that almost everybody has a Sharon Stone story. During a prepublication interview with Darian O'Toole, the self-proclaimed Howard Stern of San Francisco's KBGG radio, the hostess showed that she was more circumspect than her role model, Stern. It was only during the commercial break that O'Toole told me this whopper. In 1990, just before Stone became semifamous after the release of *Total Recall*, she proved that she was a good friend to her sister, even if it meant engaging in a little misrepresentation. Kelly was dating an attorney named Steven Adelman. O'Toole, an "ex-friend," in her words, left a "sexy message" on his answering machine while Adelman was away in Europe.

Soon afterward, Adelman's alleged legal secretary called O'Toole and asked the "nature of her business" with Adelman. O'Toole realized that it was actually Sharon Stone pretending to be Adelman's secretary. Before hanging up, O'Toole said, "You can't even play a receptionist convincingly."

Nancy Young, a teacher at Saegertown High, feels Stone continues to act like the brat in the schoolyard even now. "She's told the whole world that we're all a bunch of small-town nobodies from Nowheresville. We can't understand why she'd go out of her way to alienate the only people who care about her for who she was, not for who she is now that she's rich and famous. I hope for her sake money really can buy happiness, because someday when she's a has-been, she's going to need lots of it." No wonder Stone was a C student if teachers felt that way about her.

Teachers bad-mouthed her, and even people who should have been supportive treated her like Rodney Dangerfield rather than the sweetheart of Saegertown High. An alleged boyfriend humiliated her. Still seething at the memory, Stone told *Mirabella* magazine that one day her boyfriend dropped her off at the local Holiday Inn, where she worked as a hostess. She had just confided to him her secret dream to go to Hollywood and become a movie star. Instead of encouragement, she got raspberries. "As I walked in front of the car headlights, he stuck his head out the window and started singing. 'Hollywood, da-da-da-da-da, Hollywood.'" Her anger evaporated into a look of supreme satisfaction, the interviewer observed, as Hollywood's regnant screen queen realized the irony of the taunt by a long-ago beau.

A childhood acquaintance remembered that Stone dressed like Winona Ryder's death-obsessed teen in *Beetlejuice*. Black was her favorite color.

Stone, an unmarried American Madame Bovary, found small-town life stifling. Just how small were Meadville and nearby Saegertown? The even tinier population of Saegertown (1,045) only hints at the Rouault-like claustrophia of her roots. "I'd never been anywhere, done anything. It wasn't until I was a senior in high school that I went on an escalator for the first time. When I got to Philadelphia, I still had never been in an elevator." Even Mrs. Bovary got weekends off for rendezvous in Rouen.

Geography was the subject she hated most, and it had nothing to do with memorizing all those capitals or learning what an isthmus was. Perhaps it was because the subject gave her a galling glimpse of the greater world she feared she would never experience. "I thought I'd never get to go anywhere, that I was stuck in this small town," which she dismissed as being "the size of a shoe."

Edinboro Community College didn't dramatically enlarge her horizons. It wouldn't be unkind to say that Edinboro was not a prep school for the Ivy Leagues. Stone earned an A for an essay she wrote in an English literature class. The subject was the chair she had sat in all semester. Maybe her professor envied the lucky chair. Or maybe Stone did in fact do an excellent job ripping off a Robbe-Grillet novel.

In 1990 an interviewer for *Interview* sounded a cautionary note about all this essay mythology. The reporter mentioned that another blond bombshell came to Hollywood after winning an essay contest in high school. Frances Farmer, however, proceeded to crash and burn in a mental institution that dispensed frontal lobotomies like aspirin.

Stone will never play the victim role—unless she gets $7 million per victim. A film scholar once called her the first "Postmodern Screen Goddess." I enjoy laughing at Postmodern architecture and art as much as the next aesthete, but I had no idea what Postmodern Screen Goddess meant until the full-service studio chief, Sherry Lansing, enlightened me with an ingenious definition. "I know what that means," she said. "Sharon is contemporary and hip. She is of our generation. Sharon wasn't the victim, ever. So many screen goddesses were victims off-screen. They also played victimized women. The sensuality of a *modern* goddess like Marilyn came from softness. You felt you had to take care of her. Sharon is and always was in control. Sharon's sensuality as a screen goddess started with *Basic Instinct*.

"And she fucked the guy around rather than vice versa."

Victim or unvictimized, it's impossible to overestimate Stone's self-loathing during her formative years. She suffered from a textbook case of dysmorphic body image (Dysmorphic disorder is an affliction in which a normal-looking person is preoccupied with some imagined defect in his or her appearance.) Like an anorexic who looks in the mirror and sees fat, the beautiful teen saw a pork chop staring back at her from the vanity. Stone has never implied that she suffered from any eating disorder, but she did have the afflicted's negative self-image. She just didn't starve herself to death.

In front of the mirror was not where Stone liked to be. For years, she hated the stranger she knew all too well frowning back at her. Her dysmorphia was so profound, she literally didn't feel comfortable in her own body. "I used to look in the mirror and go, 'You are…?' And the purpose of your visit is…?' You know? And I never could get comfortable. My clothes always hurt, and my hair felt wrong, and my teeth felt bad in my mouth." She even confessed that she saw a "zaftig Semitic girl with long, curly dark hair" peering out from her mirror. To this day, some of the aftershock lingers in the interior decor of her home. In all eleven-thousand square feet of it, there are only a few mirrors.

Stone's ugly duckling phase was a matter of bad timing. Body image, psychologist Dr. Miller says, forms during puberty. The image formed at this time stays with you the rest of the life. The ninety-pound weakling who metamorphoses into Mr. Universe still sees the teen who got sand kicked in his face when he looks in the mirror.

If you're a mess with acne and pudge, as Stone contrary to photos of the time insists, that image can stay with you the rest of your life. "When the ugly duckling becomes a swan, she still sees that ugly thing from puberty," Dr. Miller says. Staring at her uncovered breasts in all their 36B glory during a photo shoot for *Vanity Fair*, Stone said, "I look like a wittle boy." A wittle boy with a testosterone deficiency. Most heterosexuals would say 36B ain't chopped liver, but Dr. Miller says, "Compared to the competition, for a movie star 36B is small."

Although Stone won beauty contests at seventeen, Dr. Miller says her negative self-image was probably formed five years earlier, at the onset of puberty. "Probably at that age she was somewhat geeky, unattractive."

Why would a woman who loathed her body show it off in film after film? "It may be overcompensation. She may have entered beauty pageants in an attempt to convince herself that she wasn't as unattractive." Seeking stardom and baring all on screen are other ways to get reassurance from millions of ticket buyers. "Showing tit on screen is compensatory," Dr. Miller says. "She does more than necessary to try and prove to herself by way of other people's reactions that she is indeed not unattractive. So getting asked to be nude in front of the camera is flattering, whereas other women might find it very invasive."

And as Stone admitted, she finds it easier to relate to an arena full of marines than one on one.

One childhood trauma justified her fear of mirrors. More than one interviewer has commented on the dramatic scar running across her neck. Until *Basic Instinct,* when the scar helped flesh out her lethal villainy, she usually hid the blemish under makeup on-screen. Stone got so tired of being asked about the origin of the scar, she admits she began to make up fanciful tales. "I've told a lot of great stories about it, organized crime stores, gang-attack stories." Sharon's mother was happy to reveal the true story of the scar to a journalist. The truth was less dramatic than a botched gangland hit but still pretty horrifying for a preadolescent. "Sharon was eleven or twelve," Dorothy said. "She was on a pony that hadn't been ridden often." (Where did the strapped Stones get access to a horse?) "And it ran under the clothesline. She passed out and fell off. Otherwise, it would have killed her. For a long time after, she never wanted anyone to touch her."

I have spent the past twenty years psychosimplifying the lives of celebrities, putting them "on the couch," as more than one book reviewer has complained. To a man (and woman), all of these supersuccessful overachievers have spent their childhood and teen years feeling, in the jargon of Alcoholics Anonymous (AA), "less than" (AA-speak for "inferior".) Stone's formative years, with all their self-loathing, fit this pattern to a tee.

Today Stone is inarguably the most beautiful woman in the movies. If she were a man, she would be a shoo-in for *People* magazine's annual "Sexiest Man Alive" cover story. But her comments in a 1995 interview in *People* suggested that her dsymorphic hell was still alive and unwell. "I have a gangly body, long arms and long legs, and a short curvy torso…and a really girlie little spot in the middle."

This is the same actress who made it utterly believable that all she had to do was uncross her legs to make hard-boiled police interrogators dream of leaving their wives—at least for the night. While she continues to trash her looks, Stone is not unaware of her impact on men. She just doesn't call it beauty. For this supremely insecure bombshell, she's merely turning tricks in a magic act. "I've never thought I was a great beauty," she has said. "Just a great magician. You can create an illusion of glamour and it is very powerful. You come into a room, and people react—not to who I am but to the energy of the glamorous projection."

Her family felt that the magic was real. An uncle, as supportive as her parents Joe and Dorothy, tried to improve her self-esteem by bribing her with $100 to enter a local beauty contest, Saegertown's Spring Festival Queen, in 1975. The uncle sounds like the hard-driving Joe. Strings were attached to the bribe; Stone had to win the contest to collect the money. Stone was not encouraged by the offer and said, "I thought it was some ugly joke."

She entered the contest only because she needed the money to help her cash-strapped parents with college tuition.

Stone resented being treated like a piece of meat even back then, although her career would be jump-started playing the human embodiment of filet mignon.

"I'm like seventeen," Sharon recalled, "and it's the county fair, and they're judging cows. So I went and within the first four hours I realized the horror of my position, that I didn't have a prayer. The only way I could get through it was to act like it was funny. So I just blew down the runway, did this big spin. I had on this cape, and the audience thought it was hilarious."

Stone lost, but like so many others in her life at that time, the judges were very encouraging. One pageant official urged her to enter the Miss Pennsylvania contest. She declined and set her sights lower, winning the Miss Crawford County title in Meadville.

The whole beauty-pageant phenomenon has produced some amazing women of accomplishment, ironic, since these flesh-peddling orgies emphasize the contestant's physical, not intellectual, endowments. But such overachievers as Diane Sawyer, Phyllis George, Bess Myerson, Mary Hart of *Entertainment Tonight*, and, of course, our superstar herself have all paraded down a runway in maillots and high heels before taking on infinitely more complicated tasks, like reading a teleprompter for news and infotainment shows.

For the talent portion of the Miss Crawford County competition, Stone chose to recite the Gettysburg Address. Stone did her homework for the speech, thanks to the help she received from an ophthalmologist named W. T. Holland, her "personal trainer" for the contest.

The future superstar already was attracting fans and a support group. W. T. Holland, the retired Meadville eye doctor, recalls that Stone was no Lincoln. "It was kind of tough getting her to pull it off." His wife joined the team and described the horrors of the Civil War to add resonance to Stone's address. Mrs. Holland says, "She was hanging on my every word" until Stone interrupted and said, "May I ask you something?" Instead of a question about the influence of slavery and high tariffs on the conflict, Mrs. Holland quotes Stone as asking, "Should I wear sparkly stuff in my hair?" Whether it was the speech or the sparkly stuff, Stone aced the contest. A photo of her in full beauty-queen drag—tiara, scepter, and rose bouquet—shows the typical orgasmic facial expression of a Miss America, except, unlike most of her counterparts, Stone is not crying. She is clear-eyed, not starry-eyed.

A pageant judge saw a star in the making and suggested that the winner try an even bigger "Big Time." "Forget all this meat-rack stuff," he told the seventeen-year-old. "Go to New York and become a model. That's where the big money is."

Stone ignored her first big fan's advice. As much as she hated semirural Pennsylvania and school, she was savvy enough to know that a college diploma was her surest route out of Meadville.

It's at this point that Dorothy Stone, a high school dropout, betrayed her roots and maybe even her daughter. Dorothy was nodding off watching Merv Griffin one afternoon when she heard Griffin's guest, Jean Shrimpton, say she earned a then whopping five-hundred-dollars a day as a top model. Five hundred dollars for a day's work was unimaginable wealth in the Stone family. When she told Sharon to drop out of college and move to New York to try her luck as a model, her daughter obeyed.

It was a profession she came to loathe only slightly less than the one that followed—starlet.

2

Fashion Victim

UNLIKE SO MANY OTHER SUPERSTARS (Tom Cruise, Mr. and Mrs. Bruce Willis), Stone has never embraced grunge except for one regrettable appearance in a Gap T-shirt at the 1995 Oscars. She has expressed a taste for expensive togs that suggests she gets fashion tips from Mrs. Marcos or the Mmes. Trumps. "I have a real blue-collar mentality. I dress up to show that I am happy and grateful to be there. That's what you do where I come from, and it makes sense to me. I don't feel like saying, 'Fuck you,'" says Stone, who has frequently used exactly those words when dispatching terrified publicists and producers. "I feel like saying, 'Thank you.'"

She may have gotten her yen for couture during the unhappy years she spent modeling in New York, Paris, and Milan, with quick trips to Tokyo, Rio, Buenos Aires, and Los Angeles.

Unlike her glacial film career, Stone's rise in the world of mannequins was meteoric. After leaving Meadville in 1977, she stayed with an aunt in New Jersey, crossing the Holland Tunnel to Manhattan every day.

She didn't have to endure many crossings. Within four days, the drop-dead-gorgeous blonde was signed by the elite Ford

Modeling Agency, truly the Elite of its day. Soon she was making a Shrimptonesque $500 per day.

Stone kept her head out of the clouds and her eye on the bottom line. Modeling wasn't fun. It's a dirty job, but some beauty has to do it. And it paid the bills better than Mrs. Stone, daydreaming with Merv, could have ever imagined. "Modeling was a way to avoid being a starving artist," Stone has said.

Maybe Dorothy Stone hadn't been unwise in turning her daughter into a community-college dropout. Stone, though, wasn't so sure. Others might envy such a glamorous life, which led to runways and photo studios around the globe, mostly Paris, Milan, and Manhattan. But her dysmorphic body image kept getting in the way of any pleasure she might have taken in her portfolio. "It was endless. I was a very bad model. I had no ego fulfillment. At the end of the day, what do you have? A Polaroid."

A London newspaper said that Stone was also mortified by what she considered her "farm-girl figure." I sat next to her at a press screening a few years ago and was struck by the width of her hips. Maybe her body image wasn't quite so dysmorphic, after all. But unlike my untrained eye, the camera just seems to fall in love with Stone, regardless of her girth.

The young woman eventually moved out of her aunt's apartment and into a Ford agent's co-op, but life at Camp Ford was concentration camp-like—right down to the starvation diet.

Dorothy and Joe's salt-of-the-earth value system helped her cope with life on the fast runway. "My upbringing left me with the basic way to live. As a model, you live a really decadent life. Being a single girl, relatively naive—well, those values pretty much kept me alive. More than a few girls I worked with are dead, more than a few are junkies, and very few are still around doing anything. It's a hard life for young girls, and it's a life that's only for young girls," she said.

Sometimes her parents' values didn't help her cope, and Stone took her frustrations out on inanimate objects. In a typical story that revealed more about the magazine's sensibility than its subject, *Rolling Stone* salivated over the fact that Stone keeps a large punching bag in a garage and regularly beats the hell out of it.

The magazine writer couldn't resist reporting what sounds more like his fantasy than hers when he quoted her in a 1992 piece: "I've hit a few people, yes. I've knocked a couple guys across the room." The magazine explained her behavior by saying it was "because she needs a lot of room." The writer went on to quote a totally irrelevant source, comedian Richard Lewis, on his fantasy of what Stone's sex life must be.

Life on the wicked runway didn't start out decadent; ascetic is more like it.

"I did have to live with one of the agents," she recalled. "She was very strict. I wasn't allowed to bring soda into the apartment because soda was bad for me. I was a big farm girl, and they were trying to bounce that fat off me." Again, the embryonic anorexic was struggling to be born. Photos from her high school days show the same lean panther who scorches the screen today.

It didn't help that she also did TV commercials for the king of fat, Burger King, while having to stay slender enough for other TV gigs for Clairol and Maybelline.

"I'm still the fattest thin girl I know. But I started modeling, moved out of the agent's apartment, moved downtown, then moved to Europe to model. I lived in Europe, being tortured by Italian playboys and wondered, Why am I doing this? I really only wanted to be an actress. So I packed my bags, moved back to New York, and stood in line to be an extra in a Woody Allen movie."

Stone's version of being discovered on a soda fountain stool at Schwab's by a talent scout was even more exciting. The master himself, Woody Allen, wanted to meet her; actually, he wanted to hire her on the spot. That's what an assistant told her after Allen spotted her transcendent beauty swimming in a sea of a hundred extras. The assistant whispered into her ear what must have sounded like her ticket to stardom: "Woody would like to know if you'd like a part in the movie."

Of course, Stone agreed, but her inner critic was shocked when they poured her into a slinky evening gown complete with glamorous makeup, feather boa, and tiara—attire she had already found uncomfortable wearing as a beauty-contest winner in her high school days. Playing a bombshell on film made her even more uncomfortable than inciting the Meadville yahoos.

"I went to wardrobe, and they put me in a bombshell dress. I said, 'Wait, let me explain something. I'm not a bombshell.' They didn't see it my way. I played Woody's fantasy. And that was the beginning of the end."

3

An Indiscreet Object of Desire

THE YEAR WAS 1980, and *Stardust Memories,* Allen's disastrous salute to Fellini's *8 1/2,* did look like the beginning of the end of the director's career. The *New York Times*'s generally gentle Janet Maslin barbecued the film for a "laziness of sorts." *New York* magazine's staff barracuda, David Denby, said, "Woody is dead."

It was the beginning of Stone's decade-long climb to the middle before her last-minute Hail Mary pass as the bisexual kitten with an ice pick in Camille Paglia's favorite film. Stone was only twenty-one at the time, and it would be another fifteen years before she worked with a director of comparable talent, Martin Scorsese, although by then she would be the star, not a silent goddess with a yen for plate glass.

It's hard to say if her beginning was auspicious or portentous. Stone had eighteenth billing and a nonspeaking part smaller than a bit. All she did was kiss the window of a train. And yet her impact was so great that the lead paragraph in the *New York Times*'s review mentioned the goddess's first screen apparition, if not her name. The credit in the press kit, which was appropriated by the *New York Times*'s reviewer, understated her visual impact and described her character as "Pretty Girl on Train."

The train was filled with gorgeous people "partying like the Fourth of July" or the day before Armageddon. The railroad car opposite the party train was filled with just the opposite kind of souls. Old, ugly, deformed, Woody Allen, among others. The *New Yorker*'s Pauline Kael, the Will Rogers Antichrist of film critics— she rarely met a film she didn't hate—compared Allen & Co. to photographic subjects suitable for a sitting with Diane Arbus.

Stone bestows a kiss on the schlubby director-star, but their romance is interrupted by reinforced glass.

After the New York production of *Stardust Memories* wrapped, Stone found herself fully inoculated with the acting virus. She decided to try the mother lode of movie-star wannabes, Los Angeles.

Her optimism was misplaced or at least premature. "I arrived in L.A. at twenty-one with naive goals. I thought I'd get off the bus and everyone would go, 'It's her, our new movie star.'" Her naiveté, one writer said, would lead to ten years of career-crippling films. Or as Stone eventually realized, "I just didn't get it."

An early admirer got "it," but he unfortunately turned out to be a minority fan club of one. Her appearance in *Stardust Memories* not only caught the attention of the *Times*'s critic, but the great French director Claude Lelouch (*A Man and a Woman*) was also mesmerized by her two minutes on screen. He cast her in 1982's *Les Uns et Les Autres,* starring James Caan. Stone didn't star. In fact, she didn't even get listed in the credits. But she got an all-expenses-paid trip to the City of Light—and she got laid.

It was fortunate that the brainiac actress had picked up French during her modeling career in Paris and spoke it fluently enough to pass as a native. Stone shrugged off her Streep-like ability by saying she learned the language from her Parisian boyfriend. It was even more fortunate that Lelouch had not seen her second film—and first starring role—in 1981's *Deadly Blessing,* which followed *Stardust Memories*.

The *Village Voice* called *Deadly Blessing* a "Wes Craven

horror classic," and hailed Craven as the "John Ford of Horror." Others felt combining "classic" and the name of the auteur of *A Nightmare on Elm Street* was oxymoronic at its most moronic. As for comparisons to the almighty Ford, the *Voice*'s film critic was lucky dead directors don't sue. *Deadly Blessing* was Craven's third film. After his first two films in the 1970s shocked the Brady decade, even the director knew the public had his number. "After the release of *The Hills Have Eyes* and *Last House on the Left*," Craven said, "People were calling us scum." They didn't change their vocabulary for his third film.

The film, a modest but not Z-list production, cost $3 million, the catering budget on a production today. The trades announced Stone's first shot at stardom with their usual bullish prose. The *Hollywood Reporter,* after quoting Craven's self-denunciation, had only kind things to say about Stone's blossoming climb to the bottom. Unfortunately, the actress's first public appearance in the press by name didn't correctly identify her. "Sajron [*sic*] Stone, Woody Allen's discovery, has been snapped up by Wes Craven for the lead role." Even more typical than its bullishness, the trade publication also got the billing wrong. Stone wasn't the lead. She was listed third after Lisa Hartman and Maren Jensen. But that was considerably higher up on the pecking order than eighteenth billing in her silent-screen debut.

Deadly Blessing was made during the slice-'em-dice-'em Cuisinart era of filmmaking, the same school that gave us innumerable *Halloweens* and visits from Freddy Krueger on Friday the 13th. An unsuccessful director of teen comedies said of the genre after he embraced it, "We didn't start making money until we started killing the kids."

The plot of Stone's third film sounds like Alfred Hitchcock meets *Green Acres*: Bodies begin piling up in a small rural community, and a religious cult is suspected of going on a twentieth-century crusade to kill their neighbors in the name of God. The unfortunate neighbors are a couple (Maren Jensen and Doug Barr) from the big city and their equally unfortunate weekend visitors from California, Lana (Stone) and Vicki (Susan Buckner).

Stone gave credence to rumors that would become public a few years later during a torturous shoot in Africa when she described Lana as a "drug-crazed model, not unlike my natural self at the time."

Lisa Hartman, post-*Tabitha*, pre-*Knots Landing*, got first billing for a supporting role. (As star of the sitcom *Tabitha*, the sequel to *Bewitched*, she was the production's biggest name.)

Despite her stardom, Hartman played a villain—and a lesbian villain to boot, with a lover, Lois Nettleton. The director intuitively had his hand on the popular pulse, realizing that (straight) guys really like to see two women get it on.

As though killer lesbians weren't bad enough for real-estate values, the other neighbors, a fundamentalist sect called the Hittites, were even scarier. They are so strict, the screenplay says, "they make the Amish look like swingers." In an original twist, the Hittites turn out to be heroes, not inbred monsters. The lesbians are portrayed as devil worshipers because "everyone knows," the *Los Angeles Herald-Examiner* said, that lesbians "are in league with the Devil."

Besides its good-guy-bad-girl reversal, the film is also unique because of its cast of hundreds. The credits list a barnyard of feathered and four-legged Screen Actors Guild (SAG) members, including "115 chickens, four mules, one cow, one pig, four goats, eight horses, a flock of pigeons," plus a cheeky snake and a spider with an oral fixation. Less original was the unintentionally funny dialogue. "You are the stench in the nostrils of God," yelled Ernest Borgnine in a cameo appearance.

The costar Stone was asked to swing with was even creepier than the lesbian and religious neighbors. Her first scene in her first starring role was bargain-basement Spielberg circa *Indiana Jones*. In a barn, a spider falls from the rafters into her open mouth. A rubber spider (we presume) in her mouth was one thing, but when the director called for a real tarantula to crawl over her partially exposed chest, Stone, an unknown with no clout, would show the same independence she displayed as the superstar of *Diabolique* who told the producer to buzz off when he ordered her to strip—on-screen.

Stone was willing to suffer a close encounter of the lurid kind, but first the director, off camera, would have to let the spider have its way with him, too. Unlike Stone, Craven was a full-blown arachnophobe, but he agreed and even enjoyed his punishment. "She was a no-bullshit girl," the director said, echoing Sherry Lansing's more ladylike description of her favorite actress.

Stone had prepared for the job by studying Method acting with the famous coach Roy London. She said of her mentor, who has since died of AIDS, "He has an intellectual approach to acting. He doesn't tell you to lie down on the floor and pretend to be a piece of bacon frying."

Linda Gross, the *Los Angeles Times*'s feminist film critic, who was allowed to review only B movies for the paper, typically the kind that loved to grind women up and spit them out, was revolted by all this D-movie trash. Particularly the reptiles. "The most disturbing aspect of the film is Craven's nasty revenge on women, which are misogynist male fantasies of a women's nightmares," including, apparently, Gross's worst. "Women in *Deadly Blessing* are violated and abused by other women and slimy animals."

Jensen's husband in the film suffered a worse fate, getting run over by a tractor while driving under the influence of Satan.

The defunct *Film Journal* not only hated the film but predicted box-office disaster. *Deadly Blessing,* however, was a big hit. The box-office performance didn't impress Stone, though. More than ten years later she would dismiss it as "*Charlie's Angels Get a Scare* in a bad Wes Craven movie. As if there are good Wes Craven movies," she said, by then able to laugh at the nightmare.

The film's commercial success failed to jump-start Stone's career. She'd have to wait three years for another American film, but it would turn out to be well worth the wait. *Irreconcilable Differences* was light-years away from *Deadly Blessing* in theme, sophistication, and budget. So what if she had only sixth billing and got upstaged big time by the film's nine-year-old star, Drew Barrymore, who chews up the scenery and soaks quite a few hankies as a self-possessed youngster who decides to divorce her quarreling parents (Ryan O'Neal, Shelley Long)?

To put it kindly, the studio executive who approved the credits was no film historian. He clearly didn't have a clue that Stone had appeared in three previous films when he let the ad copy cross his desk unvetted. After Ryan O'Neal, Shelley Long, and Drew Barrymore's name, the credits read: "And introducing Sharon Stone." Adding insult to injury, the press kit calls *Irreconcilable Differences* her first major film role despite the previous *Deadly Blessing,* a big, if disreputable, hit. Then the kit copy calls her sixth-billed character a "superbitch."

Actually, her character was tangential to what was supposed to be the main, tearjerker plot, about Barrymore as the little girl lost who sues her parents for "divorce." The youngster even has a climactic courtroom scene where she gets to give a speech that aspires to Darrow. Her *E.T.* discoverer, Steven Spielberg, even took time out from his busy schedule to coach her on the scene over the phone.

But what makes this film an insider's delight and provides the Nöel Coward flavor is its subplot. If there's such a thing as *cinèma à clef,* this is it. The secondary story line is a fictional re-creation of director Peter Bogdanovich and Cybill Shepherd's romance, which was as hot as Liz and Dick's fifteen years earlier. The nasty subplot was so close to the real thing that actionable rather than fictional is a more apt description.

In the film, Stone has the Cybill Shepherd role. It would be Stone's best work up to then and better than her subsequent ten films, several TV movies, and one miniseries. Moreover, trivia buffs interested in such things will be glad to learn that the film contained her first nude scene.

In the early 1970s, the real-life avatars of irreconcilable differences were Bogdanovich, Shepherd, and the director's wife, Polly Platt, who worked as the set designer on Bogdanovich's one and only masterpiece, *The Last Picture Show*. Unfortunately for his wife, the director saw a teen model on the cover of *Seventeen* magazine in the checkout lane while he was shopping with Platt at the supermarket. The director fell in love with the image—and with the girl when he got ahold of her. The G-rated Sharon Stone of her day, Shepherd got a career-making role as the Lolita-like cocktease in his masterpiece. To the puritanical horror of the press and public of 1971, the director and his discovery carried on openly during filming while his trouper of a wife continued to design sets for the production.

Bogdanovich's Svengali would then, critics claimed, go on to destroy his career as he cast his Trilby in flop after flopola. And to a chauvinist man, they all blamed Shepherd.

If ever a piece of fiction was actionable, this film was. Although Shelley Long's character was promoted to screenwriter and muse instead of set designer, her cheating husband and his cranky starlet were dead ringers for the originals.

O'Neal's character, like Bogdanovich, is a former film-school scholar turned art-house director with a huge first hit, *An American Romance,* which is well received by the critics and the public. The similarities don't end there, either. O'Neal even looks like Bogdanovich, down to his haircut and signature aviator glasses.

Shepherd, proving her critics wrong first with *Moonlighting* and then with her current sitcom, should have been particularly upset by her fictional re-creation. Stone's Blake Chandler plays the starlet as harlot and worse, with no talent. Unlike Shepherd, a top model before Bogdanovich trained a camera lens on her, Stone's diva was a carhop before O'Neal discovers her, not a radiant icon on the cover of a national magazine.

She's also a coke whore who, after achieving questionable stardom, becomes a coke tyrant. Why did Stone keep playing drug crazies? Was she seeking out autobiographical roles "not unlike her natural self at the time"? In one of the film's many hysterical sequences, Stone throws a snit fit and screams at her assistant for having the temerity to bring her a *warm* Coke. The abused assistant also happens to be her mother in the film.

Another gem of a scene anticipated the role nudity would have as a platform in her career. Stone's starlet refuses to remove her clothes for a crucial scene in her boyfriend's film. He whispers something in her ear, perhaps "Do it for Stanislavsky?" Whatever it is, Stone becomes a convert and says, "It works for me." She drops her robe and reveals herself in glorious full-frontal nudity. Even this episode paid kinky homage to *The Last Picture Show,* where Shepherd showed she also had the right stuff; her striptease in the earlier film, however, took place on a diving board, not in a Winnebago. Yet another incident anticipated Stone's career pinnacle, in which body hair would have pivotal significance. In *Irreconcilable Differences,* her bimbo is also an earthy type who refuses to shave her armpits. Stone exposes her underarms in a gesture that anticipates Madonna's early nude poses for a photographer.

Newsweek's reviewer didn't even bother to mention Stone by name but did call her "a bimbo [O'Neal] has cast as a singing Scarlett O'Hara in a musical version of *Gone With the Wind,*" entitled *Atlanta.*

The director of *Irreconcilable Differences*, Charles Shyer, knew *Gone With the Wind*'s cinematography well. The film within a film's grotesquely humorous climax re-creates the famous crane shot from the original in which the camera slowly pulls away from Vivien Leigh to reveal thousands of Civil War dead. In the original, the scene was not only famous but heart-wrenching. In its musical reincarnation, it's hilarious, because while Stone mourns the dead, she also belts out a Broadway show tune. And she sings as badly as her real-life inspiration. (Don't argue until you catch Shepherd's alleged jazz set at Hollywood Boulevard's Cinegrill. One reviewer said she doesn't sing, "she gargles." But that's another biography.)

The critical reaction to the box-office hit was mixed. *Daily Variety* felt *Irreconcilable Differences* was too "inside" and predicted, inaccurately, that "the story is more fun for the cognoscenti than the average filmgoer." The *Los Angeles Times*'s sweet-tempered film critic, Sheila Benson, was even kind to Stone's bimbo from hell, calling her a "waitress [not carhop] waif, whom [O'Neal] nurtures." Others would use a stronger term for what Bogdanovich did to Shepherd's career and vice versa. The gentle critic didn't even mention in her review the obvious similarities between O'Neal and Bogdanovich *et al.*

Perhaps fearing the same lawsuit the filmmakers never suffered, *Time* magazine gently said, "Screenwriters Nancy Meyers and Charles Shyer…also display a familiarity with the life and films of Peter Bogdanovich."

The *Hollywood Reporter,* typically fearing the loss of advertising revenue, couldn't resist alluding to the real-life inspirations, but you can almost see the marketing director's blue pencil on the copy: "A *cinèma à clef* about a college film professor who becomes a famous director—wink, wink—and dumps his wife for a bimbo actress who proceeds to ruin his career—nudge, nudge." The only person being nudged was the luckless reviewer, kowtowing to his ad-addicted superiors. The names of the real-life inspirations were never mentioned in the review.

The scrappy *Los Angeles Herald-Examiner,* forever the Avis to the *Times*'s Hertz until it became the Dalkon Shield of dailies, out of business, didn't mince euphemisms. *"Differences* also incorporates some episodes modeled upon the celebrated early marital woes of director Peter Bogdanovich and his first wife, production designer Polly Platt." No mention was even made of the third corner of this triangle, Shepherd, whose career pre-*Moonlighting* was so moribund she fled back to Elvis' hometown and hers.

Another reviewer should have had a crystal ball next to his word processor. *L.A. Weekly*'s Michael Wilmington egregiously predicted, "Shelley Long is absolute dynamite and has my vote as the Romantic Comedienne Most Likely to Succeed." Sadly, Long is stuck in Bradyville sequels, while Stone has reached Olympian floor level. Even *Irreconcilable Differences'* Drew Barrymore has become a critically acclaimed actress and a way-out (of-the-closet) bisexual.

The same year she made an indelible impression on film, Stone decided to go slumming on the small screen. *Magnum, P.I.* was the top rated show of 1984, and Stone couldn't resist the exposure of costarring with Tom Selleck on the season premiere.

In a greedy attempt by network publicists to attract even more attention than the show already received as the Nielsen champ, someone leaked to *People* magazine a fatuous scoop. The producers wanted Stone to appear nude, and she refused, the magazine's gossip columnist, Pam Lansden, reported, apparently from another planet. "Sexy Sharon Stone, 26, refused to show all on the set of her steamy scene with Tom Selleck in the season premiere of *Magnum, P.I.*." As if, to quote the late-twentieth-century philosopher Alicia Silverstone, TV nudity wasn't a full decade and an *NYPD Blue* soundstage away. If the producer or director asked Stone to take it all off, the footage was certain to end up on the cutting-room floor or in the private video collection of the executive producer, intended for private pleasures, not public exposure.

Goosing the publicity machine for all it was worth, Stone participated in this preposterous bit of flackery, telling *People,* "I didn't have the nerve to go topless." So how did she manage to go bottomless for *Irreconcilable Differences*? "It took me three months to get over doing that scene. When I dropped my top, my heart was in my feet." She failed to mention that she dropped her bottom, too.

Irreconcilable Differences was the break that got away. She told *Playboy* in 1992 that the film earned her the best reviews of her career, but "my career was really improperly managed at the time. The mistakes that were made cost me many years of having to make shitty movies."

In 1984, if Nielsen ratings hadn't intervened, Stone's acting career could have gone in a completely different direction. Today she'd be playing mothers of children with terminal diseases or butch police detectives on series television. *Bay City Blues,* created by megaproducer and writer Steven Bochco (*NYPD Blue, L.A. Law*), revolved around a minor-league baseball team. Stone, as Cathy St. Marie, was a member of the ensemble, but she was way down in the troupe, given fifteenth billing as a baseball "widow." Although only a year later Bochco would enjoy a critical and ratings success with *L.A. Law*, *Bay City Blues* attracted the admiration of the critics but not the viewers. The Nielsen dud was unceremoniously canceled less than a month after its debut on October 25, 1983. At the time, Stone was probably distraught at yet another big break turning into just another bust. She tersely dismissed the experience as *"Hill Street Blues* people trying to make a TV series about baseball. Didn't work."

But in the long run, her failed TV turn was a boon, not a bane.

If *Bay City Blues* had been a Nielsens champ, she might have been a one-series wonder, typecast as a "TV actress," too small a name for the big screen. Other major TV stars, like Veronica Hamel (*Hill Street Blues*) and Jill Eikenberry (*L.A. Law*), have all but disappeared into TV encyclopedias, popping up occasionally in disease-of-the-week docudramas or sitcoms that have the shelf life of *Bay City Blues*.

The same year that Stone was stripping in the movies and hiding behind a towel on TV, she turned down a starring role in a major film, *Teachers,* opposite Nick Nolte, because it, too, required some frontal nudity. Her squeamishness at this time is curious. Maybe it was just the modesty of youth. Less than a decade later, she'd be spreading her legs and showing what British journalists strangely called "all of Nebraska" in *Basic Instinct*'s iconographic interrogation scene. Stone's reluctance may not have revolved around *Teachers'* nudity but its dreary script, which became a dreary film and a box-office failure. The script could have warned off a savvy script reader turned screen star. Her management may have been lacking at the time, but Stone knew dreck when she read it. Unfortunately, sometimes paying the bills meant surrendering to it. As she sadly quoted a future costar, "[Elizabeth Perkins] once said in an interview that when she read a script and didn't feel like throwing up, she agreed to do it."

Her next two films suggest she must have had to stifle her gag response. After reading the screenplays, Stone may have been screaming, "Is there a script doctor in the house?" Perhaps even worse than nearly destroying her career, the back-to-back epic wannabes would result in the loss of the love of her life, the first and only Mr. Stone, producer Michael Greenburg, who married his leading lady on the set of their African misadventure *King Solomon's Mines*.

4

(Get Me) Out of Africa

IN THE MID 1980s, Stone hit personal and professional bottom. Her career and marriage crumbled amid the heat and mosquitoes (and crews urinating in her bathwater) of Zimbabwe. The downhill trajectory of screen work suggested she was en route to becoming a member of that doomed species, the over-the-hill screen-goddess. She could hear her biological bombshell clock ticking as Hollywood laid down its eleventh Commandment: Thou shalt not grow old—if you want to play an object of desire on-screen.

After her wicked performance as the tweaked starlet in *Irreconcilable Differences*, her next film showed she was going for the gold. Sadly, she ended up with something considerably less precious—dross.

King Solomon's Mines must have looked good on paper and, Stone presumed, on her resume. After nestling at the bottom of the credits as "introducing Sharon Stone" in *Irreconcilable Differences*, she may have found the offer of second billing after Richard Chamberlain irresistible. She'd also get an all-expenses paid trip to Africa and star in a film that hoped to capitalize on the success of two recent Indiana Jones movies.

King Solomon's Mines was a remake of the 1950 hit starring Stewart Granger and Deborah Kerr, based on the novel by H. Rider Haggard and a rip-off of Steven Spielberg's first two outings with an archaeologist from the University of Chicago.

"Capitalize" is not the term the critics used. Clone and cinematic plagiarism were. *King Solomon's Mines* was a virtual Xerox of *Raiders of the Lost Ark* and *Indiana Jones and the Temple of Doom* minus the wit, budget, and inventiveness of their director. Even the object of everyone's desire, the titular mother lode of King Solomon, came from the Bible, like Indiana Jones's Ark of the Covenant. There's also a scene where Chamberlain frees the slaves *à la Indy 2*. Stone even duplicates Kate Capshaw's curly hairdo, by way of Farrah Fawcett.

In his first adventure, Jones was dragged by a jeep on his belly. Chamberlain ups the ante. He's dragged by a train and stands up, appearing to ski on the train tracks, defying all laws of friction.

At least in its vulgarity and ultraviolence, the film didn't imitate its PG-13-rated inspirations. It was also shot on the cheap by Israeli auteurs Menahem Golan and Yoram Globus, who spent only $12.5 million, compared to *Indy 2*'s $30 million.

A disturbing homosexual rape of an elderly man by a German army officer is thwarted when Chamberlain shoots the would-be rapist in the genitals. If the film was meant to be kiddie fare, its target audience must have been ten-year-olds who bludgeon five-year-olds to death in the U.K. Also original is the hero's weapon of choice. Instead of Jones's trademark bullwhip, Chamberlain totes what looks suspiciously and anachronistically like a Saturday night special.

The hellish six-month shoot was even more troubled than the unoriginal concept. At one point, nature and the natives were so uncooperative, the director, J. Lee Thompson, reportedly called on the services of a local witch doctor, a *N'anga*, to lift the curse.

A trading-post set was built on the Zambezi River, even though locals warned the filmmakers that it was right in the middle of an elephant crossing. The watering hole was a favorite spa used by the animals for centuries. After spending six figures on the set, the crew realized its folly when a single elephant showed up and proceeded to chase them away from his personal Club Med. At great expense the set had to be reconstructed upriver.

The mosquitoes drove everyone crazy. So did the female star. In a widely reported story Stone's behavior was rumored to reflect her own description of "a drug-crazed model, not unlike my natural self at the time." Whether it was coke, as speculated, or the heat, Stone so enraged crew members that they surreptitiously urinated in a pond just before she shot a sexy bathing scene in it, according to an article by Hillary De Vries, which ran in 1992 in the compulsively vetted *Los Angeles Times*.

Stone has never commented on the contents of her bathwater, but she admitted that whatever she got she probably deserved. She blamed her foul mood on the heat, the mosquitoes and her husband, Michael Greenburg. They had married in 1984 on the set of a TV movie he produced and she starred in. Less than a year later, the relationship imploded in the African rainforest.

"My marriage was falling apart," she said in 1991, a year after their divorce was finalized, "and the pressure of that was just tremendous for me. I'm sure I was a bitch. But if you see that I spent a year of my life in Africa and that is what I have to show for it, I have a right to be pissed. So maybe they didn't like me sometimes. Tough shit."

To her mind, her behavior was a good career move. Assertiveness pays. "I've learned to get what I want by being direct and fearless. I am not a sucking-up-type person," she told *People* in 1993 for its cover story "Hollywood's Sexy Rebels." Per *People*, Stone was part of the rebels, Mao-Mao division.

At least she didn't scare the horses and got along with the animals. During an interview on the set, a leopard licked her ear. He was protected from his leading lady by a cage, however. And, like a good starlet, she lied through her teeth when she told the industry trade publication *Screen International* how much fun she was having in the middle of this tropical Hades.

"This is really a nice role where I get a chance to be outrageous and still be in keeping with the character. Lee allows me a lot of opportunity to improvise, and boy do you need that freedom considering what Richard and I have to go through. I mean, when you are being chased by a thousand cannibals one moment, fed to crocodiles the next, then dropped on to a runaway fruit carriage, there's no time for hesitation. Also trying to remain funny when in reality I've been burnt, stung, tripped, in daily temperatures of 49 degrees Centigrade before I even get in front of the camera, is no easy matter." (Forty-nine degrees Celsius translates to 120.2 degrees Fahrenheit for the metrically challenged. No wonder the actress was cranky on the set.)

Ten years later, with a Golden Globe and Oscar nomination for protection, she could drop the Julie Andrews shtick and say what a jungle it had been out there. Her character, she said, was "a bad hairdo running through the jungle."

Maybe the crew was in a bad mood for other reasons. Mostly Israeli, like the two producers, the production team had to listen to the Marxist government of Zimbabwe's radio broadcasts which regularly condemned Israel as "Zionist" and referred to Yasir Arafat as "comrade." The local PLO was even more upset, claiming that forty members of the crew were not gaffers or grips but Israeli army soldiers and security men incognito.

In *King Solomon's Mines,* Sharon Stone is no Sharon Stone. Twenty-six at the time, she looks worse than zaftig, almost chubby. Her hairdo is even less flattering than Kate Capshaw's. Trying to duplicate Karen Allen's tough broad from *Indy 1*, Stone looks about as threatening as a Barbie doll. Her acting, in fact, resembles an audio-animatronic toy by Mattel, strictly church basement. To call it amateurish is to insult anyone who ever appeared in a high school play. Her voice is also two octaves higher than her nicotine-scarred contralto in *Basic Instinct*. And she apparently hasn't yet hired the voice coach who got rid of her nasal Pennsylvania twang.

Trivia buffs and voyeurs will notice that Stone also looks considerably less ample than her current bust measurement, 36B, which was dutifully reported by *Vanity Fair*'s celebrity Woodward and Bernstein, Kevin Sessums. Happily, her physical transformation hasn't been as dramatic as those incredibly growing women like Anna Nicole Smith and Demi Moore, post–*St. Elmo's*

Fire, pre-*Striptease.* In fact, Stone may have tried to distract attention from her own personal, uh, growth by cattily mentioning in a magazine article that Moore's chest had suddenly ballooned in *Disclosure.*

Perhaps Stone just grew into her body the way she did her face. Like fine wine, she has gotten better with age—bimboish at twenty-six, beautiful at thirty-eight. Publicity stills from 1981 show a merely pretty, generic blonde you might see on any *Cosmo* cover or inside hustling Clairol. As for her anatomy farther south, not even the yellowest of journalists has ever accused the actress of seeking solace in silicone.

Cast as a rugged individualist, Chamberlain didn't fare well. Although 50 at the time, you can still see Baby Doc Kildare in an intern's smock peeking out from under his pith helmet and khaki. His beard looks painted on. An alternative newspaper, *L.A. Weekly,* homophobically wrote, "Unfortunately, the word virile isn't the first thing that comes to mind upon viewing Richard Chamberlain in his dapper explorer's clothes. He belongs in Camp Beverly Hills, not the Congo." Although Chamberlain's Allan Quatermain does look as though he shops at Banana Republic, he isn't nelly, just preppie beyond the help of an acting coach.

The plot, which the *Village Voice* called "paint-by-numbers Spielberger," is set in World War I Africa. Stone's archaeologist (surprise!) father is the only man who can decode a map that leads to the famed riches of King Solomon's digs. The Germans, who need the loot for the war effort, treat dad like Mr. Bill, beating him savagely several times in the film, which is surprisingly sadistic for an attempted farce. Stone hires Indiana Jones, uh, Allan Quatermain, to rescue her father.

The *Village Voice* called it a "shameless clone" of Indiana, and the *New York Times* said, "Even the music is as similar as is legally possible." The witch doctor should have been kept on the payroll to deal with the critical reception.

Stone's performance drew mixed reviews, from fear and loathing to heavy breathing by besotted reviewers. David Chute in the *Los Angeles Herald-Examiner* wrote, "I spent a lot of time studying Sharon Stone when I suppose I should have been drinking in the splendors of African scenery. Lots of elks and heffelumps go bounding past. Is Stone a gifted performer? I was too dazzled to judge." The *New York Times* was even kinder and considerably less sexist: "Sharon Stone is equally up to date as a spunky, sexy, smart-talking heroine with an effective right hook and a propensity for trouble. Can you imagine Deborah Kerr calling somebody a 'cheap-suited camel jockey'?" Can you imagine the classy, classically trained Brit appearing in such unintentional camp? The *Village Voice*, which slammed the movie as paint-by-number Spielberger, was downright bullish about its star, claiming Stone was superior to *Indy 2*'s heroine, the future Mrs. Spielberg.

The barbs ranged from damning with faint praise to just plain damning. The Chicago-based trade publication *Box Office* said, "Though Sharon Stone is attractive, she's no Karen Allen. She's not even Kate Capshaw, for that matter." Film scholar and *Hollywood Reporter* critic Arthur Knight, continuing in the same sexist vein, wrote: "Sharon Stone runs through the rain forests looking as if she has just stepped out of *Lil' Abner*. Fortunately, she has the figure to carry it off, which helps considerably to compensate for her lack of acting skills."

The *Los Angeles Times* devoted a single word to her performance in its review: "leggy." The *L.A. Weekly* lamely punned, "Sharon Stone's last name is a good description of her acting ability."

Worse than her acting, the sum of her performance and Chamberlain's was less than its parts. There was no sexual chemistry between the two leads, for reasons best left to the tabloids and their battalions of libel lawyers. The *Chicago Tribune* said, "The romance is stilted. When Chamberlain romances this Stone, he does so with all the passion of a rock. Stone is a rather fetching blond whose principal dramatic gift is a toothy smile."

The critics' displeasure was nothing compared to the fury it aroused among a specific minority of its audience. *King Solomon's Mines* was the first but not the last Sharon Stone film to draw pickets. But instead of Act Up rabble carrying placards revealing the surprise ending to *Basic Instinct* (X did it! Like we didn't know), business-suited members of the NAACP picketed movie theaters and threw brickbats in the press.

The Beverly Hills branch of the NAACP called the film a "gross distortion of the African people and their history." NAACP President Willis Edwards said, "We are asking the makers of this film, especially producers Menaham [*sic*] Golan and Yorma [*sic* again] Globus, to remove this filthy product from our nation's screens."

Variety couldn't resist reveling in what would one day be called political correctness. The holier-than-Golan critic called the film "no more than a cheap fantasy which exploits black people and black culture by using rich African mystique as a prop for sterile romanticism and adventurism."

Box Office was similarly outraged. "Then there's the movie's racism. It tries to treat the story's inherent racism as a joke, but fails to do anything but rehash some old Tarzan stereotypes. Maybe it's supposed to be satirical when black natives go bug-eyed, scream and flee at the merest trouble, but humor is missing."

Worse than this totemic Stepin Fetchitism in the jungle was the cannibalism of the locals despite anthropologists' insistence that no such phenomenon exists among homo sapiens. On the other hand, *King Solomon's Mines* seemed to inhabit a parallel universe somewhere on Planet Moron. One scene featured the leads making love while being boiled in a pot of stew by carnivorous people of color. The scene anticipated Stone's later solitary pleasures in *Sliver*'s bathtub while that film cannibalized its predecessor *Basic Instinct*'s blood lust.

Stone and Chamberlain came to their masterpiece's defense. "It was made as a spoof," the actor said in a column by Army Archerd, *Daily Variety*'s confessor to the stars. "The black actors all cooperated knowing what it was. We are definitely doing this all with tongue in cheek." (Can you say screen-extra scale in a country where the annual per capita income is $1.99?)

Stone felt that she and her costar came off dumber than the

dumb natives. "We are the biggest idiots in the movie," she said, her selection of this movie proving her point. In fact, the only person with brains and who saves the day is an African prince. But despite his character's royal pedigree, he is treated like Their Man Friday through most of the film.

It was too late to accede to the demands of the NAACP and pull the picture. Insanely, the producers were already shooting the sequel without waiting to see if the box-office success of the first film merited a follow-up. It didn't.

Box Office asked the questions Canon Films' stockholders were probably pondering themselves. "A silly mind-deadening sequel to a silly, mind-deadening movie. Few showed up for the first chapter, so why should this one do any better?" In fact, after three weeks in wide release, the take for number two was an anorexic $3.6 million.

It wasn't all folly. Back-to-back shooting of the two films may have frayed the cast and crew's nerves, but it was cheaper to shoot the sequel while the production was still in place in Africa. After a two-week vacation and booster shots, everyone reported back to the set of doom.

The sequel, *Allan Quatermain and the Lost City of Gold,* came out in 1987 and cost half a million dollars more ($13 million). The rip-off title echoed *Indy 2*'s *Temple of Doom* but didn't come anywhere near to duplicating its plagiarized model's success. Despite the increased budget, production values looked even cheaper. The money, as they say, wasn't all up there on the screen. The *Los Angeles Times* giggled about a sequence where a canoe speeds through rapids. "Our favorite was an underground torrent that bore an uncanny resemblance to the Pirates of the Caribbean ride at Disneyland."

Golan and Globus would eventually be laughed out of Hollywood and end up, as an Israeli director told me, "running a movie theater in Tel Aviv." At the time, despite the box-office dross, the moguls *manqué* were still seeing the two films through rose-colored glasses that needed a good cleaning. "Canon's chief executives believe the films will create a new cycle in African adventure series," *Screen International* breathlessly reported, without bothering to look at the box-office figures in its own back pages.

After the first mess hit the fan and theaters, Golan remained on manic overdrive. He announced plans for a "big remake" of *Ali Baba and the 40 Thieves*. The starstruck producer stopped just short of emulating his promoter-idol Mike Todd and promising that all forty of Baba's bad guys would be played by name stars, like the cameo stunt casting of Todd's *Around the World in 80 Days*.

Her African nightmare almost killed Sharon Stone's career, but infinitely worse, it destroyed her marriage to the only man Sharon Stone ever loved.

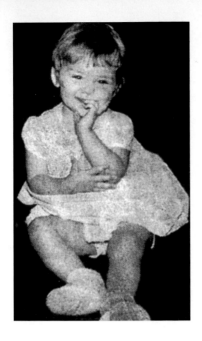

Above left: Sharon as an adorable toddler; *above right:* Her high school yearbook picture; *right:* Sharon as Miss Crawford County; *below:* Teenage Sharon in her swimsuit; *below right:* With husband Michael Greenberg. They split up after only three years.

The family Stone: sister Kelly, Sharon, and brother Michael at the St. James Club, August 26, 1994. The publicist for the Planet Hope gala said "Sharon had more security than the President of the United States."

Handsome Dorothy Stone shows where daughter Sharon got her perfect bone structure.

Stone looks like the girl next door—if Helen of Troy is your neighbor.

John Rhys-Davies threatens to torture Stone in *King Solomon's Mines.*

The accomplished actor James Earl Jones (*left*) got stuck calling Richard Chamberlain (*right*) *bwana* in *Allan Quatermain and the Lost City of Gold,* the sequel to *King Solomon's Mines.*

Sharon Stone played a beautiful carhop turned movie star from hell in *Irreconcilable Differences*.

Another thankless wife role (opposite Steven Seagal) in *Above the Law*.

Stone has often played the abused wife. In *Action Jackson*, *Coach* star Craig T. Nelson makes love to wife Stone, then shoots her in the head.

Stone's first big break, as Arnold Schwarzenegger's murderous wife, in *Total Recall*.

Stone abandoned her sex-kitten image to play an uptight architect in *Intersection*.

Twenty years ago, Stone said her biggest dream was to hold her own against Robert De Niro. In *Casino,* she did.

Stone was ecstatic at the Golden Globe Awards, which named her Best Actress for *Casino.*

William Baldwin warms up Stone's frigid character in *Sliver.* The stars reportedly loathed each other when the cameras weren't rolling.

Sharon Stone, woman of a thousand faces,
is incapable of taking a bad picture.

5

Love and Career on the Rocks

WHILE COSTARRING WITH ROCK HUDSON in the 1984 TV-movie *The Vegas Strip Wars,* Stone fell in love with the producer, Michael Greenburg. A year later, they were married. The movie didn't burnish her resumé, but it introduced her to the love of her life. She said, "I met my husband on that movie....It was a special time for me." Hudson took a fatherly interest in the insecure blonde and volunteered to be the godfather of the children the producer and his discovery never had. Stone adored Hudson. "We became very good friends," she recalled eight years after his headline-making death from AIDS. "I think Rock was an extraordinarily brave and generous man."

When Greenburg was tapped to produce two African adventures expected to do Spielberg-size business, he naturally thought of typecasting his wife as the beautiful blond bombshell in the films.

Big mistake.

The bust-up of the marriage left Stone desolate, and she seriously blamed it on the Curse. "I'm sorry about the divorce.

You learn a lot of things when you grow up, but no one teaches you about marriage or intimacy. So once you get into it you don't have a clue what you're doing. I think I got on my husband's nerves. Michael didn't have any sisters, and I think it was really hard for him to understand that premenstrual syndrome didn't mean I hated him."

Stone may not be liberated, but she is very self-aware. Fear of intimacy has plagued the actress all her adult life. Journalists note than none of her relationships with men has ever lasted more than three years. Her marriage to the love of her life didn't make it past twenty-two months.

Generously, Stone blames herself entirely. "*I* messed up! I saw him recently and thought, Boy! I can't believe I let him get away!"

At least her husband had a sense of humor about these menses-induced tantrums. Stone recalled, "My ex-husband used to say I was a combination of Zsa Zsa Gabor and Arnold Schwarzenegger. I think he was right." Although Stone never slapped a Beverly Hills cop, she did beat the shit out of Arnold—but only after he told her to. That dustup, though, was several films down the line.

The breakup clearly traumatized the actress. She went into therapy after the divorce. The relationship remains an unhealed wound. "I would lay awake at night and watch him sleep. I wonder how many heartbreaks a heart can hold. Mine's like a tightly closed little clamshell," she said.

One wonders whether Stone enjoyed the irony of the reason listed in their 1987 divorce decree for the split, "irreconcilable differences." Her biggest hit up to that time would also describe the biggest heartbreak of her life.

Divorce made her gun-shy, if not paranoid, about getting involved with men. Her relationships to this day tend to be short and the breakup acrimonious rather than amicable. One ex was publicly called a "dirt sandwich," while she implied that a fiancé was a parasite trading on her name and influence with no career of his own. One gave as good as he got. Hart Bochner, her on-and-off tube lover in *War and Remembrance,* said, "She's the Antichrist." But two other beaux, both more than ten years her junior, brought out the mother in her, and they have remained friends even after they stopped being lovers.

Friendship is easy; intimacy is nearly impossible for the emotionally aloof actress. By her own admission, Stone loves 'em and leaves 'em within three years. Psychologists call it fear of intimacy. They describe intimacy as a process in a relationship where the partners reveal themselves to each other, deeply and thoroughly. For intimacy to grow, the participants need "propinquity, i.e., nearness, trust, respect, safety, sharing, empathy and compassion," says Dr. Brian Miller. Disappearing to faraway movie locations is a recipe for disaster and fuels fear of intimacy. Dr. Miller didn't know of Stone's three-year statute of limitations or that her father was a stern taskmaster who doled out praise grudgingly, but he says that they represent cause and effect. Short-term relationships show "a major fear of intimacy," Dr. Miller says.

For heterosexuals, the main identification is with the parent of the opposite sex. "Since her dad was such a taskmaster, that could impair [her adult relationships]. If she didn't feel safe with him or that he respected her autonomy or that he lacked compassion or empathy for her, all those could cause fear of intimacy. Or that she couldn't trust him to be pleased even if she did a great job; there's always more to do. Kids who grow up with perfectionist parents have real problems of insecurity because they never feel good enough. We're human, and we never reach perfection. Perfection is an impossible expectation." Stone has made perfectionism work brilliantly for her career, which consisted of twelve years of rejection before *Basic Instinct* proved that perfectionism is a great job skill, although it's hell on interpersonal relationships. The need to top herself continues, as she picks unglamorous roles that trash her typecasting as blond bombshell. Or stretches herself by writing obscure South American fables.

Stone has also spoken of the "euphoria" she feel in relationships, both romantic and platonic. Euphoria may be great for one-night stands, but it's disastrous for long-term couplings. You just can't get it up all the time. Serenity, not ecstasy, is the crucial ingredient for durability. "You can't be too ecstatic or intense.

The relationship comes to be more about fire than feeling trust. Intimacy thrives on gradual growth. It thrives on continuity. If you think the person is going to up and leave tomorrow, you won't develop any intimacy with them. You have to trust that they will be there tomorrow and the next day and the next..." Dr. Miller says.

One of the common strategies for avoiding intimacy sounds like a chapter in the *Sharon Stone Story*. Choosing emotionally unavailable partners is typical. Dr. Miller offers examples like married men (Stone's short term liaison with married producer Bill MacDonald, chapter 12) or people of another sexual orientation (Mrs. Rothenburg felt certain that the nurse Stone was aggressing in the restroom was straight).

The actress often says she does nothing more strenuous than falling in love to maintain her dazzling shape, which is a typical put-down of herself. She pumped serious iron and learned Tae Kwon Do to beat up Arnold on the set of *Total Recall*. Perhaps tutored by her bodyguard, Kristin, a black belt in karate, she daily attacks a punching bag in her garage. She may not maintain her figure by falling in love, but she's implied it's helped her career a lot.

Actor Richard E. Grant gave credence to that theory in a diary he kept while in Rome shooting one of the worst films of all time, *Hudson Hawk*. While on location in the Eternal City, he bumped into his young old friend Stone. Grant had the temerity to ask her if she had ever slept with Joel Silver, the morbidly obese producer of *Hudson Hawk,* as she clawed her way to the middle. After all, he did cast her in 1988's *Action Jackson*. Instead of inflicting on Grant a well-deserved sample of her karate lessons, she teased him by saying that "she likes a cuddly producer," the actor wrote in his diary, excerpted in *Vanity Fair*.

Stone enjoyed a satisfying revenge on the cheeky Grant. The next day on the set, Silver had obviously talked to Stone, because he asked the quaking Grant, "Come in, come in. So I hear you were asking what it's like *to fuck a fat old Jew*."

Stone's involvement with Michael Greenburg, the producer who hired her for *King Solomon's Mines* and the sequel, tempts the cynical to suspect that the casting couch may have been in play. In the 1970s the London magazine *Time Out* circumspectly reported that she lived high on the hog and drove a chocolate-brown Mercedes with no "visible means of support."

The august *Sunday Times* (London), which has published Dickens and Shaw during its two hundred years in print, was less circumspect. "There have long been rumors about her sex life, and the role it has played in getting her to the top of her profession." The *Times's* temerity is especially noteworthy, since the libel laws in the United Kingdom are much more draconian than in the land of the First Amendment. A mendacious reporter can literally go to jail for saying Elizabeth Taylor runs a tab at Winchell's. Stone has the hide of an elephant and laughs at such stories, which she pins to a heart-shaped bulletin board she's nicknamed "Cupid." If the myths are fact, "Messalina" would be a more appropriate reference to classical antiquity.

Regardless of the casting-couch lore, in the case of Greenburg you get the feeling that Stone would have loved him if he had been a production assistant instead of the producer of her first dubious break. In fact, one of her boyfriends was just that, a gofer who went for Stone big time, driving her limousine to the set of *The Quick and the Dead* each day.

Nineteen eighty-seven, the year *Allan Quatermain* imploded and the divorce from the love of her life became final, didn't seem as though it could get any worse.

It did.

Stone apparently didn't get any cash out of the divorce settlement. She must have needed to pay the rent. How else can you explain her self-sabotage by appearing in the toxic *Police Academy 4: Citizens on Patrol*? Stone unraveled the mystery with a simple explanation: "I really needed a job, and I really needed a break."

Police Academy 4 was not the kind of movie designed to give anyone a break except studio stockholders. The savvy actress, however, explained that there are breaks and there are breaks when she said, *"Police Academy 4* changed me tremendously— for the good, really for the good. I worked with twelve stand-up comedians every day. Not actors but stand-up comedians. You've no idea what a joy it is."

Stars who want to be taken seriously rarely pop up in sequels, especially when they didn't appear in the original, unless they're being offered $25 million for six weeks of work in a Roman-numeraled rip-off like *Batman* and to put it kindly, the *Police Academy* oeuvre was no *Batman*. It wasn't even *Die Hard* or *Lethal Weapon* or other cash cows attached to numbers from ancient Rome.

Worse, after a breakthrough performance as the fourth lead in *Irreconcilable Differences* and the female lead in two big-budget movies in Africa, Stone insanely picked a comedy that makes Jim Carrey look as though he belongs on Arthur Schnitzler's list. Her billing was a cavernous sixth. Even that great screen actor Bubba Smith ranked higher up on the food chain.

The running gag, in both senses of the word, in the *Police Academy* clones revolved around misfits in training for the force. The first three installments had exhausted the losers who could conceivably pass the rookie physical. For number four, the screenwriters came up with the idea of a citizen volunteer patrol so anybody could appear in the comedy. And we do mean anybody.

Stone played a volunteer named Claire Mattson. Her performance isn't mentioned in any of the reviews, which could have all been composed by Pauline Kael.

Daily Variety: "The boobs in blue are back and *Police Academy 4* carries the banner of tasteless humor raised in the first three installments to new heights of insipidness....Although there is the usual assortment of food jokes, farts and pratfalls, this is basically material that has run out of steam."

Number four had also fallen off the gravy train. Another nail in the coffin of Stone's career, this incarnation of *Police Academy* had the distinction of being the first in the vastly successful series *not* to show a profit. It earned even less than its $13 million budget but cost more than its successful predecessors.

If there was any consolation for Stone, it was that the film did better overseas. She was big in Barcelona and Beirut. The producer of the series, Paul Maslansky, showed himself a master of understatement and dimness when he told the *New York Times,* "It's hard to understand why [the films did better abroad]. Maybe because the jokes are fast, like in situation comedies and clearly unintellectual, so you don't need to understand the references or American culture to get them."

Maslansky did not understand the nature of national humor. Like fine wine, comedy doesn't travel well. If you've ever seen Benny Hill or Marcel Marceau perform, it's clear that comedy loses something in translation, even from the Cockney. Action films know no national borders, since the dialogue typically contains the universal Esperanto of bang, bang, you're dead—all ten-thousand of you. That's why Jean-Claude Van Damme's films keep getting made, even though they flop on this side of the ocean. Across the pond, Van Damme's cigar-store Belgian is as big as Arnold's Austrian oak. Even *Sliver,* Stone's 1993 stinker, for reasons best left to film historians and dirty old men in raincoats, also lit up European screens while flaming out in the States. And *Sliver* wasn't even an action film, unless you count Stone's solitary sexual gymnastics in the bathtub.

To paraphrase Talleyrand's famous quote about his boss Napoleon, If *Police Academy 4* hadn't existed, the studio would have had to invent it. The commercial imperative amounted to manifest destiny. The first three films, however dim, grossed a glow-in-the-dark $380 million worldwide. That's *Lethal Weapon* business at a fraction of the cost. The story lines, however, kept getting *Dumb and Dumber,* without doing that movie's business. The *New York Times* said, "Each *Police Academy* film seems to shoot for a younger crowd. No. 4 is designed for a 10-year-old boy."

Despite the poor box office of the fourth installment, numbers five through seven have followed. Maybe the target audience for the follow-ups was even younger than ten-year-olds, although embryos don't seem a viable demographic.

If Stone had any delusions that starring in a hit would compensate for the failure of her Out of Africa act, she was disappointed. *Police Academy 4* was not what you would call a

"Sharon Stone" movie. In the caption for the photo of her and the star accompanying the *Los Angeles Daily News* review, she isn't even identified by name. At least in the body of the review it says, "Sharon Stone and Steven Guttenberg have more on their minds than just working together in *Police Academy 4*." Maybe their thoughts were occupied with finding day jobs.

The one-sheets for the movie didn't pump up her public profile, either. A cheesy illustration in ads for the film show all the misfits crammed into a hot-air balloon, like a fraternity outing in a telephone booth. A blonde, who looks nothing like Stone, practically falls out of the balloon, and the unbuttoned police shirt exposes more flesh than the real Stone has.

It's unkind but not inaccurate to say that the actress's film choices made her look like the Raquel Welch of the 1980s, a bad joke whose punchline always involved T & A (tits and ass). *Rolling Stone* was even crueler: "Largely, her oeuvre swims in the bowels of cable, where she can be seen as the blonde in *Action Jackson, Police Academy 4, King Solomon's Mines,* and *Allan Quatermain and the Lost City of Gold*."

Superstars who hit a bad patch like to chalk it up to a business they insist is "cyclical." Hence, Arnold's *Last Action Hero,* Travolta's talking baby movies, Willis's *Hudson Hawk,* Stallone's *Stop! Or My Mom Will Shoot,* and Burt Reynolds's cycle, which seems on permanent pause at the bottom. Stone's cycle was in Reynolds land, except that she had never enjoyed his five years at the top in the late 1970s. Sadly, *Police Academy 4* was actually the zenith of a seven-film, five-year nadir. She could have sung the Bessie Smith lament "I've been down so long it looks like up." Or as she herself sadly realized at the end of the decade of greed: "My career was going nowhere."

The descent would continue with *Cold Steel, Above the Law, Action Jackson* (three in one year, 1988!), *Personal Choice,* and *Blood and Sand* (1989). Five films in only two years suggests a certain desperation that made her throw aesthetic caution to the winds.

How else do you explain her acceptance of what amounted to a bit part in *Above the Law*?

The chop-sockey turkey marked the debut of, in *Spy* magazine's term, "paranoid" movie star Steven Seagal. *Above the Law* also represented the middle of the end of Stone's free fall. Almost as bad as being billed after Bubba was playing third fiddle here to Pam Grier, who was making a brief comeback after involuntary retirement as a dominatrix in the regrettable blaxploitation movies of the 1970s.

The Ur-WASP Seagal is miscast as Nick Toscani, a black-belt cop of Italian extraction who decides to play Charles Bronson with the coke dealers littering his neighborhood corner in Chicago's Little Italy. Stone, who played a lot of wives before picking up an ice pick, is Mrs. Toscani here.

Although *Daily Variety*'s reviewer did the courtesy of mentioning her by name and bit part, his praise underlined the short duration of her screen time. "Quiet moments like the one with Seagal and his emotional wife [Sharon Stone as Sara Toscani] comprise about one percent of the film."

The *Hollywood Reporter*'s critic had a good time in spite of himself—and at Stone's expense. "Script does offer a few unintentional laughs, however, with Seagal's wife Sharon Stone grousing about early morning phone calls from CIA agents."

The *New York Times* was already prepping its annual Ten Ickiest List: "Come the end of the year, *Above the Law* may well rank among the top three to four goofiest bad movies of 1988."

L.A. Weekly didn't even bother to mention Stone, but it damned Seagal's debut with faint praise: "*Above the Law* newcomer, Steven Seagal, comes off pretty well in this relentlessly stupid but thoroughly enjoyable rehash of every cop thriller ever made. Seagal is an intimidating and slightly greasy cross between Richard Nixon and Robert De Niro doing a Clint Eastwood imitation."

During this downtime on-screen, Stone alternated between down in the dumps and self-mocking stoicism. Although *Above the Law* made it into the pages of *Golden Turkeys: the Worst Films of All Time,* she good-naturedly agreed to write the introduction to the coffee-table book, presumably as an authority on the genre. She quipped in the foreword, "A good movie is one that allows you simply to escape within it. And then there are movies that make you simply want to escape."

In more introspective moments of despair, she would say of her ten years in Hollywood and the fifteen movies, mostly B through F, which she made during her time there, "I was like a big mannequin, a prop. I felt so compressed. It was excruciating. I often got really sick in the middle of a production, yet I went on because I was paying my dues, trying to be a good girl, trying to do the right thing."

Her despair sounds paralyzing. She described years doing "stupid B movie after B movie, where women were on drugs or alcohol or insane. After a certain point I became complacent. I had a job, worked regularly, did three pictures a year, I traveled, bought a house. It wasn't my dream. Okay but then I went, 'I HATE MY LIFE! I HATE IT!'"

Her support group failed to be supportive. During these days of wine and neuroses, she called her agent and sobbed: "I just sometimes don't know if it's all worth it and if I should go on." Her then agent reinforced her feelings of failure and said, "It's not. It isn't worth it. You shouldn't go on." This verbal slap in the face turned the whiner into a winner. "I got off the phone and I said, 'She's such a baby! I'll show her.' I think she thought I was a bimbo probably."

Stone's perseverance in the face of stupidity shows why some starlets become stars and others end up selling Beverly Hills real estate or marrying plastic surgeons. If another struggling actor had taken his idiot agent's advice to get the hell out of Hollywood, moviegoers would have been deprived of brilliant performances in *Chinatown* and *One Flew Over the Cuckoo's Nest*. When Jack Nicholson won his first of two Oscars for the latter, he couldn't resist saying in his acceptance speech, "My agent once told me I had no future in this business and to try another line of work." Stone did a "Jack Nicholson" and ignored her agent's advice to quit showbiz. Instead of selling real estate or retiring in the arms of a multimillionaire, she carved out a film career that briefly made her the hottest actress in Hollywood.

Stone's unhappiness was understandable, although *Rolling*

Stone was too harsh in writing off the entire decade. Woody Allen at the beginning of her career wasn't exactly slumming, and mid-decade *Irreconcilable Differences* was a personal showcase. Still, the magazine insisted on calling these ten years of lost weekends "a decade of a blighted career of bad moves and worse movies."

The magazine was at least right about her films at the very end of the 1980s. They would require an infrared sensor attached to rose-colored glasses to see the light at the end of this tunnel to infinity. Only a dead end appeared visible to the naked eye.

In *Rolling Stone's* unkind phrase, her films in the late 1980s did indeed swim in the "bowels of cable," but at least the cable and video distributors were willing to buy. It seems almost cruel to describe in painful detail Stone's filmography during this period, but a film historian's gotta do what a film historian's gotta do. And the girl had to pay the rent.

Maybe she should have moved to a cheaper place so she wouldn't have had to endure *Action Jackson, Cold Steel, Personal Choice,* and *Blood and Sand*. Not to mention a day trip back to TV, typecast as a wife (slut division) in the miniseries *War and Remembrance*.

In 1988, *Action Jackson* was a screen atavism, a blaxploitation movie, a genre that had supposedly been put out of its misery by bad box office and good taste more than a decade earlier.

The ludicrous plot cast Carl Weathers as a Harvard Law School graduate who decides to become a Detroit cop. Poor Sharon is listed third in the credits, after Vanity, whose biggest credit derives from the Artist Formerly Known as Prince, whom Vanity formerly *shtupped*.

Once again, Stone is playing the wife, although this time she's many rungs up the socioeconomic ladder as the spouse of an evil auto manufacturer, played by future *Coach* Craig T. Nelson. And instead of slut typecasting, a review describes her as "Nelson's naive but well-intentioned wife."

Her role in the box-office failure was so inconsequential, the usually fastidious *Daily Variety* reviewer didn't even mention her. Its competitor, the *Hollywood Reporter,* couldn't resist commenting on what at this time seemed to be her only asset, drop-dead good looks. "Nelson has Vanity for a girlfriend and a dazzler of a wife, Sharon Stone."

Stone was also starting to become the Mr. Bill of movie wives. As in the upcoming *Total Recall,* her husband in *Action Jackson* offs his wife. "Auto magnate Peter Dellaplane [Nelson] is modeled vaguely on John Delorean. He's so bad, he can kiss his wife passionately and shoot her in the heart at the same moment," the *Los Angeles Herald-Examiner* wrote, describing the first of four trashed wives she would play. (In addition to *Total Recall,* where she suffered the ultimate in wife battering, *Intersection* would subject her to an unfaithful husband and *Casino* to spousal abuse.)

Ironically, on camera Nelson played the ultimate batterer, O. J. Simpson with a gun instead of cutlery. Off camera, Stone adored her costar. "When you're making *Action Jackson,* you know what you're making," she said with resignation. "But it's awfully nice to be making it with someone who's so sweet. Thank God for Craig T. Nelson. He's such a dear, wonderful man."

When a *Playboy* interviewer immediately followed that statement with a question about another costar, Steven Seagal, Stone didn't use adjectives like "dear or wonderful." In fact, she refused to use any adjectives at all. When Seagal's wife filed for divorce, according to both *Buzz* and *Spy* magazines, she listed battery rather than the usual "irreconcilable differences." That may partially explain why Stone said of their collaboration on *Above the Law,* "I will refrain from comment."

The *Hollywood Reporter* called *Action Jackson* "a throwback to blaxploitation films" and accurately predicted "some early b.o. muscle with black audiences, but its cartoon-like plotline should trip it up fast."

Also made that year, *Cold Steel* was purely rent money. It had the eerie coincidence of starring Stone's second leading man, Brad Davis, to die of AIDS, Rock Hudson being the first.

The creepy plot is paint-by-numbers Bronson. Brad Davis is a cop whose father is gunned down by the mob. Davis is mad as hell, and he's not going to take prisoners anymore. Stone, who is truly paying her dues big time in this ultraviolent role, at least doesn't have to play a sympathetic wife. Here she's a girl who picks Davis up in a bar. She has murder, not sex, on her mind— Davis's. It's so obvious to the viewers, but not the cop, that Stone is in cahoots with the bad guys, *Daily Variety* said, "It takes Davis much longer to figure this out than it would take an average third grader." *Cold Steel* swam straight to the bowels of video. The villain alone was off-putting enough to make eight-year-olds and everybody else rush out of the theater, or more likely, push the EJECT button on the VCR. *Daily Variety* described Freddy Krueger's uglier sibling: "As in any good, cheapie cop story, the villain is deformed. This time his face has been carved up and his voice amplified electrically through a hole in his throat."

By now, the luckless starlet wasn't just paying her dues, she was being aesthetically mugged.

An interesting trivia note—actually two. This ultraviolent, misogynist mess was directed by a woman who should have known better. Dorothy Puzo, making her directorial debut, demonstrated that she was truly a Daddy's girl with none of Daddy's talent, Daddy being Mario Puzo of *The Godfather* trilogy.

Perhaps for a breath of fresher air, Stone made another quick pit stop on television, with a microcameo in the maxiseries *War and Remembrance*. Typecast yet again in the role of housewife as slattern, she plays Janice Henry, Robert Mitchum's daughter-in-law, who's getting it on with her husband's best friend while he's fighting future Honda makers in the South Pacific. Stone's one-note performance in a one-note characterization is painful to watch, the discomfort only alleviated by its brevity.

For her next film, the actress may have felt as though she were still working on TV when she read the Cannes-datelined review in *Daily Variety* of *Personal Choice* in 1989: "Sappy, heavy-handed message picture aimed at theaters but too weak to qualify as even a made for TV feature."

In fact, *Personal Choice* may be the ultimate disease-of-the-week movie transferred to a screen too big for its britches. Ancient for the role at forty-nine, Martin Sheen plays an astronaut who's been to the moon and finds life on earth a depressing anticlimax. It was loosely based on Buzz Aldrin's real-life bouts with alcohol and anomie post-Apollo. Sheen's ailments, however, go beyond clinical depression and self-medication. It turns out he was exposed to fatal radiation poisoning during his moon walk.

Stone keeps swimming deeper in those video intestines in this film as the girlfriend of a minor character whose son (Christian Slater) idolizes Sheen. *Daily Variety*'s announcement of the starting date, August 4, 1988, mentioned the three male leads but not Stone. When production wrapped, the *Hollywood Reporter* referred to a girlfriend in the film, *The Wonder Years*'s Olivia D'Abo, but not the other girlfriend, Stone.

Personal Choice did earn some press for the actress. All she had to do was materialize and light up the screen to get the libidinous attention of *Variety*'s priapic critic, who uses this throwaway phrase of praise: "the presence of beautiful leading ladies [Olivia D'Abo and Sharon Stone]."

To describe Stone's psychological evolution at this time, it's practically necessary to key-word search an electronic thesaurus. A misogynist is a man who hates women. Today our obsession with political correctness revels in male bashing, so the female counterpart is almost never mentioned.

You won't find this word in your pocket dictionary; you will find it in the *Webster's 3rd New International Dictionary*: *misandry*. If Stone was becoming a misandrist at this time, it's entirely understandable. Reviewers relentlessly treated her like a piece of meat, directors carved her up, and Hollywood spit her out in one turkey after another in ever-shrinking parts. If she began to hate the male-dominated movie industry and a handful of sexist film critics, she had cause to. Unfortunately, as she slowly crawled her way to the top and her treatment was less and less meaty, she didn't leave her misandry behind. In fact, the more powerful she became, the less enchanting she found men.

Interviews from this period reflect an intriguing duality. Female reporters would be allowed to put Stone on the couch and learn her most intimate secrets. She even invited an interviewer from *Mirabella* magazine to borrow one of her many shotguns to feel the rush of plugging iron. Male reporters got the cold shoulder, the bum's rush, and their negative reportage contributed to her growing image in the press as bitch-goddess, although the star's setside antics were also big contributors to the Sharon Stone Offense Fund.

For her next picture and a starring role, Stone had to flee the States. *Blood and Sand* (*Sangre y Arena*) in 1989 was the third version of the story of a boy and his bull. The 1922 original made Valentino's career; the 1941 remake showed how little sexual chemistry there was between the bisexual Tyrone Power and the omnivorous Rita Hayworth. The 1989 incarnation wouldn't show anything except Stone's desperation to work.

Blood and Sand was one of those films studio flacks like to describe as "years in the making," but in this case it had nothing to do with the fastidiousness of the filmmakers and everything to do with the lack of financing. Shooting began in 1984, with an alleged budget of $16 million. Later reports in the trades showed an incredible shrinking budget, from $16 million to $6 million to a then-bargain-basement TV movie's $3 million. It apparently took the moneymen five years to find the money, because *Blood and Sand* wasn't released until 1989.

Producer José Frade trumpeted in *Variety* that his *Blood and Sand* was "the first truly Spanish film version of Vincente [*sic*] Blasco Ibañez's famous novel." *Variety's* reviewer riposted, "Frade's claim turns out to be empty. His picture is about as Spanish as Coke spiked with Fundador brandy."

Frade had been hustling his project since 1978, when he placed his first advertisement in the trades. Frequently, a putative film's budget consists of nothing more than the cost of a splashy ad. The producer hopes it will attract real investors and maybe even a star. Frade's advertising gimmicks didn't pay off until 1984, when the film finally went into production, only to stall once again until shooting resumed in 1988.

It didn't help that this "truly Spanish film version" was shot in English with a largely American cast. Stone is grotesquely miscast as a Spanish aristocrat, Donna Sol, a role that a half-Spanish Rita Hayworth was unable to portray convincingly half a century earlier. The filmmakers didn't even bother to dye Stone's trademark blond curls black. A photo of her in the film makes her look about as Hispanic as Goldie Hawn. The hero, a British actor, also a blond, named Christopher Rydell, wasn't so lucky. His WASP features peer out from under the worst dye job since Redford turned brown for *The Great Gatsby*.

Bloodthirsty *Variety* damned the movie for its bloodless bullfighting. The budget couldn't afford to kill a real bull, and the filmmakers apparently had never heard of stock footage. Said the paper, "The bullfighting shown is cleansed of all blood except that shed by a couple of humans. The mortal (deadly) *espada* in the bull's neck at the moment of truth is never seen." So who's complaining? People for the Ethical Treatment of Animals must have given it two thumbs up, even if Siskel and Ebert pointed in the opposite direction.

The ad line proclaimed, "Bullfighting is his passion. She is his obsession." *Variety* said, "This blood and sand is, sad to say, pure bull," complaining that the sex scenes between the principals were too brief and G rated. *Variety's* complaint doesn't make sense. It also criticized Stone for being fat. Who wants to see Roseanne in the buff—except possibly chubby chasers?

Lack of money was not the only thing that caused production delays and turned the project into a five-year ordeal. In October 1988 shooting halted for a week while Rydell recovered from an appendectomy. At least he must have known how those poor bulls felt when they suffered the *espada* that the production mercifully couldn't afford to film.

Blood and Sand is noteworthy only because it marks the beginning of Stone's screen persona as rich bitch. The Andalusian aristocrat (by way of Meadville) cruelly dumps her *torero,* who takes to drinking and cowardly avoids his bread and butter, *torros. Blood and Sand* may be the only film ever to dramatize the pathology of *torro*phobia. There's a real howler where the half-crocked matador fights a bull in the moonlight—the only condition in which he can get it up to get it on with his half-ton phobia. And neither of them is wearing any clothes. When it comes to treating talent like lunch meat, sometimes the movie industry can be an equal-opportunity destroyer.

A stunt double's close encounters with a ticked-off bull

provided the only comic relief during a dreary shoot. One scene called for the double, Juan Herrere, to leap into the ring and "pretend" to be gored by a thousand-pound bull furious for being turned into a living pincushion—spiked off camera, of course, due to the budget deficit. When Herrere didn't get up after the director yelled cut, witnesses feared that the special effect may have turned real and deadly. According to the trades, Herrere was rushed to the bull infirmary (a hospital for bulls meant for slaughter!). There the doctor said that the stuntman hadn't been gored; he had collapsed from shock! One hopes the medic gave the man an outpatient prescription: Never go jogging with the bull's cousins in Pamplona. Word gets around about wusses.

Variety paid the actress a left-handed compliment even though it found her performance and her physique lacking. "Stone appears to be not much more than a pudgy-faced teenager with a body that one might say strips well." However sexist, the reviewer at least wasn't ageist, since Stone was a nonadolescent thirty-one at the time!

6

The Big Time, Temporarily

FOR THE DESPAIRING STARLET, 1990 was a case of good news/godawful news/weird news. Stone would enjoy a big career break, if not a career-making role, in an A-list movie. But she would also come close to getting killed. The career break would be followed by broken ribs, a shattered collarbone, and a concussion after a head-on collision on Sunset Boulevard in a red-light district of Hollywood. Plus she would make the dubious decision to do a spread for *Playboy,* a move not designed to unload her bimbo baggage.

Until he gave her her big break in 1990's *Total Recall,* director Paul Verhoeven described exactly what had been wrong with Stone's film work up to that point. "I thought she had been degraded in her career, fallen into the hands of people who abused her like a bimbo." This from the auteur of *Showgirls* who ordered actress Elizabeth Berkley to dry-hump Kyle McLachlan's leg, doggie style, in the back room of a strip joint! Verhoeven also felt that "she had lost her confidence. But what I saw with her in *Total Recall* was that there was much more possible."

Stone had been trying to tell Hollywood this for years, but she kept getting typecast in blond hell.

In *Total Recall,* Stone's Lori is hellish, but she's no bimbette. Arnold Schwarzenegger plays a construction worker in the year 2075. The little woman, Stone, is described in the press notes as "his dream wife, a Doris Day of the 21st century." She turns out to be more like *Basic Instinct's* Catherine Tramell of the new millennium. But before you start thinking, Oh, no, not another wife role, Stone plays anything but a futuristic Doris Day clone. More like Barbarella with an attitude.

One of the ingenious plot twists reveals that Stone is a government operative who's been assigned to play the role of Schwarzenegger's wife. The big guy used to be a bad guy, an intelligence agent from Mars working for the same evil people who employ Stone. His memory, however, has been erased and replaced with a happy home life in blue-collar-ville—a twenty-first-century Meadville.

Based on Philip K. Dick's 1966 short story, "We Can Remember It for You Wholesale," the troubled script went through sixty-two (!) drafts and three studios before Arnold's enthusiasm had a drooling studio head writing a check with the amount left blank.

The first draft was such a mess that it literally had no third act. At the end of the draft written by Ronald Shusett and Dan O'Bannon, both red-hot after their film *Alien,* the script simply read: "The loose ends will be tied together and the rest of the film will work perfectly." Bet *Waterworld* had a similar coda.

Disney originally optioned what would evolve into a hypersexual, hyperviolent R-rated film, then let the option run out when it realized that six-breasted mutants would not feel at home with Snow White.

Rafaelle De Laurentiis, daughter of Dino, an upscale version of Golan/Globus, fell in love with the uncompleted script and begged Daddy to make her baby. He refused unless a big star was attached. The biggest action star the out-of-her-depth De Laurentiis could find was Richard Dreyfuss, Everynerd. Rafaelle De Laurentiis said delicately that the casting "meant tailoring the script to his personality" and endomorphic body.

M-G-M agreed to finance and distribute De Laurentiis's project, but Dad decided to put his two cents in and take a lot of money out. Dino's cost cutting crazily involved excising the entire second act, the riveting trip to Mars. Now they had a script without a third *or* second act. A disillusioned Shusett moaned that Dino De Laurentiis told him, "Make it action-oriented like *Rambo,* go to a foreign country, kill a lot of people." Shusett providently had had it written into his contract that Mars stayed in the script.

De Laurentiis wasn't about to let a little thing like an ironclad contract get in his way, but he finally relented after A-list director Bruce Beresford (*Driving Miss Daisy*) told the mogul that it was the best script he had ever read. In 1983, seven long years before it finally saw the dark of theaters, *American Film* magazine hailed *Total Recall* as one of the ten greatest unproduced screenplays in Hollywood.

De Laurentiis should have been suspicious, however, when Beresford failed to volunteer to direct the greatest screenplay of all time. But he heeded the classy director's advice. Mars went back into the picture.

Even so, Shusett departed. The *Alien*ated writer just couldn't put up with the philistine from Naples. The director attached to the project, David Cronenberg (*The Fly*), also buzzed off, taking the star with him. Now De Laurentiis didn't have a star, a director, a writer, or two acts of the greatest screenplay Bruce Beresford ever read.

Patrick Swayze, post–*Dirty Dancing,* pre-*Ghost,* signed on and made the project viable, but fate and fiduciary calamity intervened. De Laurentiis's production company went belly-up in 1988. Millions already spent in Australia went down the drain as the mammoth sets were struck.

Arnold Schwarzenegger saw his opening, and he quickly closed it. Four years earlier, Arnold, one of the savviest script readers in Hollywood, had fallen in love with the property and told his *Terminator* producer, Carolco, to buy the script. "I don't care how much it costs," Schwarzenegger told Carolco chief Mario Kassar. Carolco rolled over and played banker, hiring an even hotter director than Cronenberg, Paul Verhoeven, scorching after his sleeper hit *Robocop*. Flush with cash from that hit and

The Terminator, Carolco also had a bigger wallet than De Laurentiis, putting up $70 million, Arnold's biggest budget to date. Carolco's largesse wasn't as crazy as Universal's Japanese philanthropy toward Kevin Costner and *Waterworld.* On the strength of the former Mr. Universe's name alone, the production company was able to meet the cost of the film before a single ticket was sold by preselling foreign rights worldwide. In the States, Schwarzenegger may be a steroid-bloated joke, Hans and Franz without *Saturday Night's* live laugh track. In Europe, though, he's considered the auteur of *film rouge,* the color of all the blood in his jerk-and-clean school of cinema.

L.A. Weekly got it wrong and had the tail wagging the dog. It was the bicepsual movie star's clout, not his backers, that made things happen: "All it took after a decade of aborted screenplays and frustrated filmmakers from Bruce Beresford to David Cronenberg to get *Total Recall* made was for one man, Mario Kassar, to say 'yes' to Arnold Schwarzenegger," the alternative newspaper said.

Verhoeven was a perfect match for the material. *Total Recall* was even more violent than *Robocop,* and it was as twisted sexually as Verhoeven's European adventures into semisoft porn, like *Turkish Delight* and *Keetje Tippel,* in which the heroine is graphically depicted using a toilet in full view of her family.

It's impossible to underestimate how much career mileage Stone got out of her housewife from hell (and the CIA) in this orgy of high concept, high testosterone. The women in action-adventures are typically as disposable as Kleenex. With the exception of Jane Seymour, not a single Bond girl has had a screen career after slipping under the covers with 007, and they only let Seymour do TV. *Newsweek* said, "James Bond wouldn't last 30 seconds" with Stone.

Total Recall further diluted Stone's potential impact by featuring not one but two female leads, both equal in importance to the plot. But while Stone has become one of the highest-paid actresses in the industry, I'm still trying to find out whatever happened to Rachel Ticotin, her *Total Recall* costar. Ticotin was billed above Stone since the Latina had starred as a junkie nurse in a major film, *Fort Apache, The Bronx,* opposite Paul Newman. Ticotin even got the best line in the movie.

The Latina actress hilariously understates her rival's villainy when she says, "You're such a bitch!" Okay, it's not Restoration Comedy, it's not even *When Harry Met Sally*'s "I'll have what she's having," but it got the biggest laugh in a film filled with memorable one-liners that people repeated at the water cooler at work the next day.

Stone's bons mots were mostly ughs and grunts; as she expressed herself with actions, which in her case did indeed speak louder than Ticotin's words. Stone's duplicitous Doris Day turns out to be more Messalina than Marie Osmond. Her lethal weapons include a knife, guns, and bare hands, which she uses to deliver a karate chop to the jugular of her husband. Oh, and she also tries to neuter Arnold with a kick below the waist.

Stone worked out like a workhorse for a chance at the brass ring. "I told myself I'd better get into training or people would just look at me and say, 'What's that lumpy thing standing next to him?'" Maybe she had read the review that called her fat in *Blood in Sand*. Maybe she looked in the mirror.

At a mere five feet nine inches, she would also be upstaged by Arnold's Olympian height of six feet four inches. For two months, four hours a day, Stone became a female Schwarzenegger, pumping iron, cycling, jogging, sweating through aerobics, and taking daily karate instructions from a black belt in Tae Kwon Do (not Kristin Marshall, her bodyguard.). She also refused the services of a stunt double.

Even Mr. Pumpitude himself found her obsessive-compulsive workout over the top and said, *"Basta."* A man who used to spend six hours a day at World's Gym in Venice after spending twelve hours on a movie set told Stone, "In another year, you'll be a truck driver."

Schwarzenegger lived to regret his barb. In their climactic fight scene, where he delivers his bon mot "Consider this the divorce" before he shoots his wife dead, Stone kicked the strudel out of her costar. In her defense, he asked her to. For once Sharon wasn't just being Sharon, she was following her director and star's orders. He's no De Niro, but Schwarzenegger likes to aspire to Method acting.

Stone, ladylike, kept pulling her punches during their duel. Arnold wanted realism, not coddling. Stone recalled, "Underneath that tough guy, overmuscled physique lies a really sweet guy with a terrific sense of humor. On the set of *Total Recall,* I beat the hell out of Arnold, and he never complained." Future collaborators would not be so forgiving.

"You know, you can fake punches, but slaps have to be real. At one point, the director complained that I was holding back on the slaps, and Arnold said, 'Go ahead, really slug me. I can take it.' And he did," Stone said. This may be a whole new pathology for psychologists to study: celebrity abuse.

Stone revealed more of her misandry; she seemed to drool over spousal abuse. When an interviewer asked what it was like to kick Arnold in the nether regions several times, she said without missing a beat, "It was great. I get a wonderful response from women. They tell their boyfriends, 'I'm gonna do that to you.' Let's be honest: We're all pissed about something." The subtext of her statement could fill a doctoral dissertation: "The Movie Star as Emasculatrix."

Their brawl climaxed with Arnold dispatching his wife. While feminists were enraged, the creator of the film, Verhoeven, also found the scene disturbing, but not because of any feminist sensitivity, which the infamously misogynist director has never developed a taste for.

It was Stone's transformation on camera that scared the director, since he suspected she wasn't acting. Just before Arnold shoots Stone, she tries to make nice, reminding him that although she has tried to kill him, they are still man and wife, after all. Her facial expression changed in a split second from murderous evil to wifely charm in order to stop Arnold from pulling the trigger. Verhoeven watched in horror: "That [transformation] is probably in her character. There are very rare people who can switch so easily from one to the other. It's kind of a frightening switch, actually. I don't know if I liked it because I also felt it was part of her. But as for her acting, I thought it quite amazing."

Stone replied insouciantly when this Dr. Jekyll/Ms. Hyde quote from Verhoeven was repeated to her, "I'm not the Michael Bolton of acting. I take risks."

The actress took a lot of risks and climbed mountains in order to avoid becoming just another Bond girl—here today, married to an industrialist tomorrow. One of those mountains was the Austrian Alp himself.

Male reviewers typically commented on the female lead's physical attributes. Richard Alleva, in the ultraintellectual *Commonweal* magazine, for once dished the male star's body. The critic commiserated with Stone for requiring the stamina of an Alpine mountaineer. "Watching the only bedroom scene in *Total Recall,* which must have received its R rating for violence, not sex, I understood why so many female friends have made disparaging remarks about Arnold Schwarzenegger's body. Arnold's amorous partner, Sharon Stone, seems to be exerting herself less like a passionate lover than like a mountain climber. She seems to be climbing past Schwarzenegger's muscles to get to a lither, more compact man dwelling within the pumped-up Austrian."

Schwarzenegger hinted that Stone wasn't quite the sadistic trouper during their on-screen brawl. Gamely attempting to imitate Stone's Pennsylvania twang, he quoted her as saying between kicks to the groin, "Don't touch my hair....Don't strangle me."

You get the feeling Schwarzenegger did more obnoxious things than impressions of his leading lady. Stone got on like gangbusters with his wife, Maria Shriver, and implied that Arnold behaved himself only when Maria was there to play chaperone. "Maria is lovely to be around. She came to the set quite a few times, and I was glad, because otherwise it was just Arnold and all his knuckleheads. I enjoyed being with him more when Maria was there because it makes him more grounded on a personal level when she's around," Stone said. Translation from the *Don't Dish the Superstar With Clout Book of Etiquette: He's not such a prole when a Kennedy princess is in residence.*

Stone's comments about Mr. and Mrs. Schwarzenegger reflect a recurrent strain in her interpersonal relationships. She simply gets on better with women than men. In a more diplomatic mode, she obeyed the cardinal rule of the up-and-coming: Don't bad-mouth those who are already there. She must have been gagging on her own glucose when she chirped, "Working with Arnold was great. He's a real good sport. Working with Arnold is great [again!] because he's very disciplined. Like a great athlete, he picks his coaches very well and pays attention to them. In this case, the director was the coach."

There were bigger obstacles to overcome than strangulation and bad hair days inflicted by Maria's husband. While Schwarzenegger and Ticotin, as the good girl, got all the good lines, Stone was saddled with double entendres straight out of the nighttime soaps. In the opening scene, Schwarzenegger awakens from a terrifying dream, and Stone is required to say with a leer while unbuttoning her blouse, "Come here, baby. I'll make you forget your nightmares." She paid her dues and climbed her mountain, Schwarzenegger.

Despite its years in development hell, when *Total Recall* finally came out in May 1990, it grossed a whopping $25 million during its opening weekend. Less than two weeks later it had passed the $100 million mark. Whatever you think about his Pillsbury-Doughboy-on-steroids physique, Arnold was proving he could pick hits better than high-paid development executives. Or serious actors like De Niro (*The Fan*).

The critical reaction was, as usual, mixed. Art-house critics wouldn't be caught dead admitting that they enjoyed a popcorn movie like *Total Recall*. (The best example of art-house criticism is the *Chicago Sun-Times*'s Roger Ebert, a one-time Ph.D. candidate at the University of Chicago.) The popcorn critics, who share the public taste, loved the film. (A good example of popcorn criticism is Ebert's doppelgänger, Gene Siskel of the *Chicago Tribune*, a Yale graduate and lover of crass.)

Years after the fact, clips of movie reviews are mostly interesting because of what they say about the times. They have long since stopped serving their primary purpose as consumer guide: Should I go see Movie X this weekend? Let's see what the local film critic has to say.

In 1990 there was a kinder, gentler president in the White House, a man who bombed Iraq back into the Stone Age. Violence during the thousand-points-of-light age was a no-no, to use a term that had *Time* magazine headline a cover story on George Bush "The Wimp."

Daily Variety reflected the zeitgeist, predicting that the film would do big box office, which it did in spades, but condemning it for its violence and misogyny. No matter how icky she was, it was still considered politically incorrect to blow the antiheroine away. *Variety*'s film professor *manqué* couldn't resist showing he had studied art films in graduate school. How else can you explain such a preposterous reference to an obscure (and deadly dull) film by Alain Resnais? "Sylvester Stallone or Chuck Norris, to Schwarzenegger's credit, wouldn't be caught dead in the middle of a paranoiac dream-or-reality game that somehow brings to mind *Last Year at Marienbad*[!]," *Variety*'s Todd McCarthy wrote. Right. And all those explosions in *Die Hard* clones bring to mind Resnais' *Hiroshima, Mon Amour*'s fallout from the atom bomb.

The film, he added, resembled "a *Twilight Zone* episode conceived on an acid trip." Back in film-professor mode, McCarthy couldn't resist another learned reference, however ludicrous. He compared Arnold's *Üubermensch* to Nietzsche's superman and the potboiler *Total Recall* to a Leni Riefenstahl film. Gag me with a jackboot.

As usual, Stone got short shrift from the trade, with the emphasis once again on her physical allure. *Variety* described her character as the "sexy but treacherous wife supplied by the dictator of Mars to keep [Schwarzenegger] under submission."

The *Hollywood Reporter* critic was also sexually famished, but he at least took time out from salivating to comment on her performance. The *Reporter* is notorious for paying its reporters church-mouse salaries, and the ham-fisted style of the reviewer showed he was worth every penny he wasn't paid. "As [Arnold's] knockout wife, Stone is enticing as his duplicitous wife, exhibiting some nifty martial arts moves, among others." Stone broke her hand during training for *Total Recall,* but maybe it wasn't quite the painful disaster it must have seemed at the time. At least it got one critic to focus on another part of her anatomy.

Newsweek's Jack Kroll showed he should be a casting director at a major studio instead of what he is, the greatest stylist among American film critics today. He presciently uncovered a star in the making while other critics were content to merely drool over an obscure starlet: "Stone, a beauty of Basinger-Pfeiffer caliber, seduces Arnold with sizzling efficiency and battles him like a futuristic Amazon in the ultimate body-to-body combat. James Bond wouldn't last 30 seconds with her!"

The benzoyl peroxide crowd also fell in love with Stone. UCLA's *Daily Bruin* reviewer, Michael Mordler, proved he was a film historian and should be rewarded with a casting job at M-G-M after graduation when he predicted, Kroll-like, "Stone has been around for years in supporting roles, but is known mostly for playing Schwarzenegger's deceptive wife in *Total Recall*. She's talented and has an exciting, unpredictable quality on screen, and there's more to her than is being shown. The actress has more than an outside chance of becoming a bona fide movie star." This acne-age review appeared in the November 1, 1991, edition of the *Bruin*. Only two months later, with the release of *Basic Instinct*, in January 1992, the college journalist's heavy breathing turned out to be psychic.

The all-important *Los Angeles Times*, the unofficial organ of the movie industry, also gave Stone its imprimatur on her star potential. Michael Wilmington wrote, "There are heroines too, but Rachel Ticotin's brunette rebel registers less strongly than Sharon Stone's ambiguous blond slut-wife." At last, Stone was moving out of her rut as the Rodney Dangerfield of starlets. On the other hand, New York's *David Denby*, the Al Capone of film criticism, dismissed both female leads as "mud wrestlers" armed to the teeth.

While *Commonweal* found fault with Schwarzenegger's pumpitude, Julie Salamon of the *Wall Street Journal* proved that female critics can be as catty as beauty-parlor customers. Sounding more misogynist than Norman Mailer, Salamon harumphed,

"[Schwarzenegger] lives with blond Barbie doll wife, Lori. Actress
Sharon Stone, who plays her, has the same plastic sheen and a pair
of the same pneumatic-seeming muscles as Mr. Schwarzenegger.
When they embrace, you expect to hear the click-click-click of
hard synthetic surfaces meeting." Maybe Arnold was right and
Stone had indeed metamorphosed into a Teamster. Schwarzenegger's "life is a bore. No wonder with that blank robochick Lori,"
the *Wall Street Journal* critic wrote, continuing to beat a dead
metaphor to death. Unlike the bored Salamon, the heterosexual
male critics were too busy wiping saliva from their chin to be
blasé about Stone, robochick Barbie or not.

Reviewers, like many men, love to watch two women get it on.
Every straight guy I ever questioned said lesbian sex is a real
heterosexual turn-on. In 1990 lesbianism was still verboten terra
incognita, so, as a G-rated substitute, directors for decades have
sublimated their fantasies with catfights which provide a max-
imum of body contact without incurring an X or NC-17 rating.

Confirming the theory that two good-looking women equal
hot stuff, *L.A. Weekly* salivated over Stone and Ticotin's karate
exhibitionism. "The battle royal between Ticotin and Stone is
almost as cartoonishly satisfying as its probable source—Joan
Crawford and Mercedes McCambridge vying for Sterling Hayden
in *Johnny Guitar*." (Alternative newspaper reviewers like those
of the trades, love to show that they have been to graduate film
school. The director didn't have to go all the way back to 1953 for
scholarly references about two women getting down and dirty.
Cinematic mud wrestling and its various permutations started
with the Lumière brothers and continues to this day.)

Total Recall earned Stone her best reviews and jump-started a
career that barely registered a pulse except from libidinous
critics. The film apparently didn't put much money in her pocket.
To scrape together the down payment for a measly one-bedroom,
twelve-hundred-square-foot shack, albeit in the Hollywood Hills,
she had to hold a garage sale and sell her patio furniture.

Money was still a problem, but it was nothing compared to
the nightmare that befell Stone shortly after she put all her
pennies together for the mortgage.

7

Near-Death Experiences on Sunset Boulevard

DIVA BEVERLY SILLS ONCE SAID during an interview on *60 Minutes* she believed that when something wonderful happens in your life, something godawful inevitably follows. (The otherwise brilliant soprano and artistic director of the New York City Opera also believes in astrology.) As "proof," she mentioned that the same day she received some major award like Greatest Opera Singer of All Time or whatever, her ski lodge in Aspen burned to the ground.

While skeptics might scoff at Sill's Wheel of Misfortune philosophy, Stone's triumph and trauma in 1990 bore the diva out. Shortly after hitting the big time with *Total Recall* and buying her first home, Stone almost died in a head-on collision.

She was driving home from acting class, still perfecting her craft, when a car careened over the center divider and creamed her. Stone's experience postwreck sounds more as if the accident occurred in impersonal New York than friendly Los Angeles. Maybe it was the neighborhood.

She recalled, "It was in the sleaziest part of Sunset Boulevard, with a strip joint across the street and cops picking up the hookers to take them behind the building."

The crash was bad enough, but the aftermath added insult to injury. "I was in shock, so most of the time I didn't even know I was hurt. I sat on the street for three hours. Nobody recognized me," which is surprising, since by now she must have looked just as she did after Rachel Ticotin beat the mascara out of her in *Total Recall*. "I was a crying, hysterical woman with a crashed car, sitting on a corner staring into space."

To say Stone came close to dying is not overdramatizing. She didn't realize that she had a concussion, and instead of going to the hospital, she went home to bed. As anyone who's ever taken a first-aid class knows, if you go to sleep with a concussion, you may not wake up.

Fortunately, Stone awoke the next morning, but she was all but paralyzed. She lay on the floor and cried for three days! Finally, she went to a doctor, who diagnosed a major concussion, dislocated shoulder and jaw, several broken ribs, and three compressed disks in her back. She must have been in shock to wait three days for medical treatment. The doctor put her in a back brace and cervical collar for six months. Stone apparently was friendless at the time, for she said she spent many weeks all alone in her new pied-à-terre. Physical therapy retaught her how to use her body. Her recovery was quicker than the doctor expected, although it lasted an agonizing six months. She attributed her rapid healing to the great shape she was in post–*Total Recall*, precollision. All that Tae Kwon Do had paid off.

The accident no doubt left psychological scars; it definitely left physical ones. In addition to her famous neck scar from a close encounter with a clothesline and a pony during childhood, a reporter from *Mirabella* magazine rudely mentioned a "nasty scar running down her left elbow. For a movie star famous for the volume of nudity she's done [the interview took place after the famous leg spread in *Basic Instinct*], Stone has a lot of scars. There's an even nastier one that zigzags jaggedly across her neck and a third on the back of her right thigh, visible in *Casino*." The tacky madame from *Mirabella,* accused the star of hyperbole when listing her injuries, despite all the scar tissue. Stone didn't enhance her credibility when the reporter asked if she had had any other auto accidents. She breathlessly replied, "Oh, millions!" A dramatic actress should be cut a little slack for understandable self-dramatization. Trauma victims frequently repeat the traumatic incident over and over again to anyone who will listen.

8

Take It Off, Take Almost All of It Off

IN 1975, BURT REYNOLDS took a big gamble that paid off. Some people thought he was nuts, but Reynolds's decision showed that he was crazy like a fox. A fox with only chest fur. He agreed to pose nude for a *Cosmo* centerfold. Up to that point, Reynolds had been a well-paid B-list movie star. A man posing nude in a (heterosexual) magazine was unique, and his stunt made international headlines.

It was more than a stupid dog trick. It was an ingenious promotional gimmick. Years after his *déshabillement,* I asked Reynolds why he took the risk of becoming the laughingstock of Hollywood—or at least being branded a shameless exhibitionist.

Reynolds told me that his plan was well thought out. After starring in a slew of Stone-like turkeys, he had finally appeared in the Oscar-nominated film *Deliverance,* a minor classic about grown-up boys playing in the woods and getting to know inbred Appalachians in the Biblical sense. The layout in *Cosmo* was timed to coincide with the release of his big break, *Deliverance.*

The decision was a lot more original than taking an ad out in the trades thanking his "wonderful cast and crew," the more traditional method of self-promotion.

Reynolds proved himself to be a brilliant self-promoter. Although he was only a member of an ensemble cast in the outdoor epic, his *Cosmo* spread assured that he got treated like the leading man by the press. Reynolds told me that if he hadn't had a film to hustle, he would have kept his clothes on. "If posing nude is all it takes to make a star, then George Maharis should be a superstar today," he said, referring to the parade of has-beens who followed his lead and stripped for the downscale *Playgirl,* whose readership is rumored to be largely gay despite its name. Reynolds's chutzpah paid off. For the rest of the decade, he would be the number one box office star in the world until a stunt gone terribly wrong crushed his jaw and left him for much of the next decade narcotized in a Percodan and Valium haze.

In July 1990, Sharon Stone did a very stupid thing and allowed her nude body to be draped over seven pages of *Playboy*. You might want to let her off the hook by saying that she hoped to duplicate Reynolds's game plan. Like his, her spread coincided with the release of her big break, *Total Recall*. The two events might have a synergistic effect on her career and propel it to Reynolds's heights circa 1975.

Instead, it merely reinforced the bimbo sex object image she had been trying to shed since 1980. In her defense, Stone wasn't pulling a publicity stunt. The same woman who'd had to sell her patio furniture to raise the mortgage confessed, "I had just remodeled my house. I was broke. I needed the bread."

It's a shame she couldn't have found funding elsewhere. A handful of starlets and even porn stars have found fame on TV by letting *Playboy* do a strip search with its cameras. But Stone had just finished an A-list film, and frontal nudity doesn't promote credibility. You will never see Meryl Streep even giving the sexist magazine an interview, much less showing it tit. Cindy Crawford, whose moribund film career could use a jump start, also knew better. She appeared on the cover in a tasteful chemise that showed nothing more than a dollop of cleavage. Wisely, she continued to keep her clothes on inside, wearing a couturier creation, which made her perhaps the most overdressed woman ever to appear in a skin mag with pretensions to serious journalism.

Stone, on the other, hand frolicked buck nekkid in four shower shots, which revealed that *Vanity Fair* was underestimating her dimensions when it claimed she was a 36B. Another photo of her in a lacey jockstrap suggests she should fire her bikini waxer, since the woman (we presume) didn't do a thorough job. The cover reinforced her baby-doll image and shows how much the otherwise politically liberal magazine loves to infantilize women. Stone appears topless, sucking an ice cube. Why not go all the way and ask Props for a baby bottle?

Even her manager, Chuck Binder, advised against it. "It's rare you get a working actress who is making a living who will do that," he said, noting that another client, Darryl Hannah, turned the magazine down flat. Of his other clientele, Binder said, "They just don't want to. But Sharon wanted a way to set herself apart."

More likely, she was the Ado Annie of the 1990s, a girl who just couldn't say no—in many languages, Dorothy Parker might have added.

Stone tried to justify her self-sabotaging decision. "They had been asking me to do it for a very long time, and I had all kinds of different feelings about it. I was afraid it would be exploitative, but it was a good idea to wait to do it when I had a big movie coming out," she said, à la Burt.

Her mother, the same woman who had ordered her daughter to drop out of college to become a mannequin, didn't discourage her, dismissing the issue by noting that "when streaking was popular, Sharon participated around the house."

At least Stone got to play the auteur of the photo shoot. "They offered me complete control of everything. Choice of photographer, photo approval, cover guarantee," but apparently not choice of props. Her oral fixation on that ice cube was just plain tacky. "I never thought those pictures of women laying [*sic*] around with their naked bodies greased up and big tits were sexy...so we shot in black and white, without lighting, makeup, or a big production."

The original plan was to shoot in Paris, but a time crunch kept them in a considerably less romantic photo studio in Hollywood.

The copy accompanying her layout was condescending. The interviewer treated her like a bimbo, but a bimbo who was smart as a whip. One egregious bit of patronization read: "Sharon says what she thinks—and she thinks *a lot*." The comment recalls a famous Joan Rivers joke about two men cooing over a beautiful woman who refers to peas as "those little green things." The men are impressed. "Look, she knows her colors!"

Pre–*Total Recall,* she was just another piece of meat for Hefner's raincoat-clad readers, and we all know beef isn't particularly articulate.

Stone's decision also defies the pec-ing order of *Playboy's* striptease etiquette. Unknowns must show beaver. Starlets only show tit. And the movie-star sorority, which Stone became a bona fide member of with *Total Recall,* appears in Crawford-type couture.

Two years later, after *Basic Instinct* made her the hottest thing since sliced huevos rancheros, she got a deferential fifteen-page question and answer in the same magazine that made her seem like the Sartre of screen sirens.

Besides paying the rent, why did she do it? *Vogue* wanted to know in a 1992 interview. Despite its own objectification of women and preference for the anorexic junkie look, the haute couture rag is at least edited by women. It bluntly asked Stone why she stripped if she hoped for Michelle Pfeiffer–caliber roles. The closest Pfeiffer ever came to showing anything but her ankles was in *Tequila Sunrise's* famous hot-tub scene with Mel Gibson, and the tiny bubbles kept the actress *virgo intacta*.

Stone's answer to *Vogue's* impertinent question proved, in *Playboy's* words, that she does indeed "think a lot." She also showed that she didn't take herself or her image all that seriously. That would come only after Golden Globe and Oscar honors.

"I just find the whole sex-object thing funny because I'd been so objectified in another way when I was a kid," she said, referring to her genius treatment. "I understand that none of it means anything, only that you're unusual, you create an impact that people are uncomfortable with, so they don't know what to do with you. As you get older, you realize what made life bad when you were young makes it great when you're a grown-up." Or to paraphrase Sophie Tucker's economic dialectic, "I've been ugly and I've been beautiful. Beautiful is better."

The magazine also noted that at the time she posed for *Playboy,* she left the powerhouse Creative Artists Agency for the B-list Gersh Agency. Stone claimed that the move was motivated by talent-agency agoraphobia, fear of CAA's wide-open spaces.

"I'm a small-town girl," said the girl who fled Meadville for Manhattan when she was seventeen. "I need a small, friendly environment where I can have coffee and cake and feel normal."

No actress in her right career mind would leave the home of Steven Spielberg and Tom Cruise (CAA) to go slumming at Gersh. Stone was pushed. Maybe it was the *Playboy* spread that turned her into *pudenda non grata,* the Rodney Dangerfield of CAA's stable.

The final straw that broke Stone's patience occurred when her agent, Paula Wagner, told her that she hadn't had time to see *Total Recall* because she was too busy with another client, Tom Cruise.

That was a minor humiliation compared to another incident she recalled. The recollection still angered her years later. In 1992, *Spy* magazine gleefully dramatized her discomfort at the hands of an agency that was anything but starstruck.

"Stone was treated with casual disregard," *Spy* reported. Her agent often refused to see her, and when she did, "cavalierly" rescheduled appointments at the last minute. When Stone finally got past the receptionist and the three-story Lichtenstein in the lobby, her agent kept her waiting "interminably."

At least the actress wasn't being singled out for this passive-aggressive treatment. A bona-fide superstar also found himself cooling his heels and his temper in the waiting area. Stone noticed a man whose face was hidden behind a newspaper outside her agent's office. After a half hour, he lowered the paper, and she discovered that her "fellow nobody" was Sean Connery.

If revenge is a dish best served cold, the actress must be

enjoying a frozen treat these days as CAA implodes on itself after the departure of its *éminence grise* Mike Ovitz to Disney and the man who played good cop to Ovitz' bad cop, Ron Meyer, now head of MCA-Universal. But before her denigrators dined on crow, Stone would have to eat a lot of the bird herself. (In September 1996, Stone was in a forgiving mood and re-signed with CAA after being agent-free for years. Unfortunately, the agency's reason for being, Ovitz and Meyer, were long gone by then.)

9

Star Drek— Back in the Bowel-ry

IF STONE APPEARED IN *PLAYBOY* for exposure (pun intended), she got it, but not the kind of publicity that would lead to costarring with De Niro or Pacino. Maybe her striptease was self-sacrifice for interior decor, since her spread in the skin magazine paid for the remodeling of her spread in the Hollywood hills.

But far from getting her a gig with A-list leading men and auteurs of merit, her post–*Total Recall* filmography was more of the same dreck she endured pre-Arnold. It was déjà vu all over again, as a Yogi by the name of Berra once said. The actress must have been seeing red and singing the blues. For the next two years *Total Recall* seemed more like a hairline fracture than her big break.

Even the titles of these post-1990 star drecks eerily echo her *Action Jackson/Police Academy* dip in video's intestinal tract: *Scissors, Year of the Gun, Diary of a Hitman, Where Sleeping Dogs Lie*, and *He Said, She Said* were all filmed in a workaholic whirl during a single year, 1991. In the latter film, the star of a movie that had grossed $250 million worldwide was reduced to a cameo as yet another bombshell, flight-attendant division. She was billed below Kevin Bacon and Elizabeth Perkins!

Stone must have been kicking herself for stripping if all it got her was a little stinker like *Scissors*.

Despite its slasher title, *Scissors* was not a replay of *Deadly Blessing* or all those hockey-masked jaunts with Jason. It aspired to be an art-house film. The plot sounds like a rip-off of Sartre's *No Exit*—if the great philsopher of existentialism had found himself nightmarishly on Menahem Golan's payroll. Stone is cast against type as a twenty-six-year-old virgin whose sexually repressed personality makes Marie Osmond look like Madonna or a lapsed member of the Sexual Compulsives Anonymous.

Scissors aspires to be a psychosexual thriller and gives Stone a raft of disorders that suggest writer-director Frank DeFelitta bought a copy of the Diagnostic and Statistical Manual of Mental Disorders, 4th edition (*DSM-IV*) before he hit the laptop.

There are good reasons why at thirty Stone's Angie is a virgin who sees a psychotherapist three times a week. As a child, she was molested, and her uncaring mother blamed her. Angie's adult job is fraught with symbolism harking back to childhood. She must be the only character in screen history who has a job mending broken dolls. Get it? No? Both she and her toys are damaged goods.

Stone is sent to a lavish apartment where some abused dolls need a little nip and tuck. Instead, Stone finds herself stuck, literally and figuratively, reenacting low-brow scenes from *No Exit*, a play whose characters are also locked in a hermetically sealed room. In Sartre's play it turns out that the inmates are literally trapped in hell. The critics felt that was a good way to describe the sensation of watching *Scissors*.

The *Hollywood Reporter* said, "During the second half of the film, the heroine is hermetically sealed in an apartment by an unseen, demented tormentor. [*Scissors*] has designs to put audiences through exactly the same ordeal." Then once again the reviewer got frisky. "While being trapped in a confined space with Sharon Stone may not sound like such a displeasing prospect to some of us, writer-director Frank DeFelitta makes certain that it's no fun at all."

Besides being trapped in condo hell, Stone is tormented by not one but two men, twins played by Steve Railsback. One brother is a soap star; the other, a wheelchair-bound Expressionist painter psychotic. The *Los Angeles Times* said that everyone in the film looked as though they'd rather be cleaning out latrines with a toothbrush.

The film was so bad, its distributor had to "four-wall" it at the art house Laemmle Theater in West Los Angeles. Four-wall is trade-paper patois for renting a theater because the movie house refuses to take the film on consignment. Normally, the theater earns its money not from the producer but from ticket sales, which the theater owner feared would be nonexistent in the case of *Scissors*.

Despite reviews which ranged from merely toxic to downright traumatizing, Stone's performance was singled out for praise. In fact, she earned the best reviews of her career until *Casino*.

The *Hollywood Reporter* wrote, "[*Scissors*] is actually a fine showcase for Stone. If anything, the emotional range she displays here as a victim runs deeper than the film deserves."

Its competitor, *Daily Variety,* held its nose while writing the review, then took a deep breath and gushed: "Sharon Stone as a sexually traumatized young woman trying to cope with life alone in the city is the only exception to a generally lifeless production. She deserves kudos for the sequence in which she must hold the screen alone while trapped in a high-tech chamber of horrors."

Los Angeles Weekly, usually the John Gotti of movie criticism, praised her as a "vulnerable, sympathetic presence."

Only the *Weekly*'s competitor, the *Los Angeles Reader,* sounded a sour note, slumming once again in the basement of prose stylists, punnilingus. "Since veterans of children's games should know that Stone dulls *Scissors,* director Frank DeFelitta has no excuse for casting the full, dead weight of Sharon Stone as the lead actress in this roundly bad psycho-thriller."

More cleverly, the alternative weekly described Stone's threatening environment as a "lecherous cop a feel world."

However encouraging, good reviews don't pay the rent or remodel the house. Stone soon found herself emoting for dollars in *Year of the Gun*.

At least this political thriller was directed by an established master, John Frankenheimer (*The Manchurian Candidate*), even if his star, and his box office, had waned by 1991 with films whose titles had symbolic resonance, like *Black Sunday* and *Dead-Bang*.

Screenwriter David Ambrose chose to dramatize a real-life situation from 1978 which no one by 1991 even remembered. Throughout the 1970s, Italy, home of the Renaissance and Gina Lollobrigida, had to put up with juvenile delinquents who progressed in early adulthood to Marxist terrorists known as the Red Brigade. (Their American avatar was the Symbionese Liberation Army, poor brainwashed heiress Patty Hearst's kidnappers turned comrades.)

Andrew McCarthy, hot but stinky off several weekends with a stiff named Bernie, plays a young American novelist in Rome writing a fictional account of the Red Brigade. Stone plays a busybody-photojournalist who gets ahold of McCarthy's manuscript and shows it to a university professor, a Commie fellow traveler, who submits the novel to his pals in the Red Brigade for vetting.

The terrorists may not know art when they see it, but they do recognize a *roman à clef*. And they don't like McCarthy's variation on Jackie Collins's *romans à Hollywood*, Italian style. Soon McCarthy, Stone, and his girlfriend, *Rainman*'s Valeria Golino, have made the Brigade's greatest hit list.

Year of the Gun was made on the cheap, only $15 million at a time when the average film without crowd scenes and expensive locations in European capitals cost $30 million. Stone attributed the failure of the film to finances, not the final product. "I was disappointed," she said, "that John didn't have everything he needed to make the picture."

The cast and crew suffered stoically, staying in cheap apart-
ments instead of hotels made prohibitively expensive by the
devaluation of the dollar against the Confederate currency of
Europe, the lira.

After her repressed virgin turn in *Scissors,* Stone was back in
the saddle here as an "aggressive photojournalist who isn't shy
about using her sexual appeal to get what she wants," according
to *Daily Variety*. Unfortunately for McCarthy's nerdy novelist,
Stone wants the scoop on his book, not his bod. *Variety* once
again loved the actress, hated the film. "Stone adds some interest
as the provocative photographer, though one never knows what
makes her character such a maniacal careerist....Stone puts in the
strongest performance of her career as an ambitious photojournalist who constantly puts her life on the line, even if it means
dragging others into the line of fire."

Her bedroom scenes required acrobatic feats that would have
stymied a double-jointed gymnast. She felt they were even more
implausible than the somersaults she would later perform in
Basic Instinct. The director's classic 1961 film, *The Manchurian
Candidate,* made her a big fan, and her admiration only grew
during their collaboration. Up to a point. It seemed she loved the
director but wasn't crazy about his steamroller approach to
steamy sex. Pressed by an interviewer to elaborate, Stone found
the recollection of six years ago still too painful to go into: "I just
can't think of any way to talk about it that isn't horrible, so I think
I had just better not," she said.

As the reviews suggest during this downtime in her career,
Stone was experiencing exponential growth as an actress, but she
was way behind the learning curve as a script reader who could
divine dross and drivel—and avoid them.

An industry executive said, "She probably has a personal
trainer [she does], a personal assistant, maybe even a personal
shopper. Why doesn't this woman hire a personal script reader?"
Stone doesn't have a genius IQ for nothing. She has a platoon of D
girls, development executives whose sole duty in life is to find
star vehicles for the boss, at her own production company,
ominously called Chaos Productions. Why not Titanic Inc.?

The *Village View,* a neighborhood weekly in West Los Angeles, echoed *Variety's* love-hate affair with Stone the actress versus Stone the artistic director. "Stone's troubleshooting American photographer is an adrenalin-stoked triumph, adding naturalism to the cartoony flair for camp dominatrixes she demonstrated in her career-making performance as Arnold Schwarzenegger's memory-implanted wife in *Total Recall.* Stone's performance is so believably modulated, she even manages to believably lust after McCarthy, until she actually gets him in the sack, where even her prodigious resources can't keep her from seeming to be off somewhere else, balancing her checkbook or some such." The reviewer went on to suggest that McCarthy had been taking acting lessons from the late Bernie, the corpse in *Weekend at Bernie's.* "Andrew McCarthy's Alfalfa on novocaine petulance reaches new heights of ambulatory inertia. McCarthy may be the only actor in history who actually *acquires* baby fat as he ages," the critic said in a rare instance of treating the leading man instead of the leading lady like a piece of meat.

Stone still couldn't get respect from the movie credits and a few critics of the movie. She was billed third after McCarthy, whose biggest hit was *Mannequin,* and Golino, Pee-Wee Herman's one time screen gal pal. *Los Angeles* magazine, whose editorial board I know from personal experience was staffed by male chauvinist pigs, reduced her to "*Playboy* model Sharon Stone" in its review, even though she had starred in a film that grossed $250 million only a year before.

It's hard to square the temperamental actress who had film crews unable to contain their bladders whenever they got near her African bathtub with the trouper who emerged at this time. Not only did she continue to beat the sauerkraut out of Arnold after breaking her hand during martial abuse of a punching bag, on the set in Rome for *Year of the Gun* she limped up and down the Spanish Steps for six weeks after breaking her left foot while shooting a crowd sequence that turned into a mob. Since then, the actress has become phobic in crowds, and her entourage of goons has less to do with movie-star pretentiousness and everything to do with movie-star terror.

Still recuperating from her hellish car crash on Norma Desmond Place, Stone checked into a hospital in Rome only *after* production wrapped.

Year of the Gun had a no-name distributor by the name of Triumph Releasing, which released it late in 1991, surely not for the consideration of Academy voters before the nomination deadline passed. The company wasn't reduced to four-walling like *Scissors*'s distributor, since it was affiliated with the yen-enriched Sony Pictures, but the film quickly disappeared from the front wall of theaters nationwide.

Her next film, *Where Sleeping Dogs Lie,* had a double, perhaps triple, meaning. It was a indeed a woof job, and Stone as "temptress Serena Black" suffered through a weirdly auto-biographical role based on her traumas at CAA, playing a mendacious talent agent who "has an adverse affect on her client's career"; hence, the punny "Lie" in "Where Sleeping Dogs" snooze.

Whereas at least *Scissors* aspired to pop psychology and existential despair, *Year of the Gun* tried to capture an important moment in the history of Rome's greatest hits. *Where Sleeping Dogs Lie* was pure potboiler, *Action Jackson* and *Above the Law* come back from the dead to haunt her resumé. And instead of big names like Arnold or even recognizable ones like Andrew McCarthy, her costars, billed above her, included the star of a TV series that lasted less than one year and a leading man whose biggest hit, *The Crying Game,* was more than a year away.

Perhaps the only interesting thing about the movie was the press kit! It referred to her hometown as a "two-stoplight town," greatly exaggerating cow town's urbanity. It also mentioned that her parents worked "side by side in the family tool and dye [*sic*] company," inflating her father's resumé as a hired hand and mistakenly describing Mom's real vocation as bookkeeper.

Her career trajectory couldn't seem to fall any further, but it did. *Year of the Gun*'s budget of $15 million seemed Cleopatric compared to *Diary of a Hitman*'s $2.5 million. That's Stone's hair and spandex budget on *Casino*'s $70 million mugging of Scrooge-like Universal's bean counters in a rare display of fiscal irresponsibility.

How far had Stone fallen after the twin peaks of Arnold and *Total Recall? Twin Peaks*'s Sherilyn Fenn and Forest Whitaker (*The Crying Game*) were both billed above Stone, who wasn't even mentioned in the trade reviews.

The movie's cobweb-old (and thin) story was based on a forty-five-minute off-off Broadway play. The plot sounds as though Luis Buñuel had been given two and half million bucks to make the *Discreet Charm of the Bourgeois Unabomber*. And we do mean bourgeois. The *Village Voice* nicknamed it "Yuppie's Honor." Whitaker plays a hired killer who needs just one more gig for a down payment on a condo! *Mean Streets* retires to suburbia. Whitaker's last dance with death has him commissioned to kill the wife (Fenn) of a commodities broker. The businessman claims that his wife is playing an NC-17 version of Kate to his Petruchio before Shakespeare's unliberated denouement. In fact, the broker, who sounds as though he's using the stuff himself, tells Whitaker that both his wife and their baby are crack addicts and he wants both of them dispatched. What some people will do to own their own home.

Falling in love with his target, who turns out to be crack-free and vulnerable, Whitaker finds himself playing Romeo to Fenn's Juliet as his dreams of realty dissolve into lust at first sight.

Stone starred in this no-budget stinker as a personal favor to one of the most influential men in her life and her greatest (platonic) love after her ex-husband, Roy London. As her acting coach, London may have been responsible for her notices, which suddenly went from toxic to orgasmic. London was the Lee Strasberg—Stella Adler of his generation without all the Stanislavsky-speak. His students included Oscar winner Geena Davis, Michelle Pfeiffer, Patrick Swayze, and James Belushi. He was a miracle worker who transformed Barbies and Barbarellas into Oscar honorees like Davis, who thanked him in her acceptance speech for Best Supporting Actress in *The Accidental Tourist*.

Considering how badly he used his students, London's comment on his casting may say more than he meant when he explained, "It seemed only natural and right to *use* my students."

Stone didn't feel used. She repaid his coaching favors by agreeing to do a cameo as Fenn's "tarty and obnoxious sister" in London's first and only directing effort, *Diary of a Hitman*. (London died of AIDS in 1993, one of the reasons Stone has devoted so much of her time to AIDS charities.)

"Money is not why we did it," she said with understatement, even though those pesky remodeling bills kept coming past due. "Roy London is why we did it. When you hear that he is finally going to direct a film, you crawl through broken glass to be there."

London must have been asleep at the Movieola. He failed to notice that Whitaker, allegedly a Pittsburgh-based assassin, speaks with a distinct Bensonhurt, Brooklyn, accent. The *Village Voice* called that "the Big Question. The Bigger Question was what are marquee monsters like Sharon Stone [one scene] and Jim Belushi [one and a half] doing in this tax write-off, waltzing through their marks without breaking a sweat? Answer: London is a popular acting coach, and his students…are helping out on his feature directing debut, yet another of this year's bumper crop of first timers [directors] who should be last timers."

As if her billing and tiny role weren't insult enough, she suffered the ignominy of her best asset, her blond mane, being dyed an unflattering brunet. She is almost unrecognizable in the film, which needed the help of every student turned star it could get.

The production was shot mostly in Youngstown, Ohio, which meant that Stone could cross state lines for a quick trip to Meadville had she wanted to return to her place of birth and adolescent torment.

The movie had its U.S. premiere at the ultraprestigious Santa Barbara Film Festival, mostly on the strength of London's fame as Hollywood coach to the stars. The audience, but portentously not the judges, voted it "best of the fest." At the even artier Deauville film fest, *Diary of a Hitman* impressed the same Frenchmen who worship Jerry Lewis and earned rave reviews.

Like Lewis, the film may have impressed foreigners, but it made the natives restless. *Daily Variety* nutshelled the critical consensus when it predicted it would go straight to Stone's favorite swimming hole, video bowel hell. Speaking of no-name distributors, the Continental Film Group dumped *Hitman* on Vision International during a deal at 1991's American Film Market at a beachfront hotel in Santa Monica.

The film quickly disappeared from theaters after its March 31, 1992, debut stateside. Then a little miracle called *Basic Instinct* was released, and *Diary of a Hitman* came surging back into multiplexes in May, with the newly minted superstar's billing raised to the same line as the considerably less superstarry-eyed Whitaker and *Boxing Helena*'s limbless second choice, Fenn.

While Stone made *Diary of a Hitman* for Roy London, it's hard to figure whom she made *He Said, She Said* for—other than her expensive interior decorator. Once again she landed in the billing basement, listed fifth, after Kevin Bacon and Elizabeth Perkins, another candidate for a *Whatever Happened to...?* trivia book.

The plot of the alleged romantic comedy had a brilliant conceit written and codirected by a brilliant Ph.D. from the University of Chicago, Ken Kwapis. The other director was his fiancée, Marisa Silver, daughter of Joan Micklin Silver. The reason for the double duty was the film's double story. *He Said, She Said* recounted the breakup of a relationship, first told from the man's point of view, then from the woman's. Their conflicting memories are so colored by prejudice and anger that not only do their recollections differ, but so do the costumes and personalities of the supporting cast.

Stone once again was cast as the fantasy girlfriend, a flight attendant who used to be Bacon's live-in lover when she wasn't serving coffee, tea, or herself at thirty-thousand feet.

Stone's frequent typecasting as Helen of Troy, A.D., finally merited a scientific analysis in 1996. A fascinating documentary, *Face Value,* on cable's the Learning Channel, featured a college instructor on the prowl for the "perfect face." Prof. Michael Cunningham, of the University of Louisville, Kentucky, polled film fans and compiled a list of the best facial features. On his computer screen, Professor Cunningham accessed Audrey Hepburn's large, fawnlike eyes, Brigitte Bardot's lips, Michelle

Pfeiffer's eyebrows, Meg Ryan's jawline, and Stone's cheekbones, all voted tops in their field. Surprisingly, the scientist didn't poll for best nose.

The result was a grotesque jigsaw of facial features until Cunningham typed in a few computer commands and the parts were blended into a harmonious whole. Here, he said, was the most beautiful face in the world. Although Ms. Perfect was made up of bits and pieces of stars going all the way back to the mid-1950s, the face that appeared on the professor's monitor was Sharon Stone's!

In pursuit of tenure, Professor Cunningham had found something else—the most beautiful woman in the world—and he had the gigabytes to back up his theory.

So when their script described Stone's flight-attendant Linda as a fantasy girlfriend, the writer-directors immediately thought of the modern era's Helen of Troy.

Maybe Stone agreed to do a cameo because she got to play herself twice, filtered once through Bacon's rose-colored glasses and a second time through Perkins's, tinted green for envy.

In Bacon's reverie Stone shows up for a dinner date modestly dressed in the real-life actress's favorite color and style, a black suit circa Winona Ryder in *Beetlejuice* that's all business. In Perkins's angry remembrance of zingers past, Stone in the same scene is dressed like a dominatrix, basic black again but dipped in leather and accessorized with metal hardware. Ace should have received a costume-design credit.

The conceit of two films in one was ingenious but ultimately boring, as the viewer had to sit through the same story two times. Not many people were willing to see this twice-told tale. *Daily Variety* summed up the end hybrid neatly: "*He Said, She Said* is two awful films rolled into one." *He Said, She Said* did only slightly better business than Kwapis's directing debut, *Vibes,* the *My Mother the Car* of feature films.

Once again, Roy London's Pygmalion must have worked his magic on a Galatea animated by London's intense acting workshops. The critics adored Sharon, panned her movie. Even a female critic drooled this time.

One critic called Stone's psycho novelist in *Basic Instinct* "Jackie Collins on steroids."

In *Basic Instinct,* Michael Douglas is obsessed with Sharon Stone. So is Sharon Stone.

As the sexually repressed book editor in *Sliver*, Stone was the perfect sex symbol for the AIDS-plagued nineties. No sex is the safest sex.

Sharon Stone imitates Clint Eastwood in the retro western *The Quick and the Dead*. (Ivor Davis Collection)

Stone and Isabelle Adjani plot to kill their abusive lover in *Diabolique*.
(Ivor Davis Collection)

With her newfound power, Stone rejected the producer's demand for a nude scene in *Diabolique*.
(Ivor Davis Collection)

Sharon Stone plays a multiple murderer on Death Row in *Last Dance*.
(Ivor Davis Collection)

Stone gets comfortable at a Planet Hope fundraiser for homeless children.

Why mince superlatives? Sharon Stone is the most beautiful woman in the movies today.

The *New York Times*'s Janet Maslin, never prone to Kael-type vitriol, rooted for Stone to get the guy. "Sharon Stone, as the alluring ex-girlfriend who wants [Bacon] back, steals each of her [two] scenes and makes it nearly impossible to understand why [Bacon] and [Perkins] are together."

The *Hollywood Reporter* was also in the cheering section for the Stone team. "One ultimately roots for 'He' to get together with his longtime bed partner [Sharon Stone]. There is something way afoul when one roots for the 'other' woman in a romantic comedy, especially one as thinly drawn as Stone's bimbo character."

Stone was making a habit by this time of disproving the old acting axiom that you can't rise above the material. In turkey after gobbler, she skyrocketed over junk. The critics always hated the film. Early on, they merely lusted after its starlet. As the decade wore off, her talent would grow exponentially, and the reviewers would take note.

Her next film would require a similar leap of faith, but this time her trust was not betrayed, at least not at the box office. After more than a decade of box-office dysphoria and only a year after *Scissors, Year of the Gun, Where Sleeping Dogs Lie, Diary of a Hitman*, and *He Said, She Said* seemed in danger of earning her Katharine Hepburn's 1930's title of box-office poison, Stone would "suddenly" become an "overnight sensation."

10

...And Catherine Tramell
as the Beaver

IN 1992, SHARON STONE was in trouble. At thirty-four, she could hear her biological "bombshell" clock ticking. Her face and figure—and priapic movie reviewers—stereotyped her as the goddess next door, but the sexist movie industry lived by the Eleventh Commandment, "Thou shalt not grow old"—if you want to play sex objects. Love handles and love goddesses just don't mix in the studio stew.

Until *Basic Instinct* allowed her to give "one of the greatest performances by a woman in screen history," in Camille Paglia's hypertensive prose, Stone was in danger of becoming an unknown Marilyn Monroe for Generation Geritol.

Her last-minute Hail Mary pass as the bisexual kitten with an ice pick in *Basic Instinct* came just in time—and after twelve years of clawing her way to the middle. If any actress can claim to have paid her dues, Stone put in overtime that was less than golden in screen embarrassments like *King Solomon's Cold Steel Scissors*.

Stone's big break was a fluke. Chalk it up to good luck (hers) and the good, or prudish, taste of established actresses, depending on how familial your values are.

No-name Stone fought as hard for the job in *Basic Instinct* as she did beating up Arnold. But instead of punching a bag till her hand broke, she stalked the director, Paul Verhoeven. First, Stone got ahold of a pirated version of Joe Eszterhas's script so that she could do her homework and bone up on the character she was desperate to play.

Initially, Verhoeven refused to see her. Her scary transformation from good to evil "in a split second" in *Total Recall* may have scared him off. After *Total Recall* earned more than the annual GNP of a Riviera principality, the director engaged in a bit of revisionist history, insisting his reluctance to cast Stone was simply a matter of film credit record rather than a personality clash, Verhoeven revised his original explanation that Stone was too scary to work with again and claimed she just didn't make the cut. "Basically, her name wasn't good enough," he said. "In the beginning the names that came up were Michelle Pfeiffer, Julia Roberts, Geena Davis. It was like a package. You don't think character, you think names. 'Who would work with Michael Douglas?' We had seen him with Kathleen Turner and Glenn Close. Now who?" Significantly, the latter two actresses weren't even considered for the sulfurous bombshell part. By 1992, Turner, ravishing ten years earlier in *Body Heat,* had apparently made one too many trips to Winchell's. One critic said that the sequel would have to be called *Body Fat.* As for the most talented of the bunch, Close, let's be kind and just say that no university researchers are using parts of her face to composite the perfect woman.

And a no-name actress wanted the job.

Soon Stone's no name would have to do. Every established bombshell had read the script and gagged on its nudity and violence. In addition, the politically savvy stars all turned it down because they realized that its homophobia and misogyny would bring out the pickets, which it did. Verhoeven summed up the superstar disdain. "I think a lot of stars didn't want to consider it because it was about a bisexual killer, which involved a lot of violence and explicit sex." He was understating the inflammatory nature of the final cut. Douglas also saw the writing on the wall, which read something like "You've got to be kidding. You want me to make love in a public toilet with a woman?" At least one actress didn't find that so off-putting, but her name wasn't Julia or Geena.

Douglas explained: "Between the hype of the [$3 million script, the most expensive ever] and the nudity, a lot of actresses we had hoped for were put off by the part. Women are often caught between politics and a particular role. But I thought that as dangerous as the film was, it was also that good of a woman's part. The irony is that for many male actors, playing a good heavy has made their careers." All that heavy lifting—and breathing— would make Stone's.

But first the actress who landed the role in *Basic Instinct* would have such choice assignments as sitting on a public toilet in the *men's* room of a disco while her girlfriend climbs on top and dry humps her on the potty. The script read like an animated version of the lesbian sex–obsessed *Penthouse*. The final product would resemble a live-action grooming guide for Lipstick Lesbians. Stone and her gal pals wear leather and lace with equal chic. Also, the lucky actress would have to expose her vagina not once but twice in front of a full complement of cast and crew. It's hard to imagine the exquisitely delicate Geena Davis even glancing at the script without asking her personal assistant for smelling salts. Tougher Michelle Pfeiffer and Cher probably threw the script at their agents and said, "Are you out of your fucking mind? You expect me to let Michael Douglas suck on my nipples, then make me take it up the ass?"

Before she read the script, Stone was also wary of playing yet another exploited character. She had had a decade's worth of Mrs. Bill jobs as the abused or murdered little woman in junk like *Scissors* and *Cold Steel* which did nothing for her career or the retirement of her decorating debts. "At first I didn't want the part. I've been in every stupid action picture. Then my agent said Paul was directing, and I said, 'If he's directing the phone book, I'll audition,'" she recalled after the film made her the hottest thing since diced tamales. With her overweening ambition and work-aholism, one would suspect that Stone would have volunteered to read for all 6 million parts in the greater Los Angeles phone directory.

After she digested the script's high-caloric smut, Stone wasn't about to let little things like political correctness and moral squeamishness get in the way of her career. She actually crashed the editing session for the airplane version of *Total Recall* in which Verhoeven no doubt had to cut all those scenes where Stone tries to turn Schwarzenegger into a soprano with her foot instead of a scalpel. Don't want Grandma en route to visiting the grandkids to have a coronary at thirty-thousand feet. It's a safe bet that *Basic Instinct* never even flew the friendly skies. If Verhoeven had tried to cut it to a G-string, the only frames left would have been the opening credits. Probably not even those, since they rolled over soft-focus scenes of the murderess picking at her boy toy.

Stone's in-studio invasion turned into an unsolicited audition, complete with hair, makeup, and even wardrobe. Stone wore the getup she would later insist on for her famous police-interrogation scene. The script had numerous *hommages* to Hitchock, which the savvy actress knew, since she had purloined a copy of Eszterhas's monsterpiece. So the sexiest woman alive showed up in the editing room in a plain white suit, her hair pulled back from her face and knotted in a bun—Grace Kelly, circa *Rear Window* (1954). The director was smitten. Forget Michelle, who wasn't interested, anyway.

When he saw her standing beside the Movieola and her radiant image on the Movieola's tiny screen in *Total Recall,* Verhoeven claimed he suddenly changed his mind. Up to that point, he hadn't even returned her calls.

Why don't I test her? he said to himself. He claimed it was while editing *Total Recall* that he forgot the actress's diabolical traits and fell in love with her celestial image all over again. Hunched over his lonely Movieola, he may have thought, If she can kick Arnold's butt, surely she can castrate Michael's libido. That sounds like more revisionist history. Geena and Julia had already passed, and it was beginning to look as though the lead would need a permanent stand-in. Second-string superstars like Kim Basinger and even over-the-hill Cher were being wooed. (The same avoidance syndrome occurred during casting of the even randier *Showgirls,* with the director forced to go bargain shopping in the depths of syndicated television and hire *Saved by the Bell*'s Elizabeth Berkley for a big budget production.)

Verhoeven's "recovered memory" seems limitless when he claims—after refusing to even see Stone—that he actually lobbied the moneymen to green-light the starlet. This is the same man who told a reporter, "If an ashtray could talk, it would sound like Sharon Stone." A critic disagreed, saying, "Her voice sounds like whiskey poured over broken glass."

However he felt about her pipes, Verhoeven secretly tested Stone four months before she crashed his editing room, he later claimed in a fit of Orwellian historicism. Her image on the Movieola inspired him. "I used that tape [from the in-flight *Total Recall]* continuously in the next four months before we started the real casting. I used the tape to convince everybody attached to the movie that Sharon was the best choice. You realize, of course, that at that point Sharon was not a star, and it was in the interest of the studio to find a star to work next to Michael."

Maybe the real reason Verhoeven refused to see her at first had to do with his recollection of their collaboration on *Total Recall*. Talk about a bad memory that had to be erased, but this time it was the director's, not Arnold's secret agent's. Verhoeven admitted that his was a love-hate relationship with his female star on the set of the sci-fi epic and that the battle royal would continue on their next pairing. He spoke to the *Hollywood Reporter*'s Martin Grove, whose must-read column he knew Stone would read. "There was a lot of anger and a lot of kissing and making up. The same applied to *Basic Instinct*. I knew what I was facing when I was starting *Basic Instinct*." And once more that revisionism: "On the other hand, I felt that Sharon, against nearly everybody's advice at that point, would still be the best actress by far for this part."

After the film became a box-office leviathan, Stone's star

outshone Verhoeven's, and she could stop playing the subservient starlet on or off the record. She admitted her fights with the director. "I don't know if I'd work with him again. We have a certain kind of magic when we work together, even though we fight like cats and dogs. We love each other, and we hate each other, but we make something that works. So I don't know if I'll work with him again. It might depend on whether or not I kill him first!"

If Verhoeven felt more love than hate for her, why did Stone have to crash his editing room? He started his reappraisal of Stone's merits when he was casting *Showgirls*. At that point, Verhoeven not only would have rolled out the red carpet to his editing room, he would have crawled over cut glass to secure the services of *the* hottest actress in Hollywood. But by then Stone was already in her Meryl Streep—stretching mode. Lap dancing on a B movie actor's crotch was not on her agenda. In fact, by this time, her clothes always stayed on in her pictures. It was the lesser female costars who had to strip. (See *Diabolique*. See Isabelle Adjani have a near-fatal coronary while she just happens to be stark nekkid.)

Half a decade later, Stone's supernal loveliness has become ho-hum, but it's hard to exaggerate her impact in *Basic Instinct*, which was the number-one hit of 1992. Not since Bo Derek emerged, cornrowed and bronzed from the Acapulco surf, in *10* almost two decades ago has an actress had such a scorching effect on libidos worldwide.

As recent scientific studies show, beauty knows no national boundaries. What's considered gorgeous in Andalusia (her *Blood and Sand* location) and Zimbabwe (site of her unfortunate bathwater experience) remains universally the same. *Newsweek*, in a cover story, "The Biology of Beauty," didn't need to cite scholars to prove the boundarylessness of beauty. All it had to do was run Stone's belle visage on its cover to prove the scientists' point.

Stone is transnationally and transcendently luminous on-screen. To find another woman as gorgeous, you would have to go shopping for body parts, taking the best-of-the-best anatomic features and combining them into a clone of Stone. Her beauty makes it entirely believable, without using any of her considerable acting skill, that she could reduce hard-boiled homicide detectives to quivering, perspiring Jell-o molds of adolescent lust.

At first, Stone, happy to have arrived, joked about her exposure in *Basic Instinct*, saying, "At least it proves I'm a natural blonde." As she became a more serious "ach-truss," however, she engaged in some mythmaking of her own, claiming that the director promised that Nebraska, in a London newspaper's inexplicable geographic phrase, would be seen only in a long shot, not up close, personal, and underneath a klieg light. Her story continued to evolve as her stardom rose. In another version she claimed that Verhoeven asked her to remove her jockeys because they reflected light back at the camera. The director promised that nothing would be seen. When *Playboy*, in 1992, asked her point-blank, whether she was sandbagged or a willing victim, she stonewalled the magazine's David Sheff. "I'm not going to talk about this with you. It's not because I don't respect your...right to ask. But it's resolved, and I'd like to leave it that way." By now Stone had learned the delicate circumspection of a presidential press secretary.

Verhoeven dismissed her attempt at self-rehabilitation. Every scene was discussed with the stars before filming, "separately and together. So that when we started to shoot they knew every position I wanted to use. They could comment on the shot and say if something made them uncomfortable," the director insisted. Verhoeven even claimed that every frame was storyboarded, so Stone knew exactly what she was getting into.

According to Stone, she looked at the anatomically improbable storyboards and laughed in the director's face. "I didn't have a lot of input into the sex scenes," she said. "Paul and Michael, very macho men, created them. When I read them and saw the storyboards, I thought they were ludicrous. Certainly in my experience. Do you have sex like that? Do you know women who have orgasms from these anatomically *impossible* positions? Please. In two minutes? Send them over to my house so I can learn. In the meantime, ludicrous they remain."

Stone let the clueless director know that outside of the Olympic Games, women were incapable of performing the kind of gymnastics he had committed to storyboard. "When Paul showed me the storyboards, I said, 'Jesus Christ, I'm going to be sitting on my shins! I not only have to do a complete back bend, but I also have to pull myself back up without using my hands. And then make it look as if I'm getting off.'"

The trouper actually resorted to weight training in order to physically comply with the director's impossible stage directions, and her leading man helped make their sex scenes less unpleasant. Douglas was the perfect gentleman during their intimate scenes. Stone recalled gratefully that when the director said cut, Douglas would always pull the sheets over her nude body until the camera was ready to roll again. This sort of gentlemanliness relaxed her so much, she was able to let go of her girlfriend's hand and remove the crotch patch she was given to wear for modesty's sake. (Mimi Craven lay on the floor out of camera range for all Stone's sex scenes.) Douglas made her feel comfortable in the nude, but there was a more prosaic reason she dispensed with her little Velcro of Venus. Stone explained, "Every time you have to pee, you have to unglue and reglue it, which is quite painful. Besides, Michael's a real professional, and obviously there wasn't gonna be anything untoward, so I felt very safe. And, of course, there isn't anything sexy about doing sex scenes."

Douglas was such a good sport, if that's the right word, that when Stone decided to dispense with her panty shield, he dropped his flesh-colored jock. As one breathless journalist reported, "They agreed to expose their genitals to each other for their craft with nothing between them but molecules!"

Molecules and a distinct aversion for one another. For unexplained reasons, she and Michael Douglas didn't like each other. Douglas implied that making love to Stone was more heavy lifting than heavy breathing. "I've spent some quality time with her, yes," he said. "To create the illusion of the Fuck of the Century for ten or eleven hours a day, over four or five days of shooting, I mean, you're exhausted."

By December 1992, when the *Playboy* "Q & A" ran, critics

were hailing Stone as the twentieth century's Helen of Troy and Lola Montez. Studio executives would sack cities and bankrupt Bavaria to secure her services. Stone's girlhood dysmorphic body image, however, still plagued her. When *Playboy* asked what was going through her mind during *Basic Instinct*'s sexual pyrotechnics, her sad replay showed less embarrassment than self-loathing: "Yeah, like, why is my ass as large as it is?"

Stone was ambivalent but ultimately resigned to riding Douglas like a bronco, among other gymnastic feats in the bedroom and men's loo. She said, "The sex didn't worry me at all. But I told Paul there are not a lot of people I would do this for, because they'd spray me down with Evian, photograph me with a blue light, put the camera on my leg [?], and have me moan, 'This is so fabulous!'"

Plus, she was supposed to pretend to come in four minutes, coinciding with Douglas's staying power or lack thereof. Ultimately, the trouper surrendered to the creator's macho fantasies and threw herself into his delusion like the Methodical actress she was. "Once I realized that was what the guys wanted, I thought, Oh, I get it! No matter how he touches her or where he touches her or what else he does to her, it's the most, it's the best, it's the sexiest! I want to have some more of that! That's 'the fuck of the century,' according to the macho-man mentality." Stone's words sound as though she were resigned to colluding in this masculine inanity, but her behavior spoke louder than words. The *Playboy* interviewer mentioned that as she described her sex scenes in *Basic Instinct* at the St. James Club in West Hollywood, she became so disturbed and her voice so loud that people at adjoining booths in the restaurant began to turn around and stare.

As anyone who has $7.50 or a membership card at the local video store knows, *Basic Instinct* is the most sexually omnivorous film ever made. Whether or not it does indeed contain "the greatest screen performance of all time," it certainly contains one of the sexiest. It's also a poisoned cotton-candy confection right out of Krafft-Ebing, a bowl of popcorn drenched in amyl nitrate. But instead of *Venus in Furs,* it features a panty-free Stone in Grace Kelly-drag down to the severe chignon and basic white dress. (The hair and couture were Stone's idea; actually, they amounted to a demand from the brave but cloutless starlet. As she later recalled from the top of the heap, "When I did *Basic Instinct,* I said, 'I'm not going to wear a tight dress with my tits on a platter in the police-station scenes.' So they said, 'We don't care if you wear your hair in a bun and a turtleneck.' And I said, 'Okay, that's exactly what I'll do.'"

The convoluted plot revolves around sadomasochism, serial murder, sexual compulsion, bisexuality, misogyny, homophobia, fetishism—a veritable DSM of disorders and dysfunction. Oh, and Michael Douglas's character can't stop chain-smoking, the least of his vices, which include alcohol and substance abuse and a regrettable habit of shooting innocent bystanders in the line of duty.

Stone plays Catherine Tramell, typecast one more time as the most alluring woman in this or any alternate universe. She's Jackie Collins with an attitude, a bestselling author who may or may not moonlight as San Francisco's kitten with an ice pick, a serial murderer whose victims are tied up with Hermes scarves, then dispatched with a poke of the knife.

Michael Douglas is also typecast as a sex addict, a real-life role which allegedly caused the breakup of his nineteen-year marriage, which has yet to be dissolved. (Diandra Douglas filed for divorce in June 1996. The attorneys are still calculating a fifty-fifty split of a fortune estimated at $200 million. A very rich but very irate Douglas denied in the pages of *Vanity Fair* that he sought treatment as a sexual compulsive at Minnesota's Hazelden Clinic.) In the film, he's the troubled homicide detective assigned to find the ice picker and defang her. Stone's Tramell falls under suspicion because she's written a novel whose plot is identical to the homicide Douglas is investigating. Against his will, Douglas falls under her spell. His brilliantly modulated combination of lust and guilt recalls another tortured cop sexually obsessed with a similar toxic blonde—James Stewart in *Vertigo*. Douglas will never be as good an actor as the star of *Vertigo*, but as the nude tracking shot in Stone's bathroom shows, he's got a much better butt than the ectomorphic Stewart ever had.

Unfortunately for Douglas, Tramell is a major cocktease with a decided preference for women. Douglas's cop, still recovering from the suicide of his wife and a police shooting he was cleared of, is sexually famished, but Stone's empty-calorie buffet of sex and Mandarin contempt leave him hungry an hour later. During a psychotherapy session with his counselor, Douglas confesses that he's become a compulsive masturbator. "See the calluses," he says, waving his palms in the air.

Basic Instinct is a film whose parts are greater than its whole. The film is filled with memorable scenes that strangely add up to one big mess of a denouement as unsatisfying as sex with Catherine Tramell.

Newsweek's David Ansen summed up the critical dysphoria over this dysfunctional plot: "Funniest of all is that this whodunit gets so tangled up in its twists that half the audience can't figure out who *did* dunit when it's over." The critic failed to mention an even more egregious error in direction and script. *Basic Instinct* may be the only murder mystery that has no mystery. The $3 million writer gives away the identity of the killer in the first few frames of film. Her face may be hidden behind disheveled blond bangs, but as many later nude scenes prove, the 36B-cup breasts belong unmistakably to…(Rent the video if you can't complete the sentence.)

The other half of the audience must have understood whodunit or didn't care that the surprise ending was no surprise, because they patronized it to the unpatronizing tune of $285 million worldwide.

Some condemned *Basic Instinct* as a Caucasian *Kama Sutra,* except that the film made that pious piece of Indian pornography look like the *Book of Hours* by comparison. It was derided as a live-action, illustrated companion to Krafft-Ebing. And yet others evidently welcomed the alleged pervert into their homes as video sales and rentals surpassed the theatrical take.

With an opening weekend of $15 million, the box office justified the $50 million budget, although it had some critics carping that *Basic Instinct* was basically a $50-million porno movie. The money isn't all up there on the screen either, because at least $15 million of it ended up in superstar Douglas's pocket. Stone got the coolie wage of only $300,000–$400,000, depending on which trade you read. Poster art for the film is a semiotic gold mine. We see more flesh of the established star, a handsome daddy but at forty-eight not exactly a poster child for Calvin Klein. Stone's computer-perfect face is half-hidden behind Douglas's underdeveloped rhomboid muscle. Only her eyes peer out from behind his shoulder. They seem to be saying, "Just wait. You'll be seeing a lot more of me real soon." At least they're both nude, but the poster shows that the studio was clearly banking on Douglas's box-office clout, not his costar's beauty.

Indeed, with its muscular budget, instead of the usual skags who populate skin flicks, this triple X feature boasted the participation of the most beautiful woman in the world—with the University of Kentucky computer analysis to prove it. Douglas wasn't chopped liver, either. Pushing fifty, his sexy, muscled body proved two things: Weight training is the real fountain of youth, and men do look more distinguished with gray hair and the few wrinkles beyond the power of plastic surgery.

Despite the boffo box office of *Basic Instinct* and the previous year's *Terminator 2,* the film's producer, Carolco, was in trouble soon after the film went ballistic, listing debts of $171 million. Although *Newsweek*'s Ansen was good at handicapping Stone's prospects, the critic less sagely attributed the bankruptcy of Carolco to budgetary excess—$50 million, to be exact. However, it wasn't the millions spent on the film—and Douglas— that had Carolco's Kassar suffering terminal Golan-Globus syndrome. Carolco, like Canon ten years earlier, would go bust because it paid exorbitant sums to no-talent box-office talent like Sylvester Stallone, whose films didn't come close to earning *Basic Instinct*'s quarter billion.

With this choice of film, Stone's ability to handicap box-office potential finally caught up with her growth as an actress, and post–*Basic Instinct* paydays would balloon to $7 million. She must have breathed a sigh of relief when she finally retired her interior-decoration debt. It turned out to be money poorly spent. All those *tchotchkes* and chintz were for naught in her twelve-hundred-square-foot hovel in the hills of Hollywood. With her *Basic Instinct* fortune, she moved higher up the hill to an eleven-thousand-square-foot faux château fit for a fake Bourbon. This time the decorator was probably paid in cash.

The critics, of course, were not impressed with her box-office performance. They didn't care if Stone could afford to move to Valhalla. Republicans have always accused the press of being liberal, and for once they're right. Polls show that most journalists are far to the left on issues like gun control, abortion, tax breaks for the rich, and gay rights. And the press reserves its special venom for political incorrectness, especially when it's sexist or homophobic.

Basic Instinct was accused of being both. Of course, the media were right. Every lesbian in the film is a serial murderer—from Stone's girlfriend, who tries to run Douglas over with a Ferrari, to sweet, grandmotherly Dorothy Malone, who took a razor to her husband's and baby's throats years earlier. (Now she's dating Catherine.) Even the female psychologist, played by Jeanne Tripplehorn, is a tormented bisexual stalker.

David Ansen criticized this lesbian-vampire camp but found the film an equal-opportunity misogynist: "Every woman in this bizarre male fantasy—straight, gay, bi or undetermined—is or has been a killer. Indeed, the female roles in *Basic Instinct* are so peculiarly conceived, you'd swear the men who made the movie had never met a woman." Lucky for Ansen he hadn't seen Verhoeven and Eszterhas's collaboration on *Showgirls,* four years in the future. He would have written that the Abbott and Costello of feminism had never met an ecdysiast, either. How else do you explain Elizabeth Berkley's psycho stripper?

The only good guys are, well, guys. Douglas's cop may be a near rapist who drinks, snorts coke, and accidentally shoots tourists and his girlfriend, but he feels guilty about it. In fact, it's a testament to Douglas's acting skill that he can take such a flawed character and make us feel sorry for him rather than appalled. As written, the role would have been unbearable to watch if Stallone or even Eastwood had played such a bad good guy. Rambo and Dirty Harry have never evoked the sorrow and the pity Douglas manages to create. You feel genuine sympathy for the angst-ridden Douglas. He's not a bad man, he just does bad things—accidentally. His clumsiness with weapons and women makes him Don Knotts's Barney Fife after a decade pumping iron at Gold's.

The film's treatment of women was enough to make the *male* reviewers burn their wives' bras. Kenneth Turan of the *Los Angeles Times* criticized the filmmakers' ignorance of the difference between eroticism and exhibitionism, but *L.A. Weekly* saved its thunderbolts for industry misogyny and homophobia in general and *Basic Instinct*'s in particular: "Insulting various groups and genders has always been business as usual in Hollywood, and anyone who expects that to change is either out of town or just likes to hear the sound of their own voice." The critic, Michael Ventura, did derive one benefit from sitting through its 127 minutes of carnal carnage. It gave him a clean bill of mental health. With his usual guerrilla prose, Ventura wrote, "If you think you're fucked up and you go see this movie and you're *not* sexually aroused by it, then you're probably not as fucked up as you think you are. I'll confess that I found my lack of arousal positively comforting."

David Denby of *New York* magazine trashed the film and its star while marveling over the merchandising potential. *Basic Instinct,* he wrote, "will do wonders for the sale of headboards and Hermès scarves." Just as Clark Gable's G-rated frontal nudity in *It Happened One Night* more than sixty years ago caused the sales of T-shirts to plummet, Denby saw a bonanza for Bloomingdale's as bored *belles du jour* bought scarves with which to tie their husbands to the bedpost. It is hoped that sales of ice picks didn't also skyrocket.

Although bullish on the marketing possibilities, Denby felt that the female lead's performance was just bull. No handicapper of star potential, he inaccurately predicted, "The movie's forgettable star, the former model Sharon Stone [not for twelve years, David] is made up to resemble such blonde Hitchock ideals as Tippi Hedren. She's also dressed up in one scene to look like Kim Novak in *Vertigo*." Denby was right about the *hommages* to Hitchock, but they weren't limited to the look-alike female star.

Douglas' character shares the same occupation and sexual obsessions as James Stewart's cop in *Vertigo*. Plus Stone was exponentially more lovely than the plastic-wrapped Hedren or even Novak, who was typical 1950s zaftig.

Despite his heavy-handedness with female sexuality, Verhoeven showed that he had a light touch when homaging Hitch. Douglas's burned-out detective is Stewart in *Vertigo*, only kinkier. The staircase in *Basic Instinct* is an iconographic salute to *Vertigo*'s vertiginous bell tower. The antiheroine's weapon of choice, especially when she appears suddenly out of nowhere and stabs Douglas's partner with it, is a more svelte rendering of Tony Perkins's silverware in *Psycho*. Respectful is the operative word here when it comes to ripping off the master. George Dzundza's murder in the elevator honors but doesn't plagiarize Martin Balsam's backward tumble down the staircase of the Bates home. For all his ham-handedness, Verhoeven is no Brian De Palma, who has made a career out of plagiarizing Hitchock's greatest hits. (See De Palma's *Obsession, Blowout, Sisters*. On second thought, don't see them. Rent the superior originals—*Vertigo, Psycho*—they rip off.)

Surprisingly, amid all the critical venom, no one mentioned the film's real surprise ending. The surprise had nothing to do with the identity of the culprit, since she was ID'd in the very first frame. After all the hard-core sex and cynicism, genuinely surprising was the sentimental ending. Skip the next two paragraphs if you haven't rented the video.

At the climax, Douglas once again, in his lyrical words, enjoys the "fuck of the century," courtesy of the acrobatic Stone, who likes to be on top in bed. A psychologically consistent script would then have had Stone deliver the coup de grâce, an ice pick to the jugular and everywhere else.

Instead, she drops her weapon, rolls over, and hugs him. The implicit and preposterous message seems to be a reworking of the adage "Music hath power to soothe the savage beast." In this case, Douglas' devotion miraculously cures Stone of an encyclopedia of psychosexual pathology, which would have taken a mere psychoanalyst ten years and three days a week on his couch, not to mention a thirty-year-stretch in an institution for the criminally insane. (But a prison role for Stone was four years and an Oscar nomination away.)

The critical barbs were nothing compared to the reaction of gay and lesbian pressure groups. Sixty protesters from Queer Nation and the Gay & Lesbian Alliance Against Defamation turned out at a location shoot in a San Francisco back alley. For nonmembers who wanted to join the gang, Queer Nation left this helpful message on its answering machine: "You have reached the Queer Nation Emergency Hotline....GEFFEN, Gay Extremists Fighting Fascistic Entertainment Normalcy—a focus group of Queer Nation—urges you to join them at a protest of the filming of the lesbophobic, biphobic movie *Basic Instinct* [which] features a razor-wielding man-killer dyke and an ice-pick-happy man-killer bi woman, both scary stereotypes." Other activists damned the film's misandry and demanded the addition of female victims to prevent the film from becoming a male basher's fantasy. *As if,* to quote the late-twentieth-century pop philosopher Alicia Silverstone, enough teenaged girls hadn't already been sliced and diced in countless permutations of *Friday the 13th* and Clive Barker plasmathons.

Producer Alan Marshall had providently obtained a restraining order to keep the straight bashers 100 feet away from the crew. Queer Nation spokesman Jonathan Katz insisted that his group complied with the order. Marshall disagreed and further inflamed the situation by making a citizen's arrest of thirty-one pickets at another location. The pickets had ignored the assistant D.A.'s order of "quiet on the set" and noisily chanted, yelled, and blew whistles, according to *Daily Variety*. Executing Marshall's arrest, police loaded the protesters into paddy wagons for a trip downtown, where they were immediately released and returned to the set to further disrupt production.

Screenwriter Eszterhas expressed remorse after the denunciations and the police *aktion,* which he felt resembled stock footage from *Schindler's List*. "I was sorry about the arrests. I've always believed in trying to communicate with people, not arresting them. I admit it's a perverse situation because I'm fighting to change my own script with a director who doesn't want change," Eszterhas said. Many of his scripts, not just *Basic Instinct,* suggest he hates women, but his films' rampant lesbianism suggests even more strongly that he likes to watch two women get it on. He's a misogynist but not a homophobe. To mollify the protesters, he submitted seventeen pages of gay-sensitive changes in his script, all of which were summarily rejected by producer-star Douglas and the director, who, at fifty-eight, remains unaffected by Generation Stonewall. (See *Show-girls*'s killer-lesbian-heroine.) Douglas defended his rejection of the revisions and bashed the screenwriter. He insisted, "Look, it's a hot, sexy thriller. That's why I wanted to do it. Joe [Eszterhas] claimed it was a matter of principle, and now we know this man has no principles." Douglas's latter assertion is puzzling, since Eszterhas had yet to sit down at his laptop and compose his "lesbophobic" epic to the dance of lap, *Showgirls*.

The *Washington Post* described one rewrite that was patronizing but at least better intentioned than Verhoeven, who has a doctorate in math and physics but apparently flunked Political Correctness 101. Douglas's partner on the force, George Dzundza, who has a vaguely homoerotic resentment against his best friend's infatuation with Stone, was given a new line by Eszterhas. In the original draft, Dzundza asks if Stone's Catherine is gay. In the rewrite, Douglas flies off the handle and says, "A lot of the best people I've met in this town are gay." That condescending attitude resembles a famous diptych of disingenuousness: "Some of my best friends are Jewish," and, "The check is in the mail."

The writer also lobbied the director, to no avail, to cut one of his own lines, where Dzundza says in reference to Tramell's degree from Berkeley, "That magna cum *lawdy* pussy on her done fried up your brain."

In the pages of *Vanity Fair,* Eszterhas revealed the minutes of a story meeting with the director preproduction: "Verhoeven's first comment when he walked in was 'How can we put more tits and cunt into this movie?' [Verhoeven] made a gigantic argument for a lesbian sex scene on screen. [Then producer] Irwin Winkler and I both felt that the sole reason to put this kind of scene on the screen was for titillation value and for prurient as opposed to artistic reasons."

Eszterhas, some reporters cynically suggested, had more cogent reasons for suddenly trying to raise everyone's consciousness, since his original draft showed his taste was also in the gutter. The writer's wife and newborn baby lived in the Bay Area, and he feared the retribution of Queer Nation's more bloodthirsty sans culottes.

After the director ignored all his entreaties to change the script he had originally submitted, Eszterhas begged that at least this disclaimer run before the film began: "The movie you are about to see is fiction." By this time, producer Winkler had quit in disgust. So had Eszterhas, but he came back in one last vain attempt to domesticate his own homophobic creation. Douglas put on a second hat as producer after Winkler's departure. As the new producer, Douglas summarily dismissed Eszterhas' plea. "Sure, why didn't we have a disclaimer before *Wall Street* that said, 'This doesn't mean that every Wall Street banker is a crook or before *Fatal Attraction,* 'This doesn't mean every single woman is a psycho.'"

Douglas, of course, was being disingenuous with his desperate analogies. There have been plenty of positive role models on-screen for rich people. Ditto for women, although not in any Verhoeven-Eszterhas collaborations. Until *Philadelphia* came along and collected a few Oscars, gays, when they appeared in movies at all, were leather-jacketed psychopaths in *Cruising* or crazed bank robbers in love with drag queens (*Dog Day Afternoon*).

Finally, Eszterhas reached the last stage of Elisabeth Kübler-Ross's famous stages of dying, the stage called acceptance, although his was a moral death. "I don't want to be part of anything that lends itself to gay bashing," said Eszterhas, who would later write the most evil lesbian role in the history of cinema, played by Gina Gershon in *Showgirls.* "But minority groups of any kind have to accept the possibility that among them is a sociopath. Is it wise that the only villains we ever see on-screen be white male WASPs?"

In a last gasp before expiring morally, Esztheras resorted to self-mockery, telling a journalist, who reported it as fact, that his next script would be about a liberal Democratic president who is photographed having sex with a Holstein. The film would be entitled *Sacred Cows*. Lamely, Eszterhas joked, "This time it may be the animal-rights groups doing the protesting." Today, amid disclosures of the president's top adviser's foot fetish, close encounters of the bovine kind in the White House might seem as wholesome as milk by comparison.

Trouper that she was, Stone didn't have any moral second thoughts and came to her big break's defense in an interview with the *New York Times*'s Bernard Weinraub. "Certainly this is a time when people have a lot of fear about sex, and the film brings up that issue." That's like saying *Bambi* is anti–National Rifle Association. The film in fact offers an equivocal message about safer sex when Douglas, after his first "fuck of the century," says to his partner, "Next time I'll use a condom." That's the hero, not the villain, pushing unsafe sex.

Stone brushed aside all objections, whether over safe sex or unsafe lesbians. "To me, this is really a very dark and twisted love story. The character is, let's face it, kind of loony tunes."

Stone was troubled that the condemnation of her character's sexual orientation got all the attention when Tramell's sideline should have caused more outrage. She complained, "I am infinitely less comfortable with the fact that the public is more concerned with whether or not I was nude or gay than whether or not I was a fucking serial killer. Excuse me very much, but where are your priorities, people?"

The actress found it amusing rather than troubling that her performance was so convincing that strangers reacted in real life as though she had an ice pick in her Louis Vuitton handbag. "People who have seen the movie stand two feet away from me. They speak to me in careful tones. They don't condescend to me at all anymore." That, of course, had nothing to do with the fear of fatal jugular wounds and everything to do with her newfound box-office clout.

London's avant-garde magazine *Time Out* agreed with Stone,

not me. "At times it is difficult to work out where 34-year-old Sharon Stone ends and her character Catherine Tramell starts. They both have self-confidence and candor that borders on brazen." The big difference, of course, is that Stone doesn't sleep with an ice pick.

In fact, much more than the nudity and X-rated sex, the ice pick troubled her the most. Slashing victims was infinitely more disconcerting than making love to them, despite all the anatomical incorrectness. Stone described her hatchet job as "traumatizing beyond relief." She was no Catherine Tramell, whatever the pathology-oriented press in the U.K. said. In fact, she required personal and professional assistance just to cope with the trauma. Besides the comfort of best friend Craven on the floor, out of camera range, during the lethal sex scenes, paramedics stood by with an oxygen tank and mask because she came close to passing out several times, Stone claimed.

The director's behavior didn't help. Stone's public statements about his cruel misogyny gained credibility after his work on *Showgirls* showed he won't be attending any thirtieth-anniversary cocktail parties for *Ms.* magazine. If Stone's account is true, Verhoeven treated her like pond scum during scenes where he should have been holding her free hand between takes while Mimi held the other.

Stone said, "I had such a hard time with the killing scenes that Paul screamed at me the entire time we were doing them. He screamed like a lunatic, to evoke or provoke or, I don't know, he just generally badgered the shit out of me."

His abuse so frazzled the actress, her dialogue, what there was of it, had to be dubbed postproduction. During the looping session, Stone added, the editor and sound recordist were as traumatized by handling the footage as she had been shooting it.

Although it seemed like a love story to her, Stone was politically aware enough to know what really sold the movie to lubricious men around the world. *Basic Instinct,* she agreed with *Time Out,* was a "murderous male wet dream." She refused to take seriously what Douglas's cop calls their "fuck of the century." From a woman's perspective, Stone felt that the direction showed just how little the filmmaker knew about female sexual response. "How can it be the fuck of the century when a woman has to pretend to have three orgasms in four minutes from anatomically incorrect positions? I mean, that's a total male fantasy."

The erotic power of this bedroom duet proved the stars' ability to fake—whatever. According to *People* magazine, the on-screen chemistry between Stone and Douglas was purely test tube. "Michael and Sharon didn't even like each other," the magazine stated, quoting as usual an unnamed source "close to the film." Like director, like (male) star. Stone corroborated the lack of offscreen chemistry in a *Playboy* interview in 1992. In an industry where the First Commandment is Never dish a superstar you may be desperate to work with again, she said, up-front and personal, "I was never comfortable around him, and I don't think he was comfortable around me."

One wonders how the cameraman felt when Stone allegedly showed up on the set packing lead. Don't sue me. Sue *Esquire,* which claimed she waved a gun in the cinematographer's face and said, "If I see one ounce of cellulite on the screen, you're a dead man." Fortunately for the director and the cameraman, Stone wasn't armed when she saw the dailies of Nebraska.

Consummate professional that she is, Stone used their between-takes tension to enrich the on-screen antirelationship. Since Stone's character spends 90 percent of the film tormenting Douglas's tormented cop, the fricton they felt for each other in real life enriched their reel life. Or as Stone succinctly put it, "I think that kind of discomfort lends itself to this kind of movie. Tension is good."

When I watched the film on video, I was struck by two things in the bedroom scenes. Maybe just to save time, the director suggests that Douglas is a premature ejaculator. Unrealistically, he suggests the same thing about Stone.

But hey, *Basic Instinct* paid all those pesky decorating bills. "But that's what the script called for. So that's cool," said Stone, the cheerleader she never was at Saegertown High.

Her dissection of Tramell's character shows that she didn't consider herself a traitor to her sex. Catherine may be a man's woman, but she's also Stone's kind of gal. "It felt right for me to play Catherine. She not only embodies a male fantasy, but she also knows what she is doing. So she is not a victim of a male fantasy. It is her decision to do that to gain power."

Tramell is all powerful in the film. She's the John Wayne of estrogen. After *Basic Instinct* came out, Demi Moore publicly castigated herself for turning down the role. She was particularly smitten with the police-interrogation scene, which she felt brilliantly demonstrated that the movie was about female empowerment, not male masturbatory fantasies, as Stone suggested. They were both right. You *can* have it both ways sometimes.

Just ask Catherine Tramell.

Defenders of the movie, including quite a few critics, insisted that everybody in *Basic Instinct,* not just the homosexuals, were weirdos. Chris Fowler, executive director of the media-savvy Gay & Lesbian Alliance Against Defamation (GLAAD), didn't buy that argument. "We're opposed to the film's depiction of lesbians as ice pick–wielding, man-hating murderers. It's not that we want to be portrayed only in a positive light. We want balance and fairness. The first time there's a gay hero in a major studio film, then I'll accept gay villains." Fowler would have to wait three years for Tom Hanks's AIDS-afflicted litigator to win an Oscar.

The protesters didn't confine their protests to production. When the film hit the theaters, so did the pickets. One ingenious gimmick involved carrying placards that claimed to give away the identity of the culprit. "...Did It," the *Los Angeles Times* reported the sign's contents, delicately refusing to spoil the surprise and ally itself with the protesters.

Picketeer Anne Gaudino told the *Times,* "Our major focus is to keep people from going to the film. We want to tell everybody as much about the movie as possible. We're not trying to prevent them from making a movie, but [by revealing the murderer] we would certainly like to cut into the obscene amount of money they intend to make." Rumors, unfounded, also spread that the more Bolshevik elements of Queer Nation planned to release stink bombs in theaters nationwide. Only leaflets revealing the ending, however, made it inside theaters. Plans to rent billboards with

similar revelations didn't materialize on the Sunset Strip, as
threatened. One armchair critic said of the stink-bomb threat,
"That would have been redundant. There was enough stench on
the screen." Fortunately for the filmmakers, Smell-o-Vision went
out of fashion in the 1960s along with Cinerama and Mamie Van
Doren. The rumors of sabotage began to reach gerbil levels of
preposterousness. One claimed that activists planned to release
moths in theaters so that they would buzz around the movie
projector and cloud the image on the screen.

The pickets and the *Times* need not have wasted their time
over the identity of the murderer. As *Newsweek* said, by the end
of this whodunit, you still didn't know who did it. Some even felt
Henry Ford was once again proved right that there's no such thing
as bad publicity. The picketers guaranteed that local TV news
cameras would show up and provide free advertising for the film's
opening. And as its first weekend gross of $15 million showed,
the protesters were unwitting promotional tools for the film.
Danny Mangin, arts editor for the gay weekly *Bay Area Reporter,*
thought that the brouhaha was much ado about not a whole lot.
"It's amusing, when you consider how bad the film is, the amount
of publicity it's getting. I didn't leave feeling angry, particularly. I
just thought it was a waste of two hours. There are definitely
stereotypes in there. Some kind of message that either bi or
lesbian characters are liable to commit mayhem. But it's not at
some crisis point and I would want to make sure people realize
this. There are worse examples of 'lesbian treachery' in Hollywood films." It would take a more knowledgeable trivia buff than
this writer to name a film containing more psycho lesbos than
Basic Instinct. More frequently, gay activists complain about
"lesbian treachery" committed offscreen by celebrities who
refuse to come out, even though their sexual orientation is the
worst-kept secret in town. A two-time Oscar winner and a top talk
show host are both said to be chomping at the bit to come out of
their gilded closets, but handlers and publicists have shoved them
back in, claiming it would be career death. Since no leading man
or lady has ever come out, predictions of their death seem greatly
exaggerated. One studio executive believes box office, not bisex-

uality, determines a star's longevity. "If you make a good movie, nobody's gonna care if you're doing it with a llama or a lesbian," the executive says. If a major actor came out, industry observers would hold their breath until his or her next film opened. If it was a stinker, even the star's gay fans would stay home. If it were *Independence Day 2*, homophobes from Dubuque to Boise would queue outside theaters opening day.

Stone couldn't have agreed with the writer for the *Bay Area Reporter* more. *Basic Instinct* was much ado about kinky sex with no more profound implications than whether things go better with Jack Daniels and Coke. (Her character in the film insists they do.) "I keep telling people this movie is not profound, not important. Everybody wants me to say all these things about the deep psychological effects of this movie," Stone said in exasperation. "This movie is a thriller! You know, I do these interviews, answer all these questions, and try to be really thoughtful. And I go home at the end of the day thinking: What's the big deal?"

Activist Anne Gaudino, who had only seen the trailer, thought it was a very big deal. She didn't share Stone or the *Bay Area Reporter's* sangfroid. She shouted from her place in the picket line, "Dykes in Spandex!" referring to Stone and her girlfriend's clothing in the bathroom of the pansexual disco. "Where do they get these ideas from—the Playboy Channel?" Gaudino obviously doesn't watch the cable channel, which is squeaky heterosexual. The film's sapphic fixation owes more to *Penthouse* publisher Bob Guccione's preoccupation with digital vaginal stimulation than Hefner's obsession with preposterous cup size. As for the risible display of spandex, Gaudino would have probably been angrier if the film had used a more common stereotype and outfitted the girls in flannel shirts and combat boots from L. L. Bean.

Gays weren't the only ones upset over *Basic Instinct's* message and Stone's crimes of fashion. Many straight critics felt that the film was even more misogynist than homophobic despite the fact that all the lesbians were monsters. Unlike gay activists and Gaudino, who had only seen the trailer, Tammy Bruce, president of the Los Angeles chapter of the National Organization for

Women (NOW), hadn't been denied admission to a preview screening. After she saw the film, Bruce left the theater and joined the picketing lesbians outside. Bruce said, "It's a textbook example of the backlash against women in the media. We've found the problems of the film larger than simple homophobia." Bruce saw a bigger conspiracy than gay-bashing. "There was clearly a larger agenda at work targeted against women. *Basic Instinct* was clearly woven to send messages about women in general: that women are dangerous liars who are not to be trusted and who are to be used sexually. The objectification in the film was overwhelming."

Naomi Wolfe, author of *The Beauty Myth*, had also seen the film. Wolfe is the kind of rabid feminist Rush Limbaugh loves to call a "feminazi." Feminazis call him a fat Fascist pig. Amazingly, Wolfe disagreed with Bruce and NOW. Like Paglia, who has been disavowed by feminists, she felt that *Basic Instinct* was about female empowerment, not subjugation:

"What was so cathartic about *Basic Instinct* was here was not a cartoon villainess like in *Fatal Attraction*—not a misogynist two-dimensional nightmare—but a complex, compelling Nietzschean *Überfräulein* who owns everything about her own power. She's rich. She's not ashamed of being rich, which is transgressive in the ideology of femininity."

Wolfe's comments praising the depiction of a serial murderess as "empowered" says more about the lack of strong screen roles for women than it does about the "power" of Tramell's personality. A serial killer isn't empowered. She's nuts.

Wolfe was a minority of one among a larger minority. At least she had seen the film, unlike the gay and lesbian pickets.

TriStar's distribution chief, William Soady, felt that was the source of the problem. Protesters based their barbs on hearsay, not on the film's contents, which many of them had not seen, thanks to Soady's colleagues in publicity and the security muscle they hired for the press screenings. The executive claimed that the anger was based on word of mouth rather than reel experience. "There was a constant barrage from the gay community as to their dissatisfaction for this film. When [the media] investigated further, they found people who were protesting had not even seen the film."

Wolfe's analysis seems to back up Soady's contention. The women in the film may be liars, dangerous and untrustworthy, but Tramell is never, ever, "used sexually," in Tammy Bruce's phrase. Stone's spider waiting for the male fly is the biggest user in the history of female screen characters. She uses people sexually and in every other way for pleasure and book research.

TriStar wasn't taking any chances on amusement or outrage by gays. The press screening in San Francisco was hush-hush and its location a closely guarded secret with security thugs all over the undisclosed place. The invitees were also kept to a minimum at the less-than-all-media screening. A writer for the *New York Times* Syndicate at the time, I attended a press preview in Beverly Hills at the Academy Theater that was notable for its lack of studio paranoia. No security guards, although the unarmed studio publicists as usual seemed more threatening than moonlighting cops packing lead. And the press list was anything but limited; the cavernous Academy auditorium overflowed with representatives of supermarket-coupon publications and gay-bar rags. Since the 1920s and Ramón Navarro, the 1930s and George Cukor, Los Angeles and the gay community have always exhibited a live-and-let-live symbiosis as long as the gay life was lived discreetly in the closet. The conspiracy of silence by both sides remains alive and well to this day.

The articulate Gaudino commented on this conspiracy while deploring Stone's bathroom fashion sense. "We never get to see anything but the creatures of male fiction. In *Fried Green Tomatoes,* you had Mary Stuart Masterson playing the cutest baby-butch dyke I've ever seen. But the film was so coded that nobody knew she was lesbian but us. And now *Basic Instinct.* We're either invisible or crazed. That's not good enough."

It was good enough for the general population. They still kept coming until a quarter billion had piled up. The film succeeded despite a major handicap created by the studio's own paranoid fumbling. In all of its newspaper ads for the movie, TriStar failed to list the movie theaters where it was playing, not to mention its playing times. How were people to know when and where to catch the ice-pick capades at the multiplex? Somehow they knew. And they came.

An executive at a rival studio didn't feel that the pickets helped market the film. He actually praised his competitor's marketing team, insisting that the trailer showing "sex like they haven't seen on the screen before" accounted for the swollen box office, not annoying women in flannel and men in tank tops waving plot points on cardboard signs. For his studio's sake, let's hope this myopic mogul is kept out of the marketing department. Trailers are mandated by the Motion Picture Association of America (MPAA) to be G rated. If they showed anything of Stone and Douglas' sexual gymnastics, the shots had to be from the neck up. And the trailer makers would have had to reshoot the scene to remove the blood from Stone's face.

The MPAA unwittingly, as usual, contributed its own advertising bonanza by threatening *Basic Instinct* with an NC-17 rating if cuts other than the murderer's weren't made pronto. The studio was terrified. NC-17 meant that kids sixteen and under wouldn't get to watch Stone suck on her girlfriend's nipple or witness bondage scenes that would have made De Sade blush.

The studio's phobia of NC-17 has always mystified anyone who pays attention outside theaters. Basically, if you're tall enough to push $7.50 under the cashier's window, you can get in to see Triple X epics like *My Burning Bush* and *Debbie Does* the largest city in Texas.

Surprise! The film ultimately got an R rating, as Verhoeven's contract stipulated. But not before the director turned into a First Amendment Nazi and decried the censorship of his "art," which managed to keep its R rating despite lines like the one uttered by a homicide detective examining the mutilated body of a murder victim postcoitus: "There's cum stains all over the sheets. He got off before he got offed." Followed by giggles from the happy guys in homicide. The film went up or downhill from there, depending on "how fucked up you are," in the lambent prose of the *L.A. Weekly*'s Michael Ventura.

Verhoeven didn't have to cut any dialogue to get the coveted

R. He just had to delete forty-seven seconds of Douglas and Stone engaging in cunnilingus and fellatio, respectively.

Another dim-bulb studio executive, who probably makes half a mil a year, felt that the success of the film had nothing to do with Stone simulating orgasm more times than a Traci Lords video epic. People paid their $7.50 to see Michael Douglas's tush, which *was* firm but not nearly as sensational as the view offered up by Stone. The unnamed marketing executive, who probably worked on *Howard the Duck,* said, "Explicit sex scenes are not that good at promoting a film. Michael Douglas guaranteed a good show." The unnamed executive sounds hypogonadal. Or maybe he donned a mask and joined his brothers picketing the theaters.

Sharon Stone's stardom was confirmed with the official anointing of yet another *Playboy* cover, except that inside the only thing she showed was F & N (face and neck) rather than 1990's T & A. A question-and-answer interview, which has been accorded to everyone from Jimmy Carter to Donald Trump, replaced the copy of two years ago when the magazine marveled, "Sharon says what she thinks—and she thinks a *lot*."

Instead, *Playboy's* interrogator, David Sheff, would discuss more thought provoking topics, like the influence of "Chekhov, Shakespeare, Wilde, and Mamet" on her acting. Stone added, "I had worked on every great part for women there is. Then I did every great part there is for men" in acting class.

Despite its nudes, with their Valium-lidded eyes and "greased tits on a platter," to use Stone's phrase, the skin magazine is a crackerjack armchair psychoanalyst. The confessions their interviewers manage to wring from tight-lipped stars like De Niro and Pacino make you suspect that they hook their subjects up to lie detectors as well as an electroshock machine that punishes them with 100 volts whenever they stonewall.

Except for her refusal to discuss the Nebraska footage, Stone didn't need electroconvulsive therapy to shock readers with her self-revelations. The interviewer got her to reveal a fear of intimacy that may explain why her relationships with men have never lasted longer than three years.

Asked if simulating intimate sex in front of millions of

moviegoers felt "odd," Stone said, "I suppose I reveal some sort of disturbed part of my personality when I tell you that I'm more comfortable in that situation than in a real intimate situation." She mentioned an upcoming emcee job at Camp Pendleton's fiftieth anniversary. "There will be thousands of marines. I know exactly how to have that relationship. That's easier for me than being alone with one man in my living room."

Even Stone had her limits when it came to self-revelation in the pages of *Playboy*. As the intrepid interviewer pressed on about her fear of intimacy, she jumped off the psychiatrist's couch and said firmly, "That's all I have to say about that. I don't want to discuss the psychology of my personal life. Let's move on to something else." Stone demonstrated a self-possession and reticence that even more closemouthed stars like Richard Gere have felt themselves impossible to maintain under the relentless interrogation of the magazine's randy Grand Inquisitors.

And she didn't have to show anything below her neck to get a fifteen-page spread in the magazine. Not even her psyche.

The interviewer revealed perhaps more of himself than he cared to, since his job was to do that to his subject. Her stonewalling made him testy, and he tried to guilt-trip her about baring all when he quoted Bernadette Peters's claim that once you take your clothes off, "you stop being your character. The character's clothes make you the character." In effect, Sheff dismissed a great deal of *Basic Instinct* as stripping rather than acting.

Stone remained nonplussed by this trashing of her screen work and let rip an epigram worthy of Wilde or Coward. "I've never found my character in the closet," she said. When the interviewer pressed on with his theory, Stone stopped being Wilde and turned into Rambo. "I think that's all bullshit," she said. End of inquiry.

No longer the Mr. Bill of starlets, Stone now had clout, and her new attitude influenced her choice of films. *Basic Instinct*'s quarter billion box office would give her the power to pick her projects and keep her clothes on—when she wanted to.

11

Genghis Stone

IN 1993, SHARON STONE was at a crossroads in her aesthetic evolution as actress and script reader. The fork in the road was the width of the Grand Canyon and just as perilous.

She could turn into the Bo Derek of the 1990s, a one-hit wonder, a flash in the interrogation chair. Or she could become the new Jane Fonda after *They Shoot Horses, Don't They?*—a sex kitten who matured into a big cat, queen of the screen jungle.

Basic Instinct could be either her *10* or her *Barbarella*. Her next film could be her *Bolero* or *Klute,* a sex cartoon or a walking, talking DSM that won its leading lady an Oscar.

Sliver was something less than *Klute*. Unlike Fonda in 1971, no Oscar followed Stone home after *Sliver*'s release. Fortunately, *Sliver* was light-years away from *Bolero,* an exhibitionist's bad joke.

Expectations were enormous after *Basic Instinct*. It's a tribute to the actress's daring and perhaps her IQ that she chose not to clone her *Basic Instinct* performance and picked a role 180 degrees away from the empowered emasculatrix.

119

Her Carly Norris in *Sliver* is a sad, lonely book editor at Sutton. Coming out of a seven-year marriage punctuated by wife battering, she is afraid of men and relationships. She's as vulnerable as Catherine was omnivorous.

When the camera introduces Carly, Stone shows she is capable of De Niroesque transformations. Her sad, lost eyes look as though they belong to another woman—not the see-through-your-angst-bullshit gaze she trained on Douglas's flawed cop. As the film's director, Phillip Noyce, marveled, she starts out like Grace Kelly and ends up "like, well, Sharon Stone."

In *Sliver,* Stone works a self-trashing miracle. She manages to look plain. Almost. She will forever remain handicapped by her bone structure. Our Helen of Troy has morphed into—Okay, not Medusa, not even Redgrave could do that—but maybe a sad-eyed Niobe, to beat a mythic Greek metaphor to death.

Stone also reveals herself to be the least narcissistic beauty on-screen. She doesn't pull a Barbra Streisand in *Nuts,* playing a patient who's been in a mental institution for six months but who has somehow gained access to professional hair and makeup people. The same woman who voluntarily posed nude in *Playboy* with no makeup allows the costumer and hairstylist to trash her. Her usually luxurious mane is cropped short and slicked back with mousse, the whole monstrosity contained by a Hillary headband. For much of the film she wears a cloche that hides most of her hair.

Nudity in the film reflects her newfound clout and a natural reticence that is anything but exhibitionist. The much-ballyhooed bathtub masturbation sequence focuses almost entirely on her face. This may represent a first in cinema erotica. Onanism from the neck up.

Although *Sliver* was a soporific bore, Stone's character was amazingly complex, especially compared to the one-note omnivore of her preceding film. To call Stone's Carly Norris frigid is like saying the *Titanic* struck an ice cube. At the beginning of the film, Carly is a perfect Ado Annie for the disease-plagued 1990s; a girl who just can't say yes, a bathtub Molly Bloom. A more literate screenwriter would have had her murmur, "Yes, I said yes," as she used the *other* hand to flip through a paperback of *Ulysses* in the famous bathroom sequence.

At this point in her career, Stone was still a team player. On later films she might lay down the law and keep her panties on, but in *Sliver* she was still feeling her way along the corridors of movie-star power. She *asked* to keep her bra on for one scene. "That is, if we convince all the boys that it would be better," she told the costume designer, Deborah Scott. Scott, who didn't have a lot to do, since the characters spend so much of the time not wearing costumes, was delighted. At least she got to design a brassiere. Scott told Stone, "I love the idea." Referring to the star's bust measurement, the designer added mystifyingly, "I've seen 36Cs come and go in this town, but 36Bs are timeless."

When the camera does glide over her nude body like a pervert's eye, we never get near *Basic Instinct*'s full disclosure. You suspect she told the director, Phillip Noyce, the same thing she later told the producer of *Diabolique* when he ordered her to strip for the camera: Get the hell out of my face and my Winnebago. Her clout manifests itself when costar William Baldwin performs oral sex, shot again from the neck up. Baldwin's muff diver never surfaces on-screen. Maybe Stone was just heeding the warning of one critic, who said, "If I see Sharon Stone coming on celluloid one more time, I'm going to join the V-chip vigilantes!"

Even more chaste than the bathtub erotica and cunnilingus is the sole flash scene. In a four-star restaurant, Stone takes Baldwin up on his dare and exposes her breasts. But in this flash scene we not only don't catch a glimpse of her lower anatomy; there's isn't even any nipple. The writer, Eszterhas, does echo his peculiar fetish for women's lingerie. Stone, again off camera and under the table, removes her by now iconographic panties at the restaurant and hands them over to Baldwin, who waves them in the shocked waiter's face. And they say they don't write good roles for women anymore!

Sliver is based on the novel by the birth father of *Rosemary's Baby*, Ira Levin. Like the previous novel turned film, the story is set in a luxury Manhattan high-rise. This time, however, the location is a thin phallic building known in East Sidese as a "sliver" rather than the sprawling Dakota of *Rosemary's Baby*.

Also like the story of Mia's diabolical progeny, dead bodies keep falling out from behind Lalique sconces and Aubusson rugs. The potential for gore is no doubt what attracted Eszterhas, his laptop keyboard still dripping blood from *Basic Instinct,* to the novel. Not for nothing has Eszterhas been nicknamed the Antichrist Alan Alda of "women's films."

He must have been chastened by the backlash of feminists and gay activists. The world of *Sliver* is a lesbian-free zone, a unique phenomenon in the writer's sapphic filmography. For the women in the film, it's strictly a hands-off policy, while the men have their hands all over the place. Okay, women are debased and mutilated, but at least they're not evil, unless you count the coke-snorting prostitute next door, who is merely tweaked rather than no good.

Someone in the high-rise is slicing and dicing the beautiful residents. The film opens with a Stone look-alike falling to her death after being pushed by a hooded extra from *The Seventh Seal*. Will Stone's Carly be next? That question lamely propels the rest of the film's interminable two hours.

Aussie director Phillip Noyce must have been asleep at the Movieola. It's hard to square the director of the terrifying *Dead Calm* and action-packed *Patriot Games* with the auteur of this soporific thriller.

Sliver, however, was a personal triumph and showcase for Stone. It demonstrates her exponential growth as an actress from one-note omnivore in *Basic Instinct* to her brilliantly modulated creation of a woman both repelled and compelled by intimacy. (See her whirlwind affair-dump of coproducer Bill MacDonald concurrent with the film.)

The actress makes an old actor's cliché fresh. She manages to rise above the material, although that's not much of a levitation act considering the bargain-basement screenplay and discount direction. Noyce's *hommage* is marked down from Hitch's *Rear Window* and *Psycho*. Baldwin also proves he deserves a career better than the one he has, becalmed in the doldrums of adventures with Cindy Crawford. At first, Baldwin's *GQ*-quality looks are marred by little pig eyes. He soon accomplishes a Streepish transformation when his sexual charisma manages to turn his one unattractive feature into the cutest puppy-dog eyes since a transsexual male collie by the name of Lassie had a litter on-screen. This accomplishment is even more praiseworthy, since it's soon revealed that the puppy is more like a pit bull with a video camera.

If only the director and writer had shown skill equal to their two leads. Just how incompetent is this Hitchcock rip-off? As in *Basic Instinct,* the $3-million man, Eszterhas, shows himself to be a know-nothing whodunit hack. The suspects are almost immediately narrowed down to two characters: Baldwin's nerdy computer hacker and Tom Berenger's alcoholic, impotent novelist.

The story tries to conjure up *Psycho,* arming Berenger with a knife and Baldwin with a mother fixation Norman Bates would have understood.

Like James Stewart in *Rear Window,* Baldwin is also a voyeur, but he lives in the age of the computer chip, and his Peeping Tom uses hidden video cameras to spy on the building's occupants rather than Stewart's low-tech binoculars. In another nod to the master, Berenger does use binoculars, while Stone finds herself, against her will, turning into a voyeur after Baldwin gives her a high-powered telescope.

Baldwin and Stone's reported feud/fight off camera doesn't show up in their on-screen chemistry, which *Penthouse* would rate high on its Peter meter. Their multiple orgasms are even more erotic than Stone and Douglas's couplings, since they involve a minimum of blood and yucks. There is one regrettable rerun from *Basic Instinct.* Eszterhas seems preoccupied with anal intercourse in his screenplays. Just as Douglas's shrink gets taken from behind by her patient—clearly a violation of the doctor-patient relationship—Stone finds herself shoved up against a pillar in her apartment, facing the wall, while Baldwin makes a similar back-door entry.

As distasteful and disturbing as the scene is to watch, it also looks real, testament to their acting ability rather than their libidos, because Stone and Baldwin loathed each other off camera.

The friction between the two stars had a specific cause. Never go dancing with Billy Baldwin. The actor creamed his leading lady's foot. Stone had already suffered a broken ankle making *Year of the Gun* in Rome, and Baldwin's clumsiness must have been a case of adding injury to injury.

Undisclosed trouble had already been brewing when Baldwin unintentionally wreaked havoc with her instep. But his misstep was in the line of duty. Director Noyce completely absolved the actor of culpability, insisting, "It was an accident." The scene called for Baldwin to bump into Stone as he ran down the stairs. Baldwin went careening downward and landed on her foot. Noyce, a full-service filmmaker, personally ferried the disabled actress to the Paramount infirmary. "I know it hurt her because I carried her to the hospital. By the time we got there, her foot was quite swollen, so he must have landed fairly heavily on her."

Noyce bizarrely blamed the collision on nervousness over the explicit sex rather than a simple stumble: "Actors, particularly male actors, get very tense around the lovemaking scenes. Their arousal sometimes can get out of hand; they have no control over it, and they are embarrassed by it."

Paramount was embarrassed by the director's cut, which was so hot-cha-cha it made Stone's preceding film look like a sequel to the *Sound of Music* with a soundtrack by UB40 and Neneh Cherry instead of Rodgers and Hammerstein. The MPAA's ratings board summarily branded it NC-17. If Noyce wanted the coveted—and contractually stipulated—R rating, 110 separate editing changes would have to be made, the MPAA decreed ex cathedra. Noyce appealed and bargained the board down to a mere fifty cuts—forty seconds in all.

But what a filthy forty seconds they were. Noyce apparently ran such a loose ship that even he wasn't aware of all the smut on-screen. And we do mean smut. Baldwin plays a voyeur who watches all the residents of the high-rise on hidden video monitors. One monitor, which Noyce didn't notice, showed a man with his head between a woman's legs. The actor must have been improvising, because the sequence didn't come from the script or the director. Eventually, Noyce hired an assistant whose full-time assignment was to ferret out any other indiscretions. The assistant apparently forgot to draw her boss's attention to another yucky scene, because it made it into the final cut. A ponytailed recording executive clinches a business deal on a cellular phone. He's also nude and seated on a toilet.

The board got especially hot and bothered by a shot of Baldwin in full frontal nudity. While Baldwin got the meat treatment, Stone enjoyed her break from being a sex object. She said with relief to *Daily Variety,* "Billy Baldwin has more nudity than me. In one scene, he's naked and I'm dressed. It's about time." As her star rose, Stone would keep more of her clothes on. She felt so empowered making *Diabolique* that she kept all her couture on while luckless costar Isabelle Adjani had to act as though she were having a coronary in full undress. Maybe it wasn't acting.

The director of *Sliver* insisted that the ratings board was hallucinating. Or at least they weren't paying attention. There is full frontal nudity, which made it into the video version, but the *schwinging* is done by a bit actor on a black-and-white monitor. When his role was described as a "bit part," they weren't just talking about the size of the role. Noyce is no size queen.

The director did, however, feed the rumor mill when he made this ambiguous statement: "I have never understood why in Hollywood male screen sexuality is taboo but female nudity is not." The answer is simple. The industry is controlled by straight guys who like to order women to spread 'em. They don't have any interest in checking out Billy Baldwin's equipment. In fact, it makes them anxious. It's part of the atavistic homophobia which seems to be genetically encoded in the collective Western unconscious, especially the land once settled by Puritans who found Merrie Old England way too merry.

There's also a practical reason why the cinema remains dick-free and tit full. Women can simulate arousal; men to have to demonstrate, heads up.

Noyce attributed the taboo to control, not homophobia. "At its core, it has something to do with the fact that men are in

control. They're controlling the images of themselves and women. And that's why we only see women [nude]. Well, I don't want
to do that."

Noyce's logic is too deep dish sociologically when the real
answer is simple. Some phenomena don't call for psychoanalysis.
Even Freud believed that sometimes a cigar is just a cigar. Straight
guys want to see women nude, not men. Most directors are
straight; hence, we see all of Stone in *Basic Instinct,* but only
Douglas's bubble butt.

When the director is openly gay, the camera lingers over Chris
O'Donnell's codpiece and Val Kilmer's hairy pecs in *Batman
Forever* with the same joy it devotes to Demi Moore's aureoles in
Striptease.

At first, the public couldn't get enough of Stone, even from
the neck up. In its first two weeks of release, *Sliver* topped the
box-office charts. Soon the word of mouth got around that the
plot was glacial and the only genitals on display belonged to a
member of the Screen Extras Guild. The news precipitated a
flaccid third week, and the movie ended up grossing a piddling
$38 million. The sea epic (bathtub division) had cost $30 million.

The reviews ran the gamut from poisonous to biological war-
fare. London's *Time Out* compared her to a "Frankenstein goddess,
built in a Hollywood laboratory from spare parts, lying around
Central Casting." As the University of Louisville computer analysis
showed, Stone was literally the gorgeous sum of many movie stars'
best parts. While trashing the film, the British publication added to
the laundry list of physical perfections: "Jean Harlow's hairdo,
Grace Kelly's wardrobe, Carole Lombard's wisecracks, Madonna's
personal manifesto on becoming a millionairess…"

In the wake of the reviews and domestic box office, Stone
appeared to be a one-hit phenomenon, devolving into a Bo Derek
for the 1990s. The *New York Times* summed up the consensus,
but the critic sounded more disappointed in Stone than dis-
pleased with her movie. "Stone is one of the two top female stars,
the other is Julia Roberts. Stone plays strong, capable women…the exception was *Sliver's* lonely, vulnerable book editor.

Stone spent the entire movie looking confused, as if trying to figure out how to look afraid." An antifan said of her *hommage* to *Rear Window,* "She looks just like Grace Kelly if Her Serene Highness had come from the wrong side of the tracks."

Where's a postmodern goddess when you need one?

The worshipers came back to her altar soon enough. When *Sliver* washed ashore in Europe, moviegoers showed they didn't care what part of her anatomy was on display. The film grossed another $78 million overseas, and Stone's clout and asking price went ballistic. Her next film would snatch her $2 million, followed by a $7 million payday. And she became the nicest thing you can say about a star—bankable. Her name alone attached to *Hedda Gabler in Esperanto* guaranteed that bankers would sit up and beg how much for any project she wanted to star in.

Despite the international success of his baby, Noyce was coy when asked if he would ever work with Stone again. (He hasn't.) In fact, he gave a nonresponsive answer. "This was a really difficult role for her to pull off because she had to play a very different character [compared] to the one audiences would suspect her capable of. She's supposedly a mild-mannered, re-pressed intellectual who hasn't had any sexual contact with a man for quite a long time, which is tough for her, given the baggage that she brings."

Stone would pick up *tonnage* from the set of *Sliver,* specifi-cally the coproducer, Bill MacDonald, whom she would steal away from his pregnant bride of six months. She would go from box-office darling to scourge of the tabloid press and TV.

12

Home Wreckonomics

In an interview dripping with acid that was granted to promote *Sliver*, the *Times* (London) said that Stone had few enemies in Hollywood—"except for those whose sons or husbands she's had affairs with." Among them was Naomi Baka, the pregnant wife of Bill MacDonald, *Sliver's* coproducer.

In the full flush of new lust, Stone said in 1993, "I knew from the minute I met him that I completely understood him, and he completely understood me." Five months later, the blush was still on this blooming romance. As part of its August cover story, "Women We Love," *Esquire* proved it adored Stone, and Stone still adored her coproducer. "Now that I'm in a good relationship, I don't answer the phone after 6 p.m.," she said.

Perhaps she was afraid Mrs. MacDonald would be on the other end.

The actress insisted that she didn't begin dating MacDonald until after he dumped his wife, but Baka begged to disagree—vehemently. In a case of "she said, she said," Stone claimed, "I never went on a date with Bill. We talked on the phone. I told him he'd have to change his life if he wanted to see me. Which he did.

Now that his marriage is being annulled, we're living together and plan on getting married. I'd love to have a family." Although Baka and Bill had been married less than six months, Stone said she didn't begin the relationship until MacDonald filed for divorce from his wife.

On the TV tabloid show *A Current Affair,* Baka insisted that Stone had gotten her chronology all wrong. Baka noted that although she and MacDonald were newlyweds, they had been lovers for a decade. "You just don't walk away from a ten-year relationship and announce your engagement three weeks later," Baka said. That, of course, is exactly what the new couple did.

Baka didn't stop at debriefing the electronic media. She told the *Long Beach Press-Telegram* that Stone had refused to sleep with her husband until he left her. Baka was desolate. "We were very happy. We were house hunting. We were planning our future together."

Back on *A Current Affair,* Baka denied Stone's claim that the actress had waited until he dumped his bride. "Sharon gets what Sharon wants. It's like an execution. It was cold-blooded and heartless," Baka said.

Baka also mentioned that she had supported her lover-husband for ten years as an executive for American Express while he tried to get his producing career off the ground. Adding insult to injury, after he dumped her, MacDonald called and tried to perform damage control for his new squeeze. Baka was devastated, and all her husband could do was worry about his new girlfriend's public image. Baka quoted MacDonald as saying, "Sharon is worried that this might affect her career. She could look like a home wrecker." MacDonald wanted to give the superstar's fans a lesson in home wreckonomics.

Stone enthusiastically confided to friends that her psychic told her that the couple had been lovers in a past life. Mrs. MacDonald was living in the present and p.o.'ed. She continued her media hate campaign on *Hard Copy,* denouncing Stone as a "homewrecker." Her fury was fueled by her miscarriage, which she blamed on Stone's meddling. MacDonald's mother sided with his jilted wife, repeatedly calling the actress a slut on syndicated TV.

Stone remained calm in the inquiring eye of this media storm. She said of her vilification in the press, "It could walk into the room and eat you, or take you for a ride through a fabulous jungle—or it could slap the living daylights out of you, laugh and leave." Her sangfroid wasn't total. Nobody likes to turn on the TV and hear oneself referred to as Jezebel by Grandma. Stone admitted, "It was a bizarre episode. To have my life turned into a media event, to be painted to look like something I'm not, was very hurtful."

You don't have to believe in karma to see the end of L'Affaire Stone-MacDonald as a case of what goes around comes around. Within six months, it was MacDonald who was feeling hurt when Stone abruptly canceled their wedding and sent back his mother's antique engagement ring—via air mail from the Arizona set of *The Quick and the Dead*. The dismissal didn't end there. When Stone dumps a guy, she doesn't let him down easy. MacDonald was in free fall as Stone ordered all his belongings removed from her château. Their love nest in the hills had become a No Trespassing zone for her ex.

Regardless of their past-life experiences, in this life Stone told friends she felt that MacDonald was a no-talent parasite feeding off his fiancée's fame. His career, she added, was stalled, and her train was leaving him at the station. *People* magazine's favorite Deep Throat, the ubiquitous "insider," told columnist Mitchell Fink, "The actress dumped Bill at the end of January [1994] because she couldn't deal with the fact that nothing much is going on with his career."

Fink added a vicious alternative hypothesis for the split. In the July 26, 1993, issue of *People,* he reported that MacDonald and *Sliver*'s executive producer, Robert Evans, were involved in an investment scam that cleaned out eight thousand investors, including senior citizens subsisting on Social Security. Fink's other favorite interviewee, a "source," told him, "Basically, Sharon is bailing out before she becomes tarnished by his negative publicity."

Stone wasn't done with her boy toy quite yet. Amazingly, she granted an interview to the scabrous Fink and claimed all was well on the Stone-MacDonald farm. Bill was "still asking me to marry him every day, and I'm still saying yes. We wanted to be married in July, but due to MacDonald's unsigned annulment [Mr. and Mrs. MacDonald were married in a Catholic church in Rome], we are unable to. But we're going on a honeymoon, anyway." While Naomi stewed, her husband and his new mate went on a bicycle tour of Ireland's historical landmarks.

By January 1994, MacDonald was history.

Although Stone's publicist, Heidi Schaeffer, officially described the parting as "amicable," Stone undercut her flack's finesse when she told *Esquire* in March 1995, "I think of that period as like driving too fast and taking your hands off the wheel. I didn't know him at all when I got involved with him. I got involved with an idea. About six weeks in, I knew I was in serious hot water and told him so. I recognized how dangerous he was, like a whirling dervish of destruction. I explained to him that it was just going to have to stop. And that was about the time we got engaged, which was his attempt to be legitimate and make me legitimate. Oh, I really got sucked into some kind of black hole. So I made a mistake, and if you haven't, throw a rock at me."

Stone usually remains closemouthed around male journalists, revealing herself only to women writers, for whom she bares a lot. *Esquire*'s Bill Zehme was a rare exception. In a dubious case of almost getting in bed with your subject, Zehme and Stone got a massage together in her hotel suite, during which the reporter's towel fell off and Stone giggled, "Heee! I saw your butt!" The reporter responded, "I've seen yours, too." Stone one-upped him with "Anybody's who's got $7.50 has." Later, Stone dragooned the writer into making macadamia-nut cookies with her.

The reporter was wise to put up with a massage and cookie duty. Whether it was the back rub or a sugar rush, she revealed a depth of hatred for her ex-beau usually reserved for the ears of a therapist, not a conduit to a magazine's 2 million subscribers. "From the moment some of my girlfriends laid eyes on him, they hated him," Stone said. Obviously, her gal pals were more psychic than her psychic. "One used to say that I had Patty Hearst syndrome—that I was like a kidnap victim. He was constantly working on me psychologically to make me feel like I was always in danger and weak, and that without him constantly there I was vulnerable. So at a certain point, I had a very complex cohabitation agreement drawn up. After that, it still took me six months to get out of it."

When Zehme informed Stone that MacDonald was planning a tell-all on their six-month relationship, her delighted response actually told a lot more about her than a MacDonald autobiography ever would. To date, MacDonald's memoirs remain unpublished.

Throughout her life Stone's romantic entanglements have come unraveled by her fear of intimacy. The document she made her boyfriend sign wasn't a prenuptial agreement, understandable, since she was financially endowed and he wasn't. The agreement was something much more telling—a confidentiality clause. Asked about MacDonald's book, she said, delighted, "Does he have one? I hope he does sell it and makes billions of dollars on that story, because there's a confidentiality clause in our agreement. So it will be all mine!" She should have had Joe Eszterhas sign a similar pact. He sold the story of the MacDonald mess to *Vanity Fair* for $50,000. It wasn't screenplay or poison-pen-biography money, but it could pay for almost half a Mercedes 500SEL.

At the start of the affair, Stone told Liz Smith that she felt that MacDonald completely understood her from the moment they met but didn't want him spreading his knowledge all over a bestseller. That she made the love of her life sign a confidentiality clause suggests that, going in, she expected ultimate betrayal. Or maybe she made him sign on the dotted line after she dismissed him with a tidy settlement. Whatever the motivation, MacDonald, unlike his ex-wife and girlfriend, has maintained an un-Stoney silence about their six-month liaison.

People magazine had to go all the way back to the Civil War to find a metaphor for Stone's romantic modus operandi: "If love is a battlefield, then Stone is General Sherman, scorching the earth as she marches over men."

A sideshow to the main event added a fourth corner to this

messy romantic triangle. Screenwriter Eszterhas pops up in this immorality play as a major player. After her miscarriage and divorce, Baka sought refuge with her best friends, Joe and his wife of twenty-five years, Geri Eszterhas, fifty-two. As a good friend of Baka's, Eszterhas tried to make MacDonald uphold his marriage vows and dump Stone. *People* magazine described the screenwriter as "aghast," telling MacDonald, "You can't fucking do this. Don't blow your marriage over this."

A few days later, MacDonald dumped Naomi and announced his engagement to Stone. Baka took cover at the Eszterhas's luxe suite at the Four Seasons Hotel in Hawaii. During their island sojourn Eszterhas took his wife and Naomi dancing. While dancing with the distraught Baka, he fell in love with her. Eszterhas didn't let any grass grow under his lust. The very next day, he dismissed Mrs. Eszterhas, explaining, "I've fallen in love with Naomi," then marched into her adjoining suite and said, "I love you. We're leaving."

Baka's marital nightmare had a happy ending. She stopped dissing Stone and said, "You spend years thinking you're happy. And then you meet someone and you realize: I didn't even know what happiness was."

Eszterhas came clean to *Daily Variety*'s Army Archerd, Boswell and psychoanalyst to the stars. Contradicting his lecture to MacDonald, which was like Dr. Mengele teaching ethics at Harvard Medical School, he confessed to Archerd that he actually introduced Stone to MacDonald "to get Naomi for himself." Dr. Archerd also reported that Eszterhas admitted that his behavior had created a "circle of pain" because Naomi and his wife had been best friends for the past quarter century. Still, Eszterhas couldn't resist the screenplay fodder this messy romantic quadrangle had created. (Or is it a pentagon? Let's see: Stone, Mac-Donald, Baka, Joe and Geri Eszterhas.)

Describing this painful pentagon, Eszterhas said, "It would either be a dark comedy, a human tragedy, or—a great love story. The pain that went into this was gigantic across the board." Eszterhas never got around to fictionalizing the multiple partner swapping, but tellingly, he did name the psycho antiheroine of his

Showgirls "Nomi," after his new love, omitting an "a" perhaps to protect the guilt-ridden.

Baka didn't feel guilt. She was rapturous, hailing her new husband as "king [because] he's a master at having people come to him." She rewarded her forty-eight-year-old monarch with a dauphin, a baby named Joseph Jeremiah.

There were winners and losers. In the winner's circle, Joe and Naomi stood madly in love. Everybody else got the booby prize. Even Stone. The affair not only hurt her public image, it messed with an already poor body image when she discovered she had gained a whopping sixteen pounds during the filming of *Sliver.* The onset shenanigans made Stone the target of the tabs, which sanctimoniously condemned her as a home wrecker. The tabloids had a lot of nerve casting the first Stone, since the gutter press is to journalism what Elvis on black velvet is to art.

Shooting *Sliver* was apparently so nerve-racking, she must have reached for the Dexatrim when the scale showed how much weight she had gained. "Working on *Sliver* was hell," she said. "It was like swimming upstream in an ice floe." She added that "creatively" it was a "disaster" for her, "but it's making over $100 million overseas at this very moment." The actress didn't sub-scribe to *Variety,* which reported that *Sliver* grossed $36.3 million in the United States and $78 million abroad.

But its two weeks at the top before word of mouth got around that it was a stinker proved one thing: Stone could "open" a movie. The studios, for reasons best left to CPAs and the IRS, collect a higher percentage of ticket sales during the early run of a film's theatrical release. Their cut tapers off as the weeks pass. The more money a movie makes early on, the better for the studio, the worse for its exhibitors.

Stone's box-office performance with *Sliver* put her in rarefied company, an acting sorority of two. The *New York Times* re-ported, "At 35, Stone is one of the two top female stars, the other is Julia Roberts," who can open a movie. Plus *Sliver*'s foreign figures, the *Times* added, were higher than domestic megahits that year, like *In the Line of Fire* and even *A Few Good Men,* which enjoyed the services of America's box-office emperor, Tom Cruise. Offshore, Stone was bigger than Tom and Clint.

Despite hellish reviews in America, Stone played the trouper and flew to Europe to hustle the film with a blizzard of interviews and public appearances. Stone's marketing enthusiasm is one of the many reasons Sherry Lansing, the chairwoman of *Sliver*'s distributor Paramount, worships her postmodern goddess. "Everyone who makes a movie should do that," Lansing said of Stone's European victory tour. "But Sharon is one of the few who does it. Arnold does it. Michael [Douglas] does it. That is what makes you an international star."

London's *Time Out* only saw the zinc lining in Lansing's silver cloud, even though the magazine used Stone's European press tour to fill its pages. "In short," the essay that accompanied the interview said, "it would appear Sharon Stone is a more gifted talker and self-publicist than she is an actress."

Stone not only had a genius IQ; she was genuinely street smart. Not for her the press aversion of Sean Penn or Robert De Niro. She hadn't been swimming in the bowels of video for twelve years to suddenly throw it all away and say, "I don't do press." When Lansing asked her to do a hard sell, Stone was as bullish on the product as the hostess of a Tupperware party.

At about this time, the people at Harry Winston's in Beverly Hills didn't think the actress was such a gem. During her promotional tour for *Sliver,* Winston loaned her a diamond necklace worth $400,000. The operative word is "loaned." Perhaps Stone wasn't listening, or the Winston people were lying. She insisted that the bauble was payment in return for free publicity. "Sharon Stone, jewels by Harry Winston." (An interesting trivia note: Almost every star you see at the Oscars wearing a $35,000 rag hasn't paid a penny for it. All they are asked to do for the *loan* of the dress is mention the designer's name when *Entertainment Tonight* shoves a microphone in their décolletage.)

Diamonds cost more than haute couture—$365,000 more in this case. Winston thought $400,000 was a bit steep for a little plugola. The bean counters wanted their beads back. Stone felt that she was underpaid and filed a $12 million lawsuit against the company, alleging misrepresentation and breach of contract. A spokesman for the jeweler called the claim "mind-boggling" but settled out of court. Stone's heart was in the right place even if her hands were clinging to a $400,000 chunk of ice. She returned the jewelry but, as part of the settlement, forced Winston to make a large, undisclosed donation to her charity *du jour,* AmFar, the American Foundation for AIDS Research, Liz Taylor's $5,000-a-plate chomping ground.

Ron, son of Harry, couldn't resist one last dig as he reluctantly cut a check for a charity that seeks a cure for AIDS. "I really wanted to sue the pants off her, but she doesn't wear any."

Infotainment news footage at the time of the Affair of the Diamond Necklace suggests that Winston *fils*'s cynicism was not misplaced. One film clip in particular provides a mother lode of subtext for semioticians. At an AIDS fund-raiser, Stone weeps at the podium as she speaks about friends she's lost to the disease. Her hands, however, tell a different story. Between teardrops, Stone's fingers claw at the bauble encircling her scarred neck, distracting from the genuine pathos of her words. Her gestures seem to be unconsciously fending off Harry Winston's demand for the return of all that ice.

The Affair of the Diamond Necklace didn't register with the same magnitude as the original messy Marie Antoinette scam, which Napoleon, courtesy of Stefan Zweig, described as the "thunderclap of the Revolution." Stone's karatosis was more a tempest in a sexpot, but the self-aggrandizement didn't look good on her resumé.

Her next film wouldn't do anything for her resumé, either.

13

Asleep at the Wheel of Misfortune

AFTER ALL THE *DESHABILLAGE* of *Basic Instinct* and *Sliver,* Stone wanted to stay buttoned up. She picked a script with a heroine who was even more buttoned up and repressed than the burned-out case in *Sliver*. Moreover, at thirty-six, Stone's biological bombshell clock was turning into a tolling bell tower. The actress wanted to stretch in a role that was 180 degrees away from the omnivorous Tramell and the masturbatrix from Sutton.

Unfortunately, the role she picked was in the film *Intersection,* whose director didn't even want to see her! Paul Verhoeven had snubbed her while casting *Basic Instinct* because her quick-change act from angelic to diabolical scared the heaven out of him. *Intersection*'s director, Mark Rydell, rejected her for a less complex reason: He thought she couldn't act.

Now a loyal fan who refused to talk to me about his once and hopefully future star, Rydell, back then, admitted during a major *mea culpa* in the *New York Times,* "I never had her in mind. I suffered the prejudices that many people suffer in relation to

Sharon. They think of her without admiration because of her image and all that publicity." Rydell may have been watching Mrs. MacDonald on *Hard Copy*.

Stone wouldn't take "go to hell" for an answer. Rydell remembered her pit-bull perseverance, although he used a more handsome canine analogy. "She pursued this part so avidly, she was like a schnauzer on my pant leg," he said. "She was in the middle of shooting *Sliver,* but she went after the role with a hunger I've rarely seen."

Rydell still refused to see her, confessing that he found *Sliver* "appalling." Finally, Stone invited herself over to Rydell's house, where she auditioned with Gere for the director. "She begged for the opportunity to spend Saturday with Richard and myself....She was not to be denied."

In a piece headlined "The Ultimate Question: Can Sharon Stone Act?" the *Times* consoled Rydell by saying his opinion "was shared by many that [Stone] was not particularly talented, that she couldn't go beyond doing Catherine Tramell and that she was best suited for parts involving lots of sex and nudity."

In her campaign for the *Intersection* job, it was déjà vu all over again. Instead of crashing the editing room during the airplane cut of *Total Recall,* Stone besieged Rydell by phone. After more than a dozen of these crank calls, Rydell agreed to see her, but with one proviso. He wanted her to play the mistress of Richard Gere, not his betrayed wife.

Gere plays an architect as burned out as Stone's book editor in *Sliver*. But instead of getting hooked on video voyeurism for a boost, he neglects his icy wife, a partner in their firm, and has an affair with a beautiful journalist. The film's plot was unusual. The hero dies in a drowning accident within the first five minutes. As he expires, trapped in his spiffy roadster, flashbacks dramatize the events that led to his watery grave. At least that's what the script implies, although his previous actions did not contribute to his accidental death. His reckless affair didn't lead to reckless driving. His death isn't his fault. It seems injected by the moralistic screenwriters (*The Firm*'s David Rayfiel and Woody Allen's alter ego Marshall Brickman) as punishment for cheating on his wife. *Intersection* was light-years away from *Basic Instinct* and *Sliver*'s casual sex and relative morality. "You fool around, you die" seemed to be its object lesson. Sometimes it seems that the Hays Code still rummages around in the collective unconscious of filmmakers.

Stone was feeling Streepish and wanted to be cast against type as the older woman whose husband has left her bed for another. No amount of acting—or makeup, for that matter, short of prostheses—could make anyone believe a man would leave Sharon Stone for another woman.

At least Rydell thought so as he pushed the most beautiful woman in the world toward the role of the younger other woman. When Stone read the first page, she must have seen red and all the pink flesh she would once again have to bare. The opening sequence takes place in the bedroom. At least it wasn't in her usual watering hole, *Basic Instinct*'s disco john. The script says that the mistress is naked. The déjà vu must have seemed like a nostalgic nightmare for Stone by now.

Sherry Lansing was set to produce the film, and as Stone's biggest fan, she might have persuaded the director without Stone's telephone supplications to give her the wife's role. But fate and career intervened, and Lansing found herself promoted to chair-woman of the Paramount Motion Pictures Group. As chief of the studio bankrolling *Intersection,* Lansing could have arm-twisted Rydell into giving Stone what she wanted, but Lansing doesn't twist arms. She's no Michael Eisner. She's Will Rogers in Chanel and Donna Karan. Instead, the executive played coach and told Stone to go for the old—the old being the over-the-hill wife, Sally. Lansing remembered: "I showed her an early version of *Intersection,* and I told her: Don't go for the obvious, the girlfriend. Look closely at the wife's role."

When Stone finally got the director to audition her for the wife, he suddenly felt sheepish that he had refused to let her be Streepish and stretch her acting tendons.

As far as stretching, Rydell felt she had turned into Elastic Man. After he finally allowed her to read for the role of Sally, he confessed, "I expected a moderately talented piece of work. I didn't know the range she has." Stone's tryout immediately convinced him to cast against type, but he apparently enjoyed the audition so much, he made the superstar keep on reading for five hours! Only then did he say yes after all her begging. The role of the naked journalist went to the title star of *Blaze,* Lolita Davidovich, who put on thirty pounds for that stripper, then took it all off for her opening striptease with Gere.

The story moved at a glacial pace that made *Sliver*'s frozen speed seem positively lavalike. Maybe Stone was artistically hot for Rydell rather than his movie. He had directed Henry Fonda to his first Oscar and Katharine Hepburn to her third in *On Golden Pond.* But that was back in the early 1980s, when Stone was still swimming in the video depths of *Deadly Blessing* and close encounters with a Spanish bull. Since then, Rydell has chalked up disastrous women's vehicles like *For the Boys.* In defense of Stone's savvy, Bette Midler's stinker of a salute to the USO hadn't yet hit theaters, putting the penultimate nail in the coffin that Midler's career had become. But while the orgy of misandry called *The First Wives Club* has performed miracle resuscitation on Midler's resumé, *Intersection,* alas, was no Lazarus act.

To play a fully clothed ice queen required a lot of concentration, and Stone was distracted by the nudity and NC-17 sex in *Sliver,* which had come back to haunt her on the Vancouver set of *Intersection.*

According to the *Sunday Times* (London), *Sliver,* which was being edited during the shooting of *Intersection,* was turning out to be a nightmare for the filmmakers, who found it needed more than a nip and tuck. The major surgery required to get the coveted R meant that Stone and Baldwin would have go back to the soundstage and into the bathtub to reshoot scenes beyond the aid of the editor's scalpel. Stone regretfully abandoned Vancouver to fly back to Los Angeles to reshoot her love scenes with Baldwin.

Paramount was ticked off because the new footage cost a fortune. Director Noyce couldn't resist the opportunity to turn the studio's *tsuris* into additional hype for his flashterpiece. "Sexually," Noyce said, "*Sliver* makes *Basic Instinct* look like a

Sunday school training film." Not quite. Only if Jimmy Swaggart is teaching class.

Back in Vancouver, Stone found herself enjoying a unique on-the-set experience. She actually got on with her leading man, maybe because they got it on so chastely. Sometimes familiarity breeds hostility, and the two stars didn't get very familiar in front of the camera. No Velcro of Venus or flesh-colored jocks for this G-rated film. Stone may have adored Gere because their sole sex scene takes place in a private (for a change) library and their wardrobe stays on.

Their mutual-admiration society was so mutual, she accepted his invitation to lend her star clout to a big beach party for the Dalai Lama, the pope of Tibet and Gere's personal spiritual trainer. The "Big Feast on the Beach," as it was billed, was held in South Miami on November 6, 1994. Stone not only attended, she cooked up a storm, personally preparing *deysee,* a lamasery dessert of sweet rice and plain yogurt. The confection tickled so many sweet tooths that it ended up in the Tibetan cookbook compiled to commemorate the beach gala. The *New York Times* went so far as to imply that Gere had converted his leading lady to Buddhism, although her conversion didn't seem to last longer than *Intersection*'s running time.

Preview audiences didn't share in the lovefest. A Benedict Arnold at *Intersection*'s Paramount ratted to the hometown paper, the *Los Angeles Times,* "Some of the early test screenings about Sharon were brutal. They didn't like seeing her play the wife. She's very cold in the picture where Lolita is very warm, which is why Lolita's Olivia attracts Gere in the first place." Hopefully, this anonymous studio exec wasn't in the casting department at Paramount. Men didn't patronize *Basic Instinct* to the tune of $400 million because Catherine was cuddly. Her iciness added to the masochistic moviegoer's frisson of fear and loathing—and heavy breathing. The preview audience came to a Sharon Stone movie for sex, not G-rated cuddling in a paneled library. Even worse, two R-rated scenes between Gere and Davidovich so turned off the audience, they were excised from the final cut.

In a rare slip of journalistic *impolitesse,* the *Times* also quoted "an anonymous source" suggesting postpreview that if "the Stone character wants to keep her husband (and the attention of the audience) she should pick up a few explicit leg-crossing cues from Catherine Tramell."

Before reading the preview audience's postmortem, Stone cooed, "It's the best work I've ever done. It's the best movie I've ever been in. I can't imagine how it could not be a success." Paramount didn't have to call on its imagination. The sulfuric poison-pen preview cards pointed to the writing on the walls of all the empty theaters showing *Intersection*.

Rydell predicted that Stone's performance would be the "Second Coming," *Basic Instinct* presumably being the First. Before he read the preview cards, Rydell said, "What I recognize is a quite astute and craftsmanlike talent. She has real resonance as an actress, and she's blossoming in this situation because she's being treated like an actress and not a sex object. She's ready for that." Basically, Rydell desexualized the sexiest woman alive—with her full collusion. The American fans of *Basic Instinct* and *Sliver*'s European cohort felt that the collusion amounted to felonious celebrity abuse.

Although Stone was thinking Oscar, Paramount yanked the film from its scheduled Christmas 1993 release, the last period which would make it eligible for Academy voters' consideration. Serious, Oscar-worthy films are released late in the year because Oscar voters have the attention span of a gnat. Paramount dumped the film in the icy month of January 1994—fifteen months before the next Oscar poll and long past the memories of the aging, memory-challenged academy.

Rydell tried to put the best face on the situation. He claimed that the studio had demanded he finish the film for a Christmas release and Oscar purview. Rydell gallantly insisted that Stone's asexual performance had nothing to do with the delay. Besides the editing crunch, Rydell also claimed that Yuletime was not the best time to release a film about a man drowning in his Mercedes after dumping his wife. "This picture is not about Christmas entertainment, anyway," Rydell said. "It is full of performance and is an examination of an extremely mature, delicate, adult subject matter." For Rydell, denial is a river in the Fertile Crescent of Egypt.

In his unofficial role as organ of the film industry (the smoochable organ being just south of the base of the spine), Army Archerd propagated Rydell's propaganda in his *Daily Variety* column: "It's a quality pic and they didn't want to rush it." Obviously, Paramount's General Arnold didn't have Archerd's ear.

The critics felt that the film was full of something a little more alimentary than delicate. But before the critics weighed in, the *Los Angeles Times* handicapped the film's handicaps: "This is a tough picture to sell because they're telling an audience, 'Hey, watch this guy go into a skid for the first 15 minutes, then hold that thought for the next $1\frac{1}{2}$ hours while we flash back through his life.' The audience knows the ending before the picture even gets started. That's a big commitment to ask from any audience." The *Times* shouldn't be accused of being too yellow journalistically. It was merely quoting Paramount's in-house quisling.

Another source claimed that the film's dialogue sounded like a rip-off of *Basic Instinct*'s overripe repartee. Paramount's stockholders could only hope that *Intersection* would resemble *Basic Instinct* where it really counts, at the box office and in video stores. The *Times*'s source was clearly grasping for straws when he said that the two films shared similarities. As proof, the insider lamely compared Stone's response in *Basic Instinct* when told not to smoke at police headquarters ("What are you going to do, arrest me?") to *Intersection*'s exchange between Stone and a nurse who lays down the same law in an even less appropriate place, the hospital ER: "What are you going to do, hurt me?"

Cinemascore's audience poll gave the film a C plus. The critics gave it an F. A sampling of the critical reaction demonstrates that it doesn't have to be Christmas for the press to act like Scrooge. Where to start in this cornucopia of nightmarish criticism:

Sounding as though he had been Pauline Kael in another life, the *Los Angeles Times*'s Kenneth Turan began his review, " 'Hell is other people,' one of the characters in *Intersection* allows in a philosophical moment, but that isn't quite accurate. Hell is other people in movies like this. Midlife crises are inevitably a bore on screen," added the middle-aged reviewer, "and this one is worse than most."

L.A. Weekly borrowed—okay, plagiarized—Turan's turn of phrase and said that hell wasn't other people. "Hell is *this* group of other people." Since Gere dies at the end (and the beginning), the *Weekly* helpfully suggested all the sequel possibilities. The next installment, it said, should be entitled *Intersection II: In Purgatory*. An armchair critic contributed a casting suggestion for this sequel. "In Purgatory, Gere should be forced to choose between Roseanne and Rosie O'Donnell."

The reaction to Stone's Streeping was mixed. The usually kind and cuddly Roger Ebert of the *Chicago Sun-Times* and syndicated television said, "Stone plays the wife like a woman with a migraine." He felt she had abused her clout by demanding to be miscast as the older, unattractive woman when she and Davidovich clearly shared similar dates of birth on their driver's licenses.

The *New York Times*'s Maslin objected even more to the role-playing. "*Intersection* couldn't have been more crazily miscast if those responsible had worn blindfolds and pulled names out of the hat."

Cattily, the *Wall Street Journal*'s Julie Salamon, author of the on-set tell-all *The Devil's Candy,* resorted to *ad feminam* attacks. "It has been said that Ms. Stone, with the right script, might just be this generation's Grace Kelly. There is some physical resemblance. However, it's more likely that Ms. Stone will be remembered as this generation's Tippi Hedren, the blank actress Alfred Hitchcock turned to after Grace Kelly left show business to become a Princess."

The abuse streched all the way across the Atlantic. The *Sunday Times* (London) inaccurately said that Stone's salary of $2.5 million made her "the highest-paid female star in the world." The squeaky-clean newspaper, which has excerpted Joyce and Eliot, then made a claim no American journal has ever dared. "Not bad going for an actress who was still doing porno in 1989." Does the *Sunday Times* know something the *Enquirer* would pay millions to acquire?

Not all the critics acted as though Stone had sold West Point to Vanessa Redgrave. *Box Office* loved Stone, hated her choice in scripts: "She handles her not very likable character with appropriate frigidity and aloofness. She isn't given a chance to exhibit much personality—her Sally likes to dress well and comb her long blond hair a lot, but that's about all Stone's given to work with."

David Ansen, *Newsweek*'s polished prose poet, must have dried Stone's eyes, which were soaked with tears after reading the majority of critiques. "The one very pleasant surprise of *Intersection* is Stone's sharply etched portrait of Gere's wife and business partner, a brittle, unspontaneous woman in whom one can see the spoiled, giggly rich girl she once was. Stone alone creates a character—Gere and Davidovich just want to win us over."

The *Village Voice* felt that Gere was guilty of more than cuddliness. He was hogging the key light. "This movie's real object of desire is the Silver Fleece himself. Once when [cinematographer] Vilmos Zsigmond backlights Gere's locks, I actually believed a new woman had entered the plot. *Intersection* is what used to be called a woman's picture [Bette Davis, Joan Crawford], but from a man's point of view."

The *New York Times*'s Maslin was more encouraging about Stone's career, if not her current project: "One of the film's few revelations is that Ms. Stone may really make the transition from sex goddess to movie queen if she ever finds the right role. Ms. Stone shows the kind of photogenic fortitude that was everything in the '40s and is only a memory today. If there's any contemporary actress who is equipped to reinvent that kind of stardom, it's Sharon Stone." Or in *Vanity Fair*'s reckoning, "a goddamned goddess for the post modern era."

The actress would gamely try in several films to live up to the *New York Times*'s expectations, but first there would be a little box-office polishing in the shower with Sylvester Stallone.

14

Specializing for More Money

INTERSECTION WENT TO A WATERY GRAVE after collecting only $20 million in the United States. In the wake of critical condemnation and public indifference, Stone temporarily halted her Streeptease and returned to the font of previous glories, the bathroom and bimbohood.

The Specialist might be slumming, but at least this corner of Hell's Kitchen was inhabited by a superstar whose muscular box office she hoped would pump up her shrinking ectomorphic body of work.

If *Intersection* was a woman's picture in the 1940s sense of the term, *The Specialist* was pure male testosterone and timeless. In yet another psychological dissection of a burned-out case, Sylvester Stallone plays an ex-CIA explosives expert who free-lances, blowing up buildings and people in Miami.

Stone is May Munro, an Armani-clad vigilante intent on destroying the Cuban drug cartel, headed by Rod Steiger and son Eric Roberts, who murdered her parents while she hid in the closet and watched as a child.

James Woods plays his patented psycho role, Stallone's ex-

146

partner at the CIA, now on Steiger's payroll. To wreak her revenge, Stone insinuates herself into the Miami-based drug syndicate and becomes Eric Roberts's moll. Roberts plays an eerily auto-biographical role as a wacko who beats his girlfriend. Stone is positively Mr. Billious here, suitable for laming. She's punched, kicked, slapped, and treated like dirt. The *Village Voice* complained that she gave up all the "pussy power" she earned in *Basic Instinct*. The *Voice's* female critic underlined the on-screen spousal abuse: "Virtually the film's only woman, the sultry Stone, gets yanked, pawed, told off and slapped silly, only to slink back for more." Indeed, the actress spends most of her screen time being tortured by Roberts and Woods—not to mention the torture of trying to find motivation for showering with the Great Stone Face and Bod himself. Does Miami have a water shortage?

Amazingly, the unliberated script was written by a woman, Alexandra Seros, who penned *La Femme Nikita,* about a female as-sassin as active as Stone is reactive. Seros was also hired for the dis-astrous American remake of *La Femme,* starring Bridget Fonda. The Greek-born writer makes it clear in the film that English is a distant second language. The script is ESL (English as a second language) for illiterates. Even the farewell note the screenwriter composes for Stone is subliterate, a Germanic hodgepodge of upper and lower case: "I'm NOT A WoMAN You CAN TRUST" (*sic, sic, sic*). Kidnappers compose neater notes from newspaper cuttings.

Stone's thankless role is upholstery for the men's reclining pleasure. Instead of "Turn the Beat Around," Gloria Estefan should have sung over the closing credits, àla Eastwood, "Play Misogyny For Me."

Unlike *Basic Instinct* and *Intersection,* this was one role she didn't have to crawl over broken glass to get. In fact, His Pectitude solicited her personally. During casting, Sly told the producer he was looking for "somebody like Sharon Stone." Stallone, via producer Jerry Weintraub, sent the script to her manager, Chuck Binder, known as Buddha Binder for his girth. "She read it immediately and signed on right away," Weintraub said.

Stone may have agreed so quickly because in all fairness May meat by the director, Peruvian unknown Luis Llosa, but at least she's an empowered piece of meat, propelling the gossamer plot as an enigmatic operative who hires Stallone to blow up her batterer. She's a female Rambo, a harlot with a heart of plastique. Off camera, Stone showed she not only could play Rambo but the Terminator as well. When one of her bodyguards asked for the day off to attend the funeral of his former boss, Richard Nixon, Stone said, "If you go, don't come back." He went and didn't.

The film is most interesting to industry observers not for its caffeinated plot or Styrofoam characterizations but for the off-screen drama of two superstar egos colliding like giant balloons that got separated from Macy's Thanksgiving Day parade.

Stone's self-sabotage has already been examined. The Specialist represents a variation: Costar sabotage. Roberts's bad guy isn't the only batterer. She's trashed by the director, makeup, wardrobe, and hair.

Her luxuriant natural hair color is dyed an unflattering dishwater blond. In a film filled with them, her most risible moment comes when she turns up at a funeral dressed in mourning—in black hot pants, which makes her grief suspect. In most of the film, however, she wears white. It is, after all, subtropical Miami, but white accentuates her hips, just another example of the flak attack made on her in the film.

The shower scene says more about Stallone's clout and narcissism and shows little of the natural wonders of Stone.

In *The Specialist,* Stone seems to exist only from the neck up. Her clothing-not-optional turn in the boudoir should be rated SS for the ultimate in safe sex. Who needs a condom when you're fully protected by an Armani tube skirt? Fashion buffs will enjoy the answer to a question destined to turn up in Trivial Pursuit. Does Giorgio design hot pants? Couture doesn't get anywhere near Stallone's body, which requires regular pumping at the gym and the rumored occasional trip to Tijuana's *pharmacias* for synthetic muscle. Stallone's striated pectorals and grapefruit-sized deltoids preoccupy the director. The camera's infatuation with Stallone's physique reveals a homoeroticism not seen since Steve Reeves climbed into a toga at Cinecitta's Hollywood on the Tiber.

Not surprisingly, Stallone thoroughly enjoyed himself sudsing up for the cinematographer. He said in a TV interview to promote the film, "We're both standing in our robes like, 'You first. Make my day, babe. Drop that linen and start grinning.'" Stallone has inherited Muhammad Ali's guide to poetry: Float like a butterfly, sting like a bee, rhyme like a five-year-old.

The audience didn't share Stallone's good time under the tap. More than one audience pre- and postrelease tittered during the shower sequence, which took four hours to shoot for a paltry two minutes on-screen. Even syndicated columnist Liz Smith, that suckup to the stars wrote, "I've rarely heard an audience hoot, howl and applaud so merrily as the one that attended Thursday's screening." Typically, Smith hated the actor, loved the actress. She praised Stone's new gym-trained body, her "movie-queen charisma and her genuine acting talents." She had one word for Stallone's acting: "cyborg."

The pubescent MTV crowd wanted their Sharon, not a Borgeous Sly. Two minutes was too long for disappointed filmgoers who wanted to get Stoned, not Stalloned. The *Village Voice* reported, "A couple of bronze posing-torso sequences between Stone and Stallon had a screening audience hooting." The *Boston Globe* was also laughing. "The sex scenes between her and Stallone are funny, with all the energy going into posing and anatomical arranging, without an ounce left over for eroticism."

The *New York Times* said their lovemaking was a pose, not passion. "*The Specialist* is less a movie than a celebrity photo session with special effects." Annie Leibovitz with a Leica.

The Specialist is ninety minutes of torture for film lovers; an hour and a half of frustration for Stone fans who don't care to shower with Stallone.

Producer Jerry Weintraub said, "The exciting thing for me is to watch those actors acting together." Weintraub didn't appear to have seen the final cut, because he also claimed, "I don't think you've ever seen Sly like this. He's in a suit and shirt most of the movie and not running around naked." Okay, there's no jogging in the shower or bedroom, but the film still looks like an animated *Playgirl* spread.

Only the *New York Times*'s Caryn James found the objectification of the male star a refreshing switch. The "nude shower scene [reveals] that Ray and May [their names rhyme, as do the actors'] must spend a fortune on personal trainers. The camera makes sure to get a good shot of Ray's bare buttocks. Finally, Hollywood is turning men into sex objects for a change. At least it's a start."

The glacéed posing was nothing compared to the glacial plot. What there is of a story line suffers from a self-sabotaging conceit. For the first half of the film, Stone literally phones her role in, communicating with Stallone only by cellular and pay AT&T. She's Candice Bergen at considerably more than ten cents a minute. The conceit also allows more screen time for Stallone.

Speaking of pectorals, it wasn't only Stallone's physique that got pumped up in the film. At test screenings, his fans complained that James Woods got all the good lines. (What good lines? Stone gets the only zinger in the film when she says to Roberts in his tacky beachfront Bauhaus, "Next time you order a hit you might wanna consider taking out your decorator.") The script also has her declaim during foreplay, "I always know you focus your detonator." Much of the dialogue sounds like Nöel Coward as translated from the original Schwarzenegger. After demolishing some cholos on a bus, he offers their seat to a pregnant woman with this not so bon mot: "I believe there's a vacancy." By now, "*Hasta la vista,* baby" is beginning to sound like Strindberg.

Abs of steel. A Great Stone Face only the Mother of Mount Rushmore could love. Was ever an actor-auteur better described as *Spy* magazine did with the phrase "body by Fischer, mind by Mattel"? Since he upstaged the most beautiful woman in the world in the shower, Stallone was not about to be upstaged by his ectomorph alter ego, Woods. At huge expense ($1.5 million), the cast and crew reassembled to add two scenes. The opening one where Stallone beats Woods so badly a mere mortal wouldn't have survived to wreak havoc for the next ninety minutes. (My father, a retired prizefighter, used to giggle at film fisticuffs. "If you hit somebody that many times, they'd be dead," he said.) Another added scene suggests that both the star and director inhabit an alternate universe. Stallone can afford pricey Miami Beach–front property, but he takes the bus to work in the additional footage. Public transportation does allow him to cream four over-the-hill delinquents for the sole crime of refusing to give a black woman, ten months pregnant, one of their seats. Miss Manners meets Rambo.

After *Sliver*'s domestic and *Intersection*'s international failure, Stone's appearance in *The Specialist* showed she was crazy like an accountant. The film's opening weekend of $14.3 million did more than pump up her resumé. It directly led to a $4 million payday. *The Specialist*'s debut turned the producer of her next film from a holdout to a sellout. Stone had demanded $4 million for an upcoming film, *Diabolique*. Stingy Warner Bros., which financed both *The Specialist* and *Diabolique*, told her to take $3 million or leave it. After *The Specialist* opened, the independent Morgan Creek coughed up the extra mil and signed on as coproducer.

Both the studio and production company must have regretted their largesse. Like Stone pre-*Intersection*, Stallone can open a movie, but he can't keep bad word of mouth from shutting the box-office window. During its second weekend, the take fell by 50 percent, a calamitous freefall. The final tally domestically was an ectomorphic $57 million for a film that cost $40 million to make. And that figure doesn't count postproduction expenses. The studio rule of thumb is double the budget to include cost of prints and all those expensive newspaper and TV ads and you get the real cost of doing business. Internationally, the film earned $120 million, which meant it was lucky to break even. But by then Stone had a cashier's check for $4 million from Warner Bros. Throughout the film, Stone's perplexed look seems to be saying, "What am I doing here?" Her enigmatic smile implies that a devilish bank balance made her do it.

It wasn't only bucks that compelled Stone to play second banana to Stallone. Her dysmorphic body image was still plaguing her. After creating hypertension worldwide in *Basic Instinct* and *Sliver*, the girl from Meadville looked in the mirror and still felt fat and ugly. She claimed that there were "directors who consistently said I wasn't sexy enough. It's still true. I'm not sexy in any stereotypical way." (Just statisistically. See University of Louisville's web site.) "The sex I've symbolized in movies has not been loving, it's been about power." Stone said before the release of *The Specialist,* which she claimed would show her "softer side. This love scene is without doubt the most tender scene I've ever seen." Plastique is soft, but I wouldn't want to roll around in bed with it. As for the "tender love scene," the only tenderness is displayed by Stallone—toward himself.

For her next film, tenderness would be in short supply—on or off camera. On-screen, she'd break men. Offscreen, she'd break one guy's heart.

15

The Good, the Bad, and the Beautiful

STONE'S FILMOGRAPHY gets tricky here. Her western *The Quick and the Dead* was released after *The Specialist* but shot in Arizona before she endured the dolors of Miami.

As a career move, *The Quick and the Dead* shows Stone at her savviest, a woman who refuses to duplicate herself unless dwindling box-office clout demands it.

Stone signed on to *The Quick and the Dead* in the full endorphin rush of *Sliver*'s European success. She also donned a new hat, coproducer. The beauty with the genius IQ ingeniously reinvented herself again—as a female Clint Eastwood, Sergio Leone on estrogen. The *hommage* to Clint and Sergio was intentional. The protagonist was called the Woman With No Name, later changed to Ellen for easy morning-call purposes.

Ellen is one tough *muchacha,* although she's so butch, tough *hombre* might be more appropriate. After being victimized in countless films, in *The Quick and the Dead* she's as much a victim as Leona Helmsley.

153

Stone wasn't leaving anything to chance or Stallone's cinematograper. Stars who want longevity form their own production companies to find vehicles so they don't have to crash editing rooms or phone Mark Rydell a dozen times, begging.

The Quick and the Dead was the first film made by Stone's new company, Chaos Productions. Some might carp that the name was prophetic of her later films, but it actually came from Melville: "Before creation was chaos." *Playboy* was right after all when it condescendingly said of the starlet spread out nude all over its pages in 1990, "And she reads a lot too."

The actress's coproducer title was not just honorific, although such titles often are. As their clout grows, many stars demand extra credit, usually executive producer, although no extra work is required. Some overweening actors have even demanded a producer credit for their hairdressers or favorite makeup person, like a supertip for great hair care over the years.

Stone, however, wasn't interested in a meaningless title. She wanted the power that comes with the title. And she used it to overrule the other principals in the production. The director (Sam Raimi), Universal, and the screenwriter all wanted Liam Neeson for the role of the sheriff that ultimately went to Gene Hackman. Raimi was particularly enthusiastic. He and the star of *Schindler's List* had worked together on an offbeat horror film called *Darkman* and soon found themselves members of a mutual admiration society.

Stone didn't belong to this exclusive fraternity. She simply didn't want Neeson for the role, a legitimate artistic decision for a superstar coproducer. But the way she let Neeson down was anything but gentle. Neeson felt Stone was playing games—that he was just the pawn in some mystifying form of power chess whose rules he didn't know. It didn't help that Stone made him travel halfway around the globe when it had already been decided he wasn't getting the part.

It's rare for an actor to diss a superstar, because you never know when you might want to work with him or her again. Schwarzenegger once criticized Stallone's fashion sense in a *Playboy* interview, but quickly patched things up to the point where Arnold grabbed Sly at the Cannes Film Festival and made him dance cheek to cheek to show that everything was all right. You never know when Conan might fall on hard times at the box office and need to costar with Rocky the Barbarian. Neeson apparently didn't care if he ever worked with Stone. In a rare moment of public pique during an interview in the October 6, 1996, edition of the *Los Angeles Times,* Neeson called a spade a spoiled brat.

The well-liked, soft-spoken Irishman said, "Sam wanted me, the writer wanted me, Universal wanted me. Sharon Stone apparently didn't want me."

The rejection itself didn't tick Neeson off. From his days as an aspiring unknown, he was used to being treated like disposable Kleenex. "The annoying thing," the actor said, "was that I was having a holiday with my wife in Thailand. I was asked if I could fly to L.A. to meet with Sharon. It was a very pleasant meeting. Obviously the decision had [already] been made. I think Sharon was just going through the motions."

In a typical case of doublespeak, Stone's publicist claimed that Chaos, the production company, not the star, had vetoed Neeson. Of course, Stone *was* the production company.

Neeson wasn't interested in semantics. He was interested in venting. "I was kind of mad," the onetime prizefighter said. "Not that I didn't get the part, but because of Natasha [Neeson's wife] and this fruitless mission."

The film's back story bore a resemblance to *The Specialist*'s, but the similarity ends there. Like May Munro, Ellen, as a child, saw the bad guy, Gene Hackman, biblically monikered Herod, kill her father. As an adult, she's gunning for Hackman, mayor of the town of Redemption (more Bible babble). Hackman is so mean, he makes his Oscar turn as the psychopathic sheriff in *Unforgiven* seem like Matt Dillon—if Alan Alda were cast in the big-screen remake of *Gunsmoke*.

Once a year, Hackman holds a contest. It's a lethal country fair for everybody but the quickest draw in town, Da Maire, King Herod. For big bucks, contestants participate in the quick-draw contest, only to be gunned down by Hackman. The competition is tailor-made for Stone's revenge. And she doesn't have to hire an explosives expert who hogs the blanket and the shower head to do the deed. All she needs to do is go mano a mano with the mayor.

Along the way, she has a sexless sex scene with the male Lolita of the benzoyl peroxide set, Leonardo DiCaprio, who may or not be Herod's son. DiCaprio insists he is. Typically, Herod denies paternity. Sadly, DNA testing isn't available in the Old West.

For a change, Stone is the aggressor in her desultory lovemaking with the youth. For their boudoir pas de deux, DiCaprio wanted a little tongue. Stone only liked rough sex. The actor said, "It wasn't that great, actually. She sort of grabbed me by the back of my hair and pushed her lips against mine and then threw my head away. It was by no means a real kiss. And there were only two takes." DiCaprio should stop complaining. He could have been one of her "dates" in *Basic Instinct*—more intimate, but you have to die at the end. When Stone spends the night with the acned teen, they both remain fully clothed. For a change, the two actually sleep in a bedroom scene. This ultimate safe sex disappointed the *New Yorker*'s heavy breather, who complained, "Her round the clock task in life is to stand and glow like a lighthouse while the male species breaks on the rocks around her. Thus far, only *Basic Instinct* has allowed her to fulfill this sacred duty. *The Quick and the Dead* goes so far in the other direction that at one point she wakes up in someone's bed without having had any sex." (DiCaprio's. The actor did get screwed, however. To appear in this film, he abandoned a role in a huge hit, *Interview With the Vampire,* to Christian Slater. DiCaprio probably preferred Stone nuzzling his neck instead of Tom Cruise.)

Rolling Stone's Peter Travers also expressed disappointment that Stone never uncrosses her legs. There wouldn't have been much of a show even if she had, since leather chaps, not hot pants, dominate her wardrobe. "Sharon Stone keeps her panties on," Travers wrote, "so there are no surprises in this whacked-out Western, no matter how familiar it looks. *The Quick and the Dead* is deeply shallow and damned silly."

It took a female reviewer, the *New York Times*'s Janet Maslin, to appreciate the scope and inventiveness of Stone's stretch. "In playing to her formidable strength, [the film is] a definite improvement on Ms. Stone's other post–*Basic Instinct* career choices. It's hard to think of another actress who followed such an electrifying star turn with so many wan, unflattering roles and ineptly directed movies. This time, at least, she has the chance to taunt, mock, smolder and otherwise do what she does best." Maslin needs to check her own clippings. She panned Stone's "electrifying star turn" in *Basic Instinct* only two years earlier.

As producer, Stone was in charge. She proved one thing: no ego equals, no makeup, and no wardrobe. At least not the movie-queen drag with which she was usually weighed down. In the Old West, gunslingers of either sex didn't wear Armani hot pants or Donna Karan tube skirts. If Stone was going to be in a western, she wasn't going to play a dance-hall girl or a hooker with a heart of goo and a wardrobe by Lagerfeld.

The least vain of screen sirens, Stone willingly colluded in trashing her looks. Because of the tight close-ups, she couldn't use traditional makeup. The eyebrow pencil and mascara wand stayed in the box. Her brows and lashes were merely dyed so she wouldn't fade to white under the harsh glare of the camera. Her lips were blistered and Blisticked. Maybelline didn't get any product placement in this gritty western.

Her bad-hair day, which lasted months, would have Streisand screaming for smelling salts—and her agent, Jeff Berg. For most of the film, Stone's blond mane is combed up and tucked under a broad hat. When she uncaps, stringy, filthy hair falls to her shoulders. Hairstylist Paul Le Blanc felt for his charge. Because of all the rainy scenes, Stone's hair was made even more unattractive as her wet locks clung to her head. Fortunately, the head was gorgeous. "Thank god, Sharon has a beautifully shaped head and looks good with her hair wet. Most women don't," her hairdresser said.

Except for one scene in which she wears a gingham dress that looks as though it came from a nineteenth-century K-mart, donned to seduce Herod before she tries to kill him, Stone hasn't been shopping for wardrobe in Paris. (The closest we get to nudity here is when she hikes her dress and reveals a pistol tucked under a garter belt. Paul Verhoeven was originally scheduled to direct. As coproducer, Stone wisely chose a D director she could wrap around her Movieola. If Verhoeven had been behind the camera, you can be sure her dress wouldn't have stopped at the garter mid-thigh.) Her leather jacket was literally 100 years old, borrowed from a western museum. She also wears a man's linen shirt, cotton vest, and leather lace-up pants in the style favored by Mexican revolutionaries from the turn of the century. Her raincoat is also antique, as are her Mexican shawl and granny glasses. How does Stone look with filthy hair and gowns by Mervyn's? Still radiant.

The actress needed every ounce of clout as coproducer to handle studio executives who wanted to mess with wardrobe. One dork at TriStar suggested that she wear something a bit more feminine for her grand entrance. "Some people who shall remain nameless wanted me to wear a dress to ride into town. I thought, Oh, hey, the gunslinger's gonna ride into town sidesaddle," she said. If Donna or Giorgio designed the dress à la *The Specialist,* she could have straddled the saddle in hot pants.

Sliver had taught her the error of being a yes girl to bad-boy directors and executives. On *The Quick and the Dead,* no one would get her near a bathtub. People rarely bathed in the Old West, and Stone wasn't about to scrub down to please libidinous filmmakers.

"*Sliver* was my big learning experience," she said on the set in Mescal, Arizona. "I had the right to say no to all kinds of things in my contract that I [had] rolled over in an effort not to be difficult, to be a good girl. And everything I rolled over on became the enormous errors of that picture. So I got to the point in the production [of *The Quick and the Dead*] of fighting for everything. 'I am *not* rolling over on this. It will *not* be less than this. I *will* not go like this.' I became very adamant that the quality of the piece be maintained."

Stone wasn't being temperamental. Her will served the project, not a star ego. In fact, her behavior was that of a trouper. If the script called for her character—in character—to engage in mud wrestling, so be it. For the climactic duel with Hackman, she spent an entire week rolling around in the muck and the rain. With perhaps a sigh that her skills were underutilized, costume designer Julianna Makovsky, who excavated many original Sergio Leone costumes from a vault in Italy, said, "She's very unglamorous in this movie, and she's the one who wanted that."

Stone was stoic in more than mud. Faye Dunaway, her mentor and role model, once threw a snit fit when director Roman Polanski plucked out a single hair that kept falling in her face during *Chinatown*. "She's a menace," he wrote in his memoirs. Stone allowed a witless makeup man to tear off flesh without complaint. As he removed latex blood and scum from her arm, he began to pull away her real skin at the same time. The visitor from the *Los Angeles Times* said approvingly, "And she doesn't throw a tantrum."

The actress was willing to suffer for her art. Like Oliver Twist requesting a second helping of gruel, she said, "I just love the violence. Whenever somebody suggests cutting it back, I'm like, no, no, more violent. I want more...."

Some critics, however, refused to give a muddy girl a break. Apparently having seen a different film, the *Village Voice*'s J. Hoberman wrote, "What's most conventional is Stone's star turn," as though any movie goddess had ever dared to imitate Leone's Eastwood. Then the critic shows he should be sentenced to the Betty Friedan School of Consciousness Raising and Emasculation. "Not much pussy power here. Her character is as asexual as her daytime wardrobe." Precisely the point, Siskel-brain. It's called stretching, servicing the script instead of your vanity.

More justifiably, other critics complained that this *hommage* to Leone's spaghetti westerns was more plagiarism than pasta. A British reviewer considered the film a limp noodle, "endless parodies of Sergio Leone's style: long, dusty pauses before the draw, closeups of staring eyes and wet brows. Bullet holes are drilled so cleanly into a man's body that the sun streams gently through." That nifty special effect was actually state of the art and not a staple of Leone's low-tech westerns in the pre–silicon chip 1960s.

Janet Maslin was at least relieved that Stone had stopped playing punching bag and started shooting back. "In playing to her formidable strength, it's a definite improvement on Ms. Stone's other post–*Basic Instinct* career choices."

Stone usually acts as though Hannibal Lecter wouldn't scare her, but on this film she confessed she was terrified of the task. "It is scary" playing a female lead in a western "because there was nothing to look at. No woman has ever been given this luxury," she said on the set. Stone needs to renew her Blockbuster membership or subscribe to cable. Joan Crawford in *Johnny Guitar* and Marlene Dietrich in *Destry Rides Again* played tough broads in the Old West, while Barbara Stanwyck airs nightly in syndicated reruns of *The Big Valley*. Stone may not have known her Destry from Dietrich, but she was aware of the cantilevered straitjacket in which the classic western usually confined its leading lady. "They made them wear those unbelievably stupid hairdos, like, excuse me, but where did they get cream rinse and the curling iron? The whole depiction of women in film has been a joke. It's rarely a picture of a woman as women really are. It's more a man's perspective, a man's fantasy of woman, than it is of the way women actually do anything. I go to movies with my girlfriends and we come out of the picture going, 'Do you do that? I don't do that.'"

Stone luxuriated in being the strong arm rather than the arm decoration of the male lead. "You can be just a real person in this situation in a western. They never had that—a woman in this situation who had real humanity." (Sharon, rent *High Noon,* watch Grace Kelly's Quaker wife turn Coop into a pistol-packing pacifist—in the middle of a gunfight!)

"So it was scary. And probably a part of the reason that it came so close to my own self was that there weren't any movies, paintings, books, or places to go to build it all together," she said, sitting in her coproducer's chair. Maybe she was misquoted at length. The interview did appear in *Drama-Logue,* the Howdy Doody of trade publications.

Rolling Stone praised the film for learned references not only to Leone but to John Ford's *My Darling Clementine,* Fred Zinnemann's *High Noon,* Howard Hawks's *Rio Bravo,* Sam Peckin-pah's *Wild Bunch,* Leone's *Good, the Bad and the Ugly,* and, of course, Eastwood's revisionist classic *Unforgiven.* Unfortunately, D-list director Sam Raimi (*Darkman*) didn't imitate Leone's ugh-and-grunt dialogue. He aspired to Noël Coward visiting a dude ranch. He didn't come close with exchanges between Hackman and Stone: He: "I could give you more money than you'd ever spend." She: "I wouldn't feel like I'd earned it." He: "Oh, yes, you would." *Rolling Stone's* Travers agreed that as an emasculatrix, Stone needed a refresher course after her castrating turn in *Basic Instinct*: One saddle tramp says to Stone, "I need a woman." She replies, "You need a bath." Travers responded, "That putdown sadly represents the height of the film's verbal wit."

Dusting off his film-school degree, the *L.A. Reader's* critic thought that the movie paid homage to *Blazing Saddles,* not *Once Upon a Time in the West.* Worse, he compared it to one of those Black Angus steak-house commercials where a deranged cowpoke grabs a red-hot coffeepot with bare hands.

On the set, the *Los Angeles Times* reporter played script doctor and suggested an *hommage* to Mel Brooks, incorporating a line from the 1973 spoof. Sheriff Gene Wilder asks black African Cleavon Little, "What's a dazzling urbanite like you doing in a rustic setting like this?" Considering the grimy appearance of everyone in *The Quick and the Dead,* it's hard to say whose mouth the *Times's* reporter wanted to put the line in.

The problem with the dialogue had to do with the fact that the screenwriter, Simon Moore, was Coward's compatriot. The Brit obviously spoke western American as a second language. The *Hollywood Reporter* felt that the writer needed remedial lessons in ESL: "The one-liners are mainly limp spaghetti. Stone is reduced to the plight of dispensing snarly retorts that have all the wallop of vegetarian pasta." Reporters enjoyed making puns about the movie more than they enjoyed watching it. An on-location piece in Mescal by the *Los Angeles Times* punned, "*The Quick and the Dead* intends to be something more than '90s spaghetti. Think of it as Hollywood's first *fusilli* and *chevre* Western."

At least Stone had her finger on the pulse of Hollywood at the time, although the genre she selected was already suffering arteriosclerosis with other women-only westerns like *Bad Girls* and the unproduced *Outlaws*. Butch was big in 1995, with M-G-M–UA spending a record-breaking $100 million on *Cutthroat Island,* Geena Davis's pirate epic. Machisma, however, was pronounced dead on arrival, for the Island of Dr. Davis earned only $9 million domestically. *Bad Girls* cost less and made more.

Newsweek thought that the western gender bender was much ado about pronouns. The critic conceded that Stone looked "fabulous in dust coat and spurs" but found the gimmick just that. "The role reversal is just a gimmick: a script doctor could have turned this into a Kevin Costner vehicle in 15 minutes."

These days, westerns are hit-or-miss affairs, mostly miss. (See *Tombstone*; don't see *Wyatt Earp.*) *The Quick and the Dead* hit and missed both the critics and the public.

Stone's Monday morning quarterbacking of the film's failure demonstrated a Maoist knack for self-criticism. She said after the movie's lackluster opening weekend of $6 million (total take: $18 million), "I was absurdly naive. I had never produced a film before, and I didn't protect myself contractually." Stone was being disingenous. She didn't need her say-so engraved in stone or even in a contract. All she had to do was say to the cloutless director, Raimi, "Do it this way or it's *hasta la vista,* baby!"

In an orgy of self-blame, she added, "If I had, I could have helped create a better product. I grew up in Pennsylvania, and my father raised me to believe that a man was as good as his word. Unfortunately, that didn't prepare me for my future in Hollywood." Stone did not elaborate on her Sphinx-like exegesis of the film's failure.

The Quick and the Dead failed to burn up the box office, but it did heat up her love life.The heat and dust of the set in Mescal, Arizona, were tempered by another whirlwind affair. The one-year stand showed that Stone is not a snob; she has status to share. Fame may be a powerful aphrodisiac, per Graham Greene, but it doesn't tweak Stone's pheromones. She fell in love with a gofer who went for her in a big way.

Bob Wagner was a balding lad of twenty-seven when he showed up at Stone's Arizona pied à desert to chauffeur her to the set. Soon Stone was riding in the front seat. Or as *Esquire* slyly put it, "Some days they were very late." A coworker asked, "Why not? Bob is handsome, bright, kind, and completely enamored of Sharon." The handsome part was equivocal. Besides the prematurely receding hairline, photos of the time reveal a short, pudgy nebbish with a three-day growth of beard not seen since Don Johnson drove a Ferrari Testarossa on a cop's pay on *Miami Vice*. One stubbled photo was snapped at an elegant fund-raiser. Someone needed to tell Wagner that grunge had died with Kurt Cobain.

A native of Buffalo Grove, Illinois, Wagner, like Stone, had fled his podunk roots. The production assistant was her soul mate. She said, "I have met my match. He's just as nuts as I am. We both have a kind of feverish personality, which gives us a lot of compassion for each other."

Her description of their tortured twelve months together hints at why none of her relationships have extended beyond the self-imposed statute of limitations of three years.

"I used to go through fits in the night and kick him and punch him in my sleep," she said, sounding like a somnolent de Sade. When she was conscious, times were just as tough. "Sometimes we get going on these screaming torture improvs and say mean things to each other and laugh till we cry till we laugh."

Stone enjoyed another role, hausfrau, while reserving the title of TV tyrant. She did Wagner's laundry and cooking but kept the television remote well in hand. Wagner improved her chess game. A female reporter for *Harper's Bazaar* brought up the unliberated subject of their age difference, a decade to be exact, seventy years in the dog days of divas. "Who gives a shit?" Stone asked rhetorically. "I've never had a relationship that's lasted longer than consistently together three years. So where do you find a guy who's a peer, a guy where hypergamy isn't as clear?

Eight months later, the febrile affair hadn't cooled down. Public displays of affection are usually rare for Stone, but there she was in the paparazzi page of *US* magazine in July 1994. A photo shows her kissing Wagner at James Brown's sixty-first birthday concert in Augusta, Georgia. Reflecting her mood, Stone jumped onstage and grabbed a microphone to sing "I Feel Good." She did, but only for three more months.

Not published was evidence of another torrid affair, although you shouldn't rush down to the morgue of the *National Enquirer*. While still enmeshed with Wagner, Stone began another setside romance, but she was able to buy this guy. Like *National Velvet,* Stone, like Liz Taylor, fell for her costar, a horse named Magic. The affair, unlike her others, has continued to this day. It helps that this boyfriend knows his place—in the stable. "He was *such* a lover. He put his head on my shoulder. He kissed me on the lips," she said of her own Mr. Ed.

Unlike her unceremonious dismissal of Bill MacDonald, who was shown the door via Federal Express, Stone remained friends with Wagner postsqueeze and even kept him on the payroll of her next film.

Unlike MacDonald, Wagner had a career of his own. Unfortunately, separation didn't make the heart grow fonder. It made it stop beating. They split while he was on location second-directing Jodie Foster's film *Home for the Holidays*. At first, Stone's heart was broken. But his film work was better than the odd jobs he had done before becoming Mr. Sharon Stone. She said afterward, "I hope we can work together again, but he gets asked to do a lot of projects. It's hard. But it's easier than waiting tables, running pool halls, painting houses." Stone admitted she had performed the same dead-end jobs during her salad days.

Stone could be generous in victory after conquering a man's heart. Before Wagner went *Home for the Holidays,* Stone promoted him from gofer to second assistant director of her greatest film and performance.

16

"You Really Like Me, at Last"

AFTER A STURDY but aesthetically unspectacular buildup with *Total Recall* and *Basic Instinct*, Stone would show herself capable of Piranesian intricacy in her personal masterpiece, *Casino*.

Casino was the foundation on which Sharon built all her future hopes of surviving mandatory retirement as she neared forty—Social Security time for love goddesses.

That she was again typecast as Jerry Falwell's worst nightmare and Jimmy Swaggart's fondest fantasy didn't stop the Hollywood Foreign Press from anointing her with a Golden Globe Award for best actress— "at last," in Stone's famous acceptance phrase. Or the Academy from including her in its pantheon of glorious also-rans, a best-actress nomination. (A nomination confers automatic Academy membership and Oscar-voting enfranchisement, a handy perk when she votes for herself in future films.)

Without too much hype, you could call *Casino* Sharon Stone's *Schindler's List* and personal best. The director, the script, and most of all her performance, nailed the consensus that she was a popcorn movie star, an exhibitionist sex tool used by writers and directors to plane their kinks.

Unlike the preoccupations of Verhoeven and company, Scorsese's desert epic in Nevada contained not a soupçon of lesbian sex or anal eroticism. Stone, for a change, didn't show any flesh other than an aerobicized tummy, flat as a sit-up board. *Casino* was filled with spousal abuse, but the spouse who got trashed worse was Robert De Niro's stoic husband. Stone's hooker–housewife from hell proved that one sex doesn't have a monopoly on battery. Or as Sherry Lansing lyrically described her favorite postmodern divinity's modus operatics, "The guy gets fucked instead of vice versa."

Casino's quick three hours pass by like two, proving the adage that time flies when you're having a good time—even when the people on-screen are having a horrifically bad one.

"Bad" understates *Casino*'s little shop of big horrors: prostitution, drug addiction, alcoholism, child and spousal abuse, and codependence, the bête noire of daytime chat shows.

The film was based on an instant classic of nonfiction, *Casino: Love and Honor in Las Vegas,* by the *New York Times*'s Nicholas Pileggi. The title must have been ironic. The only "love" in the story of mob-controlled Vegas is obsessive lust. Honor doesn't exist in this alternative universe of sociopathic wise guys.

Pileggi's book chronicles the rise and fall of Frank "Lefty" Rosenthal, a Midwest bookie who comes to Vegas and realizes a nightmare version of the American Dream as the manager of the Stardust Hotel in the 1970s. His wife, Geri McGee, was statuesque, blond, and as photos in *Esquire*'s excerpt of the book show, even lovelier than Stone, as hard as that is to imagine. Geri was also a topless dancer, prostitute, alcoholic, drug addict, and child abuser. The decline of mob influence and Lefty's career parallels the disastrous downward spiral of his marriage to this Messalina of the mesa.

Stone may have played the role so brilliantly because it was so autobiographical—up to a point. Both the actress and her inspiration came from dead-end suburbia, although Geri's hometown was closer to the big time, Sherman Oaks in Los Angeles's San Fernando Valley. After high school, Stone managed a pool hall and painted houses. Geri worked at Thrifty, Bank of America, and

Lockheed in clerical jobs. Geri's sister Barbara described an unbringing that was even more deprived than Stone's. "We were probably the poorest family in the neighborhood. When we were little kids, we got all our clothes from neighbors. Geri hated it more than anything." Stone might say $100 was a "big issue" in her family. In Geri's, it was wealth.

Unlike Stone, Geri didn't go to New York, where her looks probably would have landed her a modeling contract. The Valley Girl obviously didn't possess Stone's genius IQ or "grim, blinkered determination and stark ambition," in the purple prose of London's *Observer*. Instead of runways and fashion shoots, Geri was dragged to Vegas by a pimp who got her pregnant. Soon, however, she was making more than a Ford model, earning $300,000–$500,000 annually as a prostitute and "chip hustler," a woman whose talent consists of holding a gambler's hand for good luck while he shoots craps. Her salary is tips in chips.

While Geri had turned into a self-made woman on the make, Lefty Rosenthal had found heaven at the Stardust. In the Midwest he was literally a criminal for placing off-track bets. In Vegas his handicapping skills were a gift and earned him the top job at the best hotel.

Rosenthal was smitten with Geri. He married her knowing that she didn't love him. A classic codependent, he thought lots of jewelry and love could win her. As he told Pileggi, "I knew Geri didn't love me when we got married. But I was so attracted to her when I proposed. I thought I could build a nice family and nice relationship."

For Geri, the match meant only one thing, building a nest egg. Her sister Barbara told the author of *Casino* that a girlfriend advised Geri, "Marry Frank Rosenthal. He's very rich. Marry him, get his money, and then divorce him."

Geri and Lefty's dysfunctional romance wouldn't cause ripples in the maelstrom of daytime TV dysfunction. But their relationship is worth studying because it provides a window into the mind of one of the greatest directors of all time, Martin Scorsese.

Scorsese, who worked on the screenplay with the author of

the book, fictionalized the names of the protagonists, changing them to Sam "Ace" Rothstein and Ginger McKenna. That's not all he changed. The fictional characters are most interesting because they hint at a deep misogyny that runs throughout the film and calls perhaps for an examination of Scorsese's other masterpieces with the same gloss. The differences between real life and reel life are telling, most of all, about the director, who often referred to Stone on the set as "the girl."

Robert De Niro is Scorsese's best friend. Maybe that's why he changed Lefty Rosenthal's paranoid, unfaithful wife beater into Ace Rothstein's desert Job, a man whose personal and professional calamities achieve biblical proportions.

Where to start? The real Geri never tied her six-year-old daughter to a bedpost, as the fictional Ginger does in *Casino*. De Niro's character remains faithful as his wife goes down on his best friend and anyone else who can further her goals. Stone's Ginger remains infatuated with her pimp (James Woods in psycho mode again) after marriage to De Niro. Not true for her real-life counterpart.

Yet another example of how the director brightened his protagonist's black heart: In the film, De Niro comes across as Al-Anon material, begging Stone to forswear pills and booze for the sake of motherhood. In the book, the real-life Lefty warns her as she's about to sip her third glass of Dom Perignon: "Listen, bitch, you put your lips to that glass, I'll knock you off that chair." Geri was so terrified of her husband, she stopped drinking for the moment. Reading that quote is as creepy as hearing John Gotti's audiotape threatening to blow up a capo's house for not returning a phone call promptly. Mob etiquette.

De Niro plays a faithful husband more horrified than angry at his wife's infidelity and substance abuse. In the book a retired FBI agent tells a different story. "Lefty made her life miserable. He cheated on her all the time, and he didn't care if she found out. He started to keep tabs on her like she was a Vegas version of a Stepford Wife. He even bought her a beeper so he could always get ahold of her."

The lead in the *Wall Street Journal* review only hints at what the differences between book and script suggest: a director uncomfortable with women. "Ms. Stone's Ginger McKenna is the most predictable role in Mr. Pileggi's pantheon of male dominance." That pan leads to a quick review of most Scorsese heroines and antiheroines, who seem to be one-dimensional compared to his richly detailed portrayal of men: Jake LaMotta's Brooklyn bimbo wife in *Raging Bull.* Cybill Shepherd's glacial cipher in *Taxi Driver,* not to mention Jodie Foster's twelve-year-old prostitute. *Mean Streets,* in which De Niro refers to his promiscuous girlfriend as the "town pump." The only woman with any heart or personality in another Scorsese masterwork, *Goodfellas,* is the director's real-life mom, who plays an Italian yenta.

The cerebral *Nation* was more explicit about the director's one-note symphony of women. "The only thing new for Scorsese, unfortunately, is the oldest thing of all—a hooker with a heart of tin....Stone's character is already monstrous when we first see her, and she's monstrous at the end, when she calls to mind nothing so much as a Hammer Films babe, staggering through the throes of vampirish excess."

The *Nation* was dead on about the lack of on-screen motivation for her inexplicable devotion to her pimp, James Woods's Lester Diamond, doing what the actor does best, hyperacting. To figure out why this beautiful woman with a husband who adores her and showers her in sable and Cartier prefers her abusive pimp, we have to stop watching the film and check out "Codependents and the Men Who Love Them" on Oprah or Sally. Scorsese had to borrow the Pulitzer Prize–winning insight of Edith Wharton to present fully realized women like Winona Ryder and Michelle Pfeiffer in *The Age of Innocence.*

As usual, Stone rose above the material and the swamp. While the *Wall Street Journal* found the role predictable, her interpretation was praised as startling. The "actress creates a startling portrait of a classy operator with ambition to burn who gets scuttled by neediness, greediness and cocaine."

At least that aspect of Scorsese's take was true to life. After divorcing Lefty, Geri moved to Los Angeles, where her demons killed her. Screaming on Sunset Boulevard, she stumbled into the lobby of a hotel and collapsed, dying three days later of an accidental overdose of cocaine, Valium, and Jack Daniels.

For once, reality was more dramatic than fiction. Reality would also have cost a prohibitively expensive shutdown of traffic on the Strip. To save money, Stone's Ginger dies in an inexpensive hotel hallway after being fatally injected with drugs by her biker boyfriends. Quietly, she slides down the roach motel's cinder-block walls in a coma of liquor and benzodiazepenes, Judy Garland's tragic mix 'n' match. Like so many of the other druggy scenes in the film, Stone pays unintentional homage to *Reefer Madness* as she chews every last morsel of scenery before literally dropping dead.

New York's David Denby also faulted the writer and director for this inexplicable portrait of a tramp. "She's a real actress, liquid, even volatile. It's not her fault that Ginger never makes much sense. Sam [De Niro] falls in love with her, lavishes money and jewels on her, but [Stone] never loves Sam; she loves the sleazy pimp from an earlier life...." At least that element of Ginger's personality does make psychological, if not script, sense. Obviously, the reviewer never heard of codependency. On the other hand, however psychologically accurate the character was, the pimp didn't exist in real life. Scorsese's overblown Lester Diamond was a construct of deeply held misogyny.

Like a true method actor, Woods seemed to stay in character, i.e., obnoxious, even when the camera wasn't rolling. Stone was amused rather than miffed by Woods's tendency to remain a jerk even after the director yelled "Cut!" The two had worked together before, so by now the actress was used to the madness in his method. Stone said, "In *The Specialist* his character was really mean to me, so he was really mean to me period [between takes]. In *Casino,* my character is obsessed with him and will do anything for him." No method actress herself, Stone stopped playing love slave as soon as the shot was completed.

Despite Woods's slaphappy behavior and an unfortunate tendency to compare her genitalia to sharp-edged kitchen appliances, the two actors are great friends and basketball enthusiasts. Stone accommodates her pal's schizo traits. "The first time I worked with Jimmy Woods, I wrote him a note saying, 'It was a pleasure working with both of you.' I mean, he's so nuts."

Casino was her comeback film, although many critics felt that the star of glossy trash like *Basic Instinct* really didn't have anything to come back from except a series of box-office failures. Stone hesitated to take the role. Friends warned her that Ginger's pathology would rub off on her, as though Catherine Tramell hadn't already proved Stone was the Teflon star. A professional handler counseled caution. "It's like this woman is so unsympathetic, she ties her kid to the bed, gets loaded, and does coke....Sharon, we don't think you should go there." However, best friend Mimi Craven earned her title when she told Stone, "You've got to take this. You could do this part in your sleep." You wonder what her close friend was saying about Stone's character when she implied playing the sleazy Ginger amounted to typecasting.

The actress didn't have to storm the editing room or make crank calls to the director, but she did have to audition, which wasn't quite the humiliation it would have been at the hands of a lesser director. Nicole Kidman and Melanie Griffith also had to take a screen test. Evidently, both failed the "orals."

Before he met her, Scorsese was unsure of her talent. Afterward, he was smitten. Diplomatically, he blamed his original reluctance on her body of work, not her ability. "I didn't decide she could act or not act based on her movies, since most of them are genre pictures [industry politesse for dreck]. It was her presence and her look. She has a tough-edged look that seemed perfect for Vegas at the time, the way her face is structured, something about her eyes. You can believe she is what in the book was called the real-life Ginger, 'the most respected hustler in Vegas.'" Tellingly, while praising Stone, he has also reduced her to the sum of her gorgeous parts, face and eyes.

Stone felt certain she had blown the audition with De Niro. She revealed for the first time what has become a habit—talking to dead people. To get the role, she prayed to the spirit of Geri-Ginger, saying, "You've got to pick who you want to play you and who is the truth to you. I'm available—and thanks a lot."

Geri answered her prayers, probably from hell. Stone's fears and supplications were unnecessary. She hadn't blown the audition; she had blown the director's mind. Scorsese became a charter member of the Sharon Stone Fan Club. De Niro, though, wasn't so willing to enroll. He wanted onetime underaged porn star Traci Lords to play his wife. De Niro's idea reflected the philosophy behind many of the hires for the film. It's called "stunt casting," and Scorsese hired celebrities who were considered jokes for this most serious of films. How else do you explain the participation of Dick Smothers, Don Rickles, Steve Allen, Jayne Meadows, and Frankie Avalon? Lords would have simply been an even bigger "stunt."

Once Stone got the part, she demonstrated the same steely will that had her crashing airplane edits and making phone pleas to uninterested filmmakers. Stone noticed that every day after shooting, Scorsese and best friend De Niro would disappear into the actor's trailer. She correctly divined they were discussing De Niro's motivation for the next day's scenes.

Stone felt shut out of this little boys' club and complained loudly and profanely. She wrote in her diary, "Oh, shit, oh, shit, oh shit, they're not gonna let me in." Her diary wasn't the only thing she hassled. She recalled, "I chased Marty around for three days up and down hallways while he was trying to work out scenes, going, 'Look, I didn't take half my fucking salary [a measly $2 mil] for twice the time to be a fucking prop! You've gotta help me here. I'm here because you're the best and you have to make me better.'" At the time, her asking price was $4 million. Her cut-rate salary shows how much she was willing to give up for the part. It was a curious sacrifice. Stars like Bruce Willis typically take cuts in low-budget films with no apparent commercial prospects like *Pulp Fiction*. If the film turns into a sleeper hit, they can console their accountant with an Oscar nomination and an avalanche of A-list, big-budget scripts. Plus a cut of the gross. *Casino* was a relatively big-budget film at $35 million. You wonder if De Niro also took a cut in pay to star in a film that didn't lack commercial heat.

Stone's praise of the director and doubts about her own ability failed to move him. She continued to pester him for three days, until he finally said, "Okay, what do you want from me?" Stone actually had a written list prepared of her aesthetic demands, including this masochistic one: "I want you to push me till I drop dead."

Soon Scorsese was doing double duty with trips to both stars' Winnebagos. And he more than satisfied her push-till-I-drop request. Stone rejected the use of a stunt double and endured six months of punches, slaps, and a really creepy oral sex scene with capo Joe Pesci. Pesci, as the psychopath muscle to De Niro's schmooze, gets fellated not once but twice in three hours on-screen. But just as the lapsed Catholic director has his actors keep their clothes on, Pesci's oral gratification is shot from the waist up. Or maybe Scorsese's squeamishness is actually good taste and manners. Paul Verhoeven was forced back into the editing room to cut Stone and Douglas's oral coupling in *Basic Instinct*. Scorsese was also dragged back to the Movieola in pursuit of an R rating to excise a hit man whose eye pops out after his head is sandwiched in a vice.

The *Los Angeles Times* was even more decorous describing Stone's fellatio. "In one of the year's weirdest movie seductions, Pesci beds Stone's hustler turned alcoholic hausfrau." The correct verb is "couches," because that's where they are sitting when he shoves her unprotesting head into his lap.

Stone happily suffered other indignities, although her patience ran thin after three takes. Still, the director marveled at her lack of temperament. "She was game, basically. Granted, by the third take she said, 'I think we've got it now.' But the fact that she did it at all is remarkable," he said. Scorsese gentlemanly offered the services of a body double, but the actress volunteered to be thrown downstairs, dragged the length of a marble hallway, and hurled headfirst into a parking lot. "By the end of the shoot," she said like a veteran, "I looked like a dalmatian," a dalmatian with black-and-blue spots. After six months of imitating a punching bag, she confessed that looking in the mirror was frightening. Stone spiked all rumors of being difficult when she said of the mauling, "It was divine."

As a film education, the director played F. Scott Fitzgerald to Stone's Sheila Grahame, but instead of great books, he had her watch videos of such curious classics as *Mildred Pierce* and *Whatever Happened to Baby Jane?*

Both the director and leading man treated her input with respect—and used it. Stone showed that it was simply a matter of being assertive, not submissive. "Going to Marty and Bob school is a little like getting a Ph.D.," she said. "They'll let you be a prop, or they'll let you play. It's up to you."

In the *New York Times*'s delicate phrase, Stone's chest becomes "noticeably larger" halfway through the film. It was Stone's ingenious suggestion that as Ginger's looks went the way of all flesh via barbiturates and booze, she would seek solace in silicone. The director was delighted to order push-up bras and padding from wardrobe. To flesh out her character further, she meticulously studied FBI files on the real-life Ginger-Geri.

Despite De Niro's original promotion of porn star Lords, Stone managed to melt her costar's heart of stone. Others may feel De Niro is no Gable, but his leading lady felt he was Cary Grant with Mick Jagger's lips. Known for her difficult on-set relationships with other actors, like Douglas and Baldwin, Stone fell a little in love with the five-foot-eight-inch actor. She began the shoot terrified by his superior talent. Soon she was obsessing about his mouth. "Believe me, I went into this thinking I'm not gonna choke now. I started this movie in a state of abject terror. I could barely speak. I started throwing myself at Bob—I had no choice. It didn't take much acting. He's a wonderful kisser. I'm sorry for saying it, Bob, but it's true. What people don't realize about him is how sexy he is. I know you're not supposed to say that. You're supposed to say how deeply talented, what an artist. Wow, was he sexy." The actress wasn't sucking up and auditioning for *Casino II,* since the dead Ginger wouldn't be showing up in a sequel, although there are always flashback possibilities.

Her career-making collaboration disproved the famous caveat Don't wish for things because they may come true. Way back in 1981, when her acting chores consisted of swallowing spiders, she confided to best friend Mimi Craven that her ultimate career fantasy was to act opposite De Niro and "hold my own." Soon she'd also be holding a Golden Globe and clutching the Oscar podium as presenter and nominee.

Stone's salary cut turned out to be a bargain for the actress. It bought her the one thing money can't buy, even in Hollywood: R-E-S-P-E-C-T. The reviews of *Casino* ranged from orgasmic to toxic. Stone's notices also included orgasmic praise, but the few barbs stopped at mildly disappointed. None contained the usual sexist slams. Some paid her the left-handed compliment of expressing pleasant surprise that the bombshell could act. In a pan of the film but a rave of her performance, *Time* magazine summed up her fall and rise. "Until *Casino* her career was dogged by critical derision. At last, she is about to be taken seriously. A woman so many took for a bimbo finally pulled it off."

Other critics were less damning with faint praise. Roger Ebert encapsulated the consensus: "Sharon Stone's call girl is her best performance." The *New York Times* overstated her courage in *Casino* and ignored her creepiness in *Basic Instinct*. "Sharon Stone has made a reckless throw of the dice playing a villain because actors usually love to be loved, even when playing villains. Ginger is appalling." Apparently, the *Times*'s William Grimes had never seen Catherine's ice pick or Hermes scarves.

The *Sunday Times* (London), which had hinted at prostitution during her starlet days and flat out claimed she had done porno, did an about-face and became an Oscar handicapper. Stone is introduced in *Casino* on a grainy black-and-white security camera monitor. De Niro instantly falls in love with the pointillist image, even though she's throwing a john's chips in the air as payback for a stingy tip. The British newspaper was enchanted from her opening scene on. "Her first scene where she throws chips in the air like confetti is a fantastic sequence. Nothing, you think, could follow that. You'd be right. Nothing could—except an Oscar for Stone—and nothing does." The *Times* (London) loved Stone; hated the film, adding, "*Casino* is a con, a cinematic sleight of hand that substitutes scope for depth. It's not a coincidence that the thing you best remember about it is the introduction it gives Stone."

The British journalist was trashing a masterpiece. Stone's intro is electric, but much of the juice comes from the script and Scorsese's feather-light camera work. De Niro's voice-over narrates Stone's introduction, calling her a "hustler." His euphemism is amusing. As Stone's "hustler" paws an old troll throwing craps, Scorsese's camera reveals that De Niro is looking at her through rose-colored glasses of instant lust. De Niro's hustler is the crapshooter's prostitute for the game and postgame wrap-up.

London's *Time Out* still refused to give a girl a break. It attributed Stone's brilliantly modulated performance to De Niro's efforts. "He…helps Sharon Stone rise to a fine performance." Stone's ability to mesmerize us by playing a monster is all the greater accomplishment because the costumes she's poured into could make the character degenerate into camp. It didn't help that Cher's Halloweenish couturier, Bob Mackie, designed much of Ginger's polyester wardrobe, although Rita Ryack and John Dunn get solo credit. Maybe Mackie was too embarrassed to be reminded of his 1970s follies with bugle beads. Her wedding dress includes the traditional virginal veil, accented, however, with hot pants. For once, short shorts flesh out her character rather than causing giggles, as they did during *The Specialist*'s funeral. Her early bouffant hairdos would recall Mary Richards if the star of the *Mary Tyler Moore Show* had moonlighted from the newsroom as a hooker. Clothes may make the man, but Stone proves they don't make the woman. As she rose in the past above so much inferior material, she manages to surmount the handicap of Brady Bunch drag. Wearing a Hillary headband, white lipstick, baby-blue leather suit, and white knee-high go-go boots, Stone still keeps her title, the most beautiful woman in the movies.

Her egolessness extended to makeup. Just as she willingly skipped all cosmetics for her 1990 *Playboy* spread and *The Quick and the Dead,* here she allows herself to be increasingly trashed as coke, pills, and Jack Daniels make her hollow-eyed, gaunt-cheeked, and puffy everywhere else. This is not Barbra Streisand in glam movie-star makeup playing an institutionalized psycho in *Nuts*. Ginger is supposed to physically deteriorate over three hours, and Stone enthusiastically surrenders to Scorsese's trashing in service of the role. Stone truly lived the "actuh's" cliché: It's all about the script.

Her jewelry was equally gaudy and much more expensive than re-creating togs from the Me Decade. Burned once by Stone's expensive concept of permanent "loans," Harry Winston stayed out of the picture. Where angels fear to trade out, Bulgari was only too happy to rush in, loaning the production a $2 million necklace, among other baubles, for one scene. The set overflowed with security guards protecting the jeweler's property. At the end of the day, there wouldn't be any confusion or lawsuits about promotion fees versus loan-outs.

Even the set decoration and design had the potential to sabotage Stone's moments of high drama and lowlife behavior. Despite the 1970s time frame, Chez Rothstein looks as though its decorator is still living in the Eisenhower administration. The "genuine" leatherette and primary-color scheme suggests that the art director also worked on John Waters's *Polyester*. Stone has to perform some of her most memorable drug-induced tantrums amid furniture Divine would have been embarrassed to sit on.

The movie's only class was the soundtrack. De Niro gets an even more spectacular introduction than Stone in the film. After he turns his key in the ignition, his Cadillac goes up in a thirty-foot-high fireball. On the soundtrack, Bach's *St. Matthew Passion* ironically underlines the stifled passion of De Niro's Job.

Scorsese is no musical bluestocking. His taste in tunes can be as gaudy as go-go boots and purple bedspreads. For Stone's jewelry-draped intro, the Rolling Stone's "Heart of Stone" hints at her character's granite aorta.

The Golden Globes and Oscars were a study in contrasts. Their respective choices for best actress said more perhaps about their membership than the quality of the performances honored. The Golden Globes are awarded by the tiny, under-100 membership of the Hollywood Foreign Press Association, a malodorous collection of Eurotrash journalists whose credentials are suspect, if not outright fictitious. The real occupations of the foreign press are often joked about. As one shut-out studio executive said, "On the night of the Golden Globes, their isn't a headwaiter in all of

Beverly Hills." Except at the award ceremony at the Beverly
Hilton. There, an off-duty maître d' often plays master of cere-
monies. The association has cleaned up its act in recent years, but
it was an Augean task, dating back to the early 1980s, when it
named Pia Zadora newcomer of the year. Since then, the cham-
pagne taste of moonlighting waiter-voters shows they own a
Cristal ball when handicapping the Oscars. Frequently, their
winners go on to more upscale glories at the Academy Awards.

In 1996 their crystal ball needed polishing. Stone won the
Globe, but Oscar went to Susan Sarandon's dead nun walking. The
Academy's elderly membership chose a saintly sister over a Satanic
slut. This isn't overly editorial. At a free screening of *Casino* for
Academy voters, one senior citizen stood up and, as he exited the
theater, asked other outraged viewers to follow him out. His
démarche was swelled by two. Despite their puritanism, the
Academy's nominees underlined Hollywood's tunnel vision of
women. Not one but two of the Best Actress nominees played
prostitutes (the other, Elizabeth Shue in *Leaving Las Vegas*).
Sarandon's win underlines the old madonna-whore complex.
Meryl Streep proved there are few well-written roles for actresses
of a certain age, but the competition was so scarce, she received a
nomination for her turgid turn in *The Bridges of Madison County*
as an Iowa Madame Bovary. Only Emma Thompson's Jane Austen
heroine escaped Hollywood stereotyping, and the British *Sense
and Sensibility* wasn't made in Hollywood.

The Golden Globes gave Stone the opportunity to do her
variation on Sally Field's "You like me! You really like me!"
acceptance speech, only much, much less embarrassingly. Her
short and elegant exclamation, "At last!" spoke volumes about
sixteen years of being treated like the Rodney Dangerfield of
divas. After some hyperventilating, she added, "This is what I
have been waiting for. This is my validation of all the work I have
gone through."

One pooper at the party rained on her parade. Commenting
on the brilliant performances by *Casino*'s amateur actors Don
Rickles and Alan King, a tuxedoed gadfly said, "Phyllis Diller
would be brilliant in a Martin Scorsese film." The gadfly was

cruel—and inaccurate. Stone earned every piece of her gilt Globe. Her acting in the wedding-reception scene alone, which she spends on a pay phone weeping to her long-lost pimp, recalls another Oscar-nominated toll call—Bette Midler's Joplinesque junkie who ODs while reaching out to touch her manager. The Globe and Oscar nod provided tangible evidence that her fifteen-year-old acting dream of holding her own against De Niro on screen had come true. Stone actually topped her dream and more than held her own. She held on to a Golden Globe statuette. De Niro wasn't even nominated for either award.

The bean counters at MCA-Universal found scant comfort in Stone's renaissance. To shut down *Casino*'s casinos and Las Vegas Boulevard cost a fortune, roughly $70 million. The brilliant film, despite crowd-pleasing, eye-popping violence, only grossed out viewers to the tune of $30 million. Even video, foreign, and cable sales would not make up the difference.

Stone's triumph at the Beverly Hilton was also diluted by an unflattering fashion faux pas. She wore a gown by Valentino with a black top and white bottom. White accentuated her ample hips. Adding insult to injury, TV star Lea Thompson (*Caroline in the City*) turned up in a mirror-image frock that offered a fashion tip to the reckless thirty-eight-year-old. Thompson's top was white, adding needed volume to her chest. Her thighs were thinned under cover of black. Thompson exhibited Kate Moss chic. Stone was doing Mae West.

The Oscars witnessed an even bigger fashion gaffe. Stone has said that because of her blue-collar roots she feels honored to be invited to upscale events and dresses accordingly. Her outfit for the Oscars was downscale and inappropriate. Even to my un-trained eye, which doesn't know Karan from K-mart, her black long-sleeved blouse stood out among all the $35,000 Mizrahis and Lagerfelds. I couldn't quite put my finger on what was wrong with Stone's blouse except that it looked more like a T-shirt. The next day, the fashion vigilantes in the press reported that Stone's "couturier" was the Gap! *Newsweek* chided the "couture commo-tion" the actress created at the gala and reported that she had commissioned two dresses, by Valentino and Vera Wang, both of which remained in the closet while she spent twenty-two dollars on a cotton turtleneck.

Sarandon, who beat Stone for the Best Actress Oscar, had spent the entire film wearing the unflattering shift of a Catholic nun. In reaction to her dreary screen togs, she showed up in a dress that recalled the hoop-skirted glory of Balmain. Stone had spent most of *Casino* dripping in jewelry and spandex. Maybe she dressed down for the Oscars in reaction to the screen glitz. Or maybe she wasn't feeling so blue collar, so honored to be there anymore.

The respect of the critics, Academy voters, and off-duty waiter-journalists proved to be contagious. Stone said, amazed, "People have started to call me Miss Stone instead of just Sharon, which I'm sure is a combination of my age and my attitude."

Age was not a problem on her next film. At thirty-eight, Stone was still the most beautiful actress in the world, per the University of Louisville, and she could top any *Baywatch* bimbo in a bathing suit, although top may not be the right word when comparing Stone's 36B to the TV show's silicone-tiered stars. The actress's attitude, however, would ruin her next film, a terrific popcorn treat that the actress's colleagues would gag on and that would send her fans in search of something more nutritious.

17

Diabolical

"IT'S AMAZING WHAT A MONSTER an Oscar nomination can turn you into," a studio source said of Stone's meddling in *Diabolique,* her first film after the Academy Awards.

As a psychopathic math teacher, Stone was typecast in more ways than one. In high school, the brainy girl tutored grade-schoolers in algebra. "When I was fifteen, I went to college half a day while I went to high school, and I tutored algebra to other kids in my school. I was like, you know, that weird girl. I cannot believe I did not know that I was a pretty girl. I was so insecure and so intimidated and so introverted," she said.

One hopes she didn't treat her youthful charges with the same contempt she shows her prep-school students in *Diabolique*. Stone's Nicole Horner isn't intimidated. She intimidates, not to mention drowning and embedding a rake in her lover's head.

Chazz Palminteri richly deserves his fatal encounter with a garden tool. The tyrannical headmaster of a boarding school for problem boys, he beats his wife, Isabelle Adjani, a weak-willed ex-nun, as well as his mistress, Sharon Stone, who plays her role so butch that her acceptance of the abuse makes no dramatic sense.

Based on the 1955 classic *Les Diaboliques* (The Fiends), directed by Henri-Georges Clouzot, the script calls for the battered women to fight back. Stone laces her tormentor's Jack Daniels with phenobarbitol. When he passes out, she and Adjani drown him in the bathtub. Then they dump the corpse in the school's unused swimming pool. The only problem is that the corpse doesn't stay put. The dead man returns to haunt his murderesses, causing Adjani to suffer a heart attack. Unfavorably compared to the French original, *Diabolique* nevertheless ditches the 1955 version's surprise ending for an even more ingenious denouement, one that involves much more blood and gore for the eighteen-to-twenty-five-year-old crowd. Unfortunately, the expensive $35 million film didn't attract that vital demographic, grossing a budget-busting $15 million.

One of the problems was that there were two films on-screen, the director's and Stone's. Jeremiah Chechik, the director of the off-kilter Johnny Depp vehicle *Benny & Joon,* wanted to pay homage to Hitchcock. *Entertainment Weekly* summed up: "Stone and Chechik always had different takes on *Diabolique*." The director saw the project as a "very, very dark thriller." Stone wanted "a black comedy." The actress dresses and acts like Joan Crawford, circa *Mildred Pierce*. Scorsese's Pygmalion had had a toxic effect on his superstar Galatea. Scorsese—and Stone—would have been better off had he recommended Tony Perkins's psycho mom rather than Crawford's hard-boiled restaurateur. Stone mimics Mommie Dearest down to the tailored suits, whose shoulders have the breadth of a linebacker's jersey. Her acting is also over the top. All the other actors shared the director's vision. They're doing *Macbeth,* while Stone is doing *Whatever Happened to Baby Jane?,* another Scorsese recommendation; only Stone wears designer frocks instead of Bette Davis's size 8 muumuus.

The actress's approval of Chechik says more about her lust for power than her sense of taste. She claimed that his sardonic *Benny & Joon* had charmed her, but she forgot to read the rest of his resumé, which included the no-brainer *National Lampoon's Christmas Vacation* and *Tall Tales: The Unbelievable Adventures of Pecos Bill*. Picking Chechik to make a film about sexual compulsion and murder was like hiring Captain Kangaroo to helm *Deep Throat II: The Tonsillectomy.*

Chechik's hire suggested that Stone had learned an important lesson from Sylvester Stallone, her *Specialist* costar. Pick a cloutless, D-list director so that the star can call the shots. Which she did. No shots of Stone uncrossing her legs. Lots of costar Adjani, who seemed to have the European's natural ease with nudity.

Stone's self-posession and clout came in handy when a more powerful figure, Morgan Creek's chairman, Jim Robinson, ordered her to strip. She had originally demanded $6 million to make *Diabolique.* Warner Bros. told her to stick her head in the bathtub. Then the studio's *Specialist* opened with nearly $15 million during its first three days, and independent production company Morgan Creek cut a check for the balance. Except now Stone had upped the ante to $7 million, to which Morgan Creek agreed. The company assured stockholders that it was being crazy like a CPA. Stone is one of the few actresses whose films do even better abroad, and Morgan Creek had a strong foreign-distribution arm.

But the company wanted some flesh in return for its largesse, a little bang for a lot of bucks. Robinson, who also produced *Diabolique,* walked into her trailer on the Pennsylvania set and said that the movie needed "something extra." He had in mind Stone's bare breasts. She threw Robinson out of her Winnebago and threatened him with a lawsuit for sexual harassment, according to *People* magazine's Mitchell Fink. Robinson immediately backed off, bowing. His frazzled press rep said resignedly, "Sharon's contract called for a nude scene. When she agreed to do this picture, she agreed to do the nude scene, and she was obligated to shoot the scene nude. She didn't want to do it, and so she didn't." Stars whose films gross nearly $400 million aren't obligated to do anything they don't want to. Stone had apparently read a different contract, which didn't require her to toss her togs. Plus, if she agreed to do a nude scene, she would retain veto power in the editing room. Too much cellulite and the offending flesh would end up on the cutting-room floor. This time she wouldn't have to pack a gun to ensure the editor's compliance, as she reportedly had on *Basic Instinct.*

The incident with the producer soured the atmosphere on the set, and Stone displaced her anger on the director, who claimed that their relationship degenerated into a power struggle. Stone denied the accusation and trashed Chechik's film at the same time. "My power game is not this petty bullshit over a marginal movie." Without offering a single example, Chechick said, "She started behaving unprofessionally." *Entertainment Weekly* offered several. The most noticeable was Stone's refusal postproduction to promote the film. This is the same woman who flew all over Europe hyping *Sliver* at Sherry Lansing's request. When it came time to give interviews at a New York press junket for *Diabolique,* Stone was a no-show. Her explanation for impersonating Sean Penn: "I didn't have enough good things left to say to fill up two days of PR." After viewing the final cut, Stone became her film's worst critic. "The original is and will remain a classic. Ours is a funny, campy, one-box-of-popcorn thriller." Chechik must have been thinking, Who needs Pauline Kael when your own star is willing to trash your work? Chechik said, "That's stupid. If she wants to characterize her own performance as campy, she's allowed to do that."

It's always good to cover your bases and butt in Hollywood. You never know when you might be working again with someone you previously badmouthed. Chechik added, "I wish her the best. I hope she becomes a bigger and bigger celebrity. I hope she just becomes God."

The public spat made waves across the ocean. Commenting on the source of the naked feud, the *Observer* in London called Stone's new found delicacy after *Basic Instinct* and *Sliver*'s exhibitionism a "prude awakening" that "had less to do with her growing sense of power and heightened consciousness and feminism than it did with her self-conscious awareness of her growing cellulite." Unlike its American colleagues, who fear blacklisting by the stars' all-powerful publicists, the mainstream British press never backs off vicious, sexist *ad feminam* attacks. If you're letting yourself go, even the august *Times* (London) will let everyone know the departure date.

The least vain beauty on the planet, Stone revels in self-trashing. She's her harshest critic when it comes to weighing in against weight gain. Her aversion to nudity was indeed a "prude awakening" to her diminished physical appearance as well as a savvy career move. She told the *Observer,* "For years I made movies because I had to put food on the table. Now I have a choice. I don't want to become a caricature of myself. I'm 37. I'm watching my butt slide down my legs. I want to extend my range. Sexpots age fast in Hollywood." German *Vogue* disagreed. It headlined one article "Sharon Stone: *Sie Ist Die Sexpot!*" Not as much as she used to be on film. Stone kept her black lacey bra and panties on for the scene where she humps costar Chazz Palminteri's leg. Poor Isabelle Adjani didn't have the clout and was subjected to full frontal nudity while enacting what has to be the least erotic event in anyone's life, a coronary followed by death!

Stone wasn't only willful about wardrobe. She refused to show up on the set until her leading man was cast. Jack Nicholson was offered $5 million, ditto Alec Baldwin, for only one week's work, since the abusive headmaster is drowned in the first twenty minutes. Both rejected the role, and Stone refused to let the production "shoot around" the absent male lead despite threatening letters from Morgan Creek's attorneys. Stone also demanded her $7 million salary up front, says press agent Howard Brandy, "because she wanted to invest in T-bills."

Brandy's firm supplied the unit publicist, Bob Levine, to babysit the press on the set. Levine refused to comment, but boss Brandy told me that Stone so terrified the publicist, he was relieved when he was asked to speak to her personal assistant instead of the star.

A veteran of Hollywood press wars, Brandy isn't so easily intimidated. He called Stone "a nutter" who is "very clever with money. She wanted to invest in T-bills because she knows this isn't going to last forever."

After she thought she blew the audition for *Casino,* Stone sat on her bed and prayed to the dead showgirl, Geri McKee. It was seance time again on the set of *Diabolique,* according to Brandy, who said that Stone claimed she talked to the dead. A columnist for Los Angeles's trendy *Buzz* magazine, Cathy Seipp, said that

Stone heard voices on the set. You wonder if the actress was consulting the spirit of Simone Signoret, who had her role in the 1955 original.

Stone dismissed all the setside rumors and insisted that everyone "ended up on good terms." That didn't stop her, after the film wrapped, from publicly trashing the producers when they tried to rip off an elderly widow. *Diabolique*'s other producer, Marvin Worth, was either lying or hadn't read the script when he said that the American remake used only the French original's title and nothing more. "Our film is a completely original version," Worth said. The script, per the *Hollywood Reporter,* which had read it, is almost a frame-by-frame, uh, *hommage* to Clouzot's pop classic. There were good legal and financial reasons for Worth's claim. Madame Clouzot had been paid pennies for the rights to her dead husband's film. When she saw the final cut, she screamed murder louder than Palminteri after Stone stuck a rake in his head.

Stone came to the widow's defense. It just so happened that she was in Mrs. Clouzot's homeland, France, promoting *Casino*. At a press conference, Stone sounded like Joan of Arc by way of Beverly Hills when she said on national French television, "I'm ashamed to be involved in a production that apparently acted improperly. I hope that Madame Clouzot will be correctly compensated and treated properly."

When Mrs. Clouzot's attorney's got an injunction against the French premiere, Stone didn't care that it was her film being blacklisted. "Too bad for the Cannes [Film] Festival," she said.

Diabolique was annoying for other reasons besides producers intent on stripping stars and ripping off pensioners. The location shoot outside a chilly autumnal Pittsburgh kept her away from her new warm home in the hills of Hollywood.

She had to supervise the creation of her personal screening room by phone. *Architectural Digest* noted in a photo spread, "Every Hollywood star has a swimming pool or tennis court, but a house with a screening room telegraphs success on a somewhat grander scale. It's the equivalent of a movie mogul's private Gulf Stream."

Stone telephoned her decorator daily from the Pennsylvania set with detailed instructions. The interior designer for a single room in the eleven-thousand-foot-square fake Mediterranean villa speaks volumes about Stone's new star status. Her decorator was more than the equivalent of a studio chief's Gulf Stream. Some maids don't do windows. It's unheard of for a top couturier to do decor, but that's exactly what Stone convinced multimillionaire Ralph Lauren to do. And she gave him only six weeks, because she wanted the room ready for a party to celebrate the opening of *Casino* and her star on Hollywood Boulevard's Walk of Fame. Only six weeks to transform cinder-block walls and a cracked floor into "a jewel box," *Architectural Digest* said.

To call the room luxe is like saying "great digs" to the curator of Versailles. First off, Lauren had to find a place to hang a Degas and a Léger which Stone bought at auction. Actually, the auctioneer accepted her bid via cellular phone. Someone suggested that Lauren hang the museum-quality pieces on the wall of a museum, where they belonged. Other acquisitions proved Pope's contention that a little learning—and a lot of money—can be a dangerous thing. Stone fatuously claimed in the pages of *Vanity Fair*'s April '93 issue that the 1930s Hollywood hack Tamara DeLempicka preempted Picasso's best period. "Tamara DeLempicka invented Cubism, not Picasso, not Braque. Cubism is not a male thing." Typically, the magazine's starstruck interviewer, Kevin Sessums, let her comment go unchallenged in print. A reader was less generous. In a letter to the editor, one Brian Abercrombie implied that the actress didn't know her art history from her elbow. "Tamara DeLempicka was all of nine years old when Pablo Picasso painted *Le Demoiselles d'Avignon* in 1907— the definitive beginning of Cubism," the armchair art historian wrote. "DeLempicka did not pick up a paintbrush until ten years later, and her first documented paintings are from the early twenties." Far be it from *Vanity Fair* to let a common fact checker contradict one of the cover subjects it grovels to.

The sycophancy of the entertainment press, which fears the wrath of PMK, is often punctured by readers who aren't so starstruck or terrified by publicists. In the March 1994 issue of

Vogue, reporter Charles Gandee unctuously wrote, "As she stepped gingerly around a metal floor sculpture by Carl André, [Stone] gave the impression of a woman perfectly at home in her highbrow surroundings, a woman comfortably conversant in history and the language of art."

One subscriber felt that Stone was speaking broken English. In a letter to the editor from the art capital of Brooklyn, New York, Jeffrey Amurao wrote, "Apparently neither Stone nor journalist Gandee are aware that Carl André's minimal floor sculptures may be walked on by viewers." The reader went on to quote Irving Sandler's *American Art of the 1960's* to support his contention that André's work was designed as a doormat.

Stone was too busy decorating up a storm to worry about art etiquette. Outside, the facade may have screamed faux château as the ghost of Louis Quinze wept amid a riot of rococo. Inside, the look Chez Stone whispered 1930s Art Deco and George Hurrell's name. *Haute* decorator Lauren suggested that the room pay homage to *Singin' in the Rain*. Stone had had too much experience ripping off a classic with *Diabolique* and demurred because Gene Kelly's projection room in the musical looked too Spanish. She picked the sleek chrome elegance of 1930s glamour photographer Hurrell. Her choice had sentimental reasons. Stone had been the last screen queen the Ansel Adams of vanity photography had shot before his death.

In keeping with the multimillion-dollar artwork, the walls were lined with platinum charmeuse, a satin-crepe hybrid and more than I ever wanted to know about interior *tchotchke*. Stone attacked decorating with the same single-mindedness she used to scale the Hollywood heap. An A-list couturier to design the place; a top producer to vet the film projector and sound. None other than the Oscar-winning producer of *Platoon,* Arnold Kopelson, was dragooned into playing sound and light technician for Stone's home theater. She sweetened the task by screening Kopelson's latest blockbuster, *The Fugitive.* The train-wreck sequence literally shook the room. Kopelson gave his seal of approval. Kopelson's verdict: "This is even better than what I've got at home. I'll have to get mine redone." Keeping up with the Stoneses.

As her finessing of Kopelson and Lauren suggests, Stone can turn on the charm when she has to. Sometimes she doesn't care whom she ticks off, including the American Cancer Society. On June 17, 1995, a few months before she showed up on the set of *Diabolique,* outside Pittsburgh, Stone was in Washington, serving as celebrity host of the National Race for the Cure, a five-kilometer jog to raise awareness of breast cancer. Stone raised consciousness during her address to the National Press Club, but it wasn't the message the American Cancer Society wanted propagated.

After movingly describing her aunt's successful battle against breast cancer, Stone let loose a howler than had cancer specialists howling coast to coast. "I hadn't planned to say this," she said at the end of her nine-minute speech. "Four years ago I was told that I had cancer. I tested positive twice for lymph cancer. I had a lump in every lymph area of my body. I knew what that meant. Very, very, very fortunately, with lots of positive thinking and lots of holistic healing I ended up testing negative for lymph cancer. But it took several months, and those months changed my life. One of the changes during that time is that I stopped drinking coffee, and when I stopped drinking coffee, ten days later I had no tumors in any of my lymph glands."

It's one thing to trash your director and his $35-million film. Or pontificate on the originator of Cubism. It's another thing to offer dangerous health tips that can also kill your career. After her speech, you could easily imagine the headline writer at the *National Enquirer* tapping out "Sharon Stone's Cure for Cancer!"

Stone's claims distressed the mainstream medical community and horrified her handlers. Claiming that your cancer is in remission is not a good career move. There's a little thing called completion bond insurance every studio pays before filming begins. All the principals involved in making the film are required to take a physical for insurance purposes. If the star has a health problem that might stall or capsize a project, the carrier either jacks up its premium or refuses to insure the production altogether. Perhaps the most egregious example of insurer terror involved Jane Fonda's *El Gringo*. The actress wanted Burt Lancas-

ter to play her leading man as the dyspeptic journalist Ambrose
Bierce. The insurance company refused to insure Lancaster
because of his history of heart disease. Gregory Peck got the job.
Lancaster sued but proved the insurer's point by dying of a heart
attack before the case ever went to trial.

Stone's announcement could have a similar chilling affect on
her insurability. Within hours, her press agent at PMK, Cindi
Berger, was doing damage control. In a rare case of a flack
contradicting a client, Berger said, "She never had cancer. She was
misdiagnosed. She actually had an allergy to caffeine, which is
what caused the lumps in her lymph glands." Pressed to elaborate,
Berger stonewalled. "She is not interested in setting the record
straight."

Dr. Andrew Saxon, head of clinical immunology and allergy at
UCLA, was equally terse but dismissive. "Makes no sense. Doesn't
compute," he told *People* magazine.

A family practitioner and alternative medicine specialist in
Las Vegas, Dr. Robert Milne, was the only "authority" *People* could
find to back Stone, sort of. Milne insisted that he treated patients
for "caffeine-related lymphatic *congestion* all the time. But the
difference between congestion and cancer is clear. You could get
a swelling from caffeine, but not a tumor."

The American Cancer Society feared that Stone's admission
would do more damage than making the actress uninsurable. The
New York Times said that her claim "caused particular concern"
for the cancer foundation. Its spokeswoman, Joanne Schellen-
bach, explained: "The concern from our organization was that
anyone diagnosed with cancer and undergoing therapy would
give it up and stop drinking coffee and start other techniques"
instead.

For espresso addicts everywhere, Schellenback added this
consumer tip: "In the 1980s, there was some research about
caffeine increasing the risk of certain kinds of cancer, in particular pancreatic cancer. All the studies since then found no connec-
tion with caffeine and any increased risk for cancer," the *New
York Times* reported in a June 21, 1995, article. Edinboro College
apparently didn't offer art history or Pathology 101, either. Stone

could have covered herself by saying, "The caffeine made me do it."

A few months after ticking off the American Cancer Society, Stone enraged all of France through no fault of her own, although the minister of culture, who awarded her a knighthood, should be impeached.

The *Times* (London) felt bad for its *confreres* across the Chunnel and condemned the relentless "Coca-colonization" of France by American pop culture. The *Times*: "French civilization suffered a double blow this week. First the American actress Sharon Stone was made a Knight of the Order of Arts and Letters by the French Minister of Culture. Second, the list of the most popular boys' names in the country was issued. The winner was 'Kevin.'"

Unlike "Sharon Stone Day" at Saegertown High, Stone showed up to be dubbed "Sir Sharon." Minister Philippe Douste-Blazzy didn't share the London *Times*'s dismay as he, lucky *garçon*, pinned a medal on one of Stone's breasts. "In the name of the president of the Republic," the starstruck pol said, "you are an absolute star. Thank you for making daily life seem a bit less routine." The minister also praised her "services to world culture. You rendered life a little less ordinary. Your game[?], your presence, your physique, troubling and captivating, have given you a special place in our cinema phantasmagoria."

Stone, who learned the *langue d'amour* from a Parisian boyfriend, made her acceptance speech in French. "I could say, like Josephine Baker [another topless American émigré], I have two loves: cinema and Paris. I am very honored by this invitation to be part of the French family."

The daily *News Soir* wanted the adoption halted. "Douste-Blazzy must think the icepick is a symbol of high culture, but that must be the reason, since Ms. Stone is not known for being an ambassador for French culture abroad....She does not speak a single word of French." To which the bilinqual star might have replied, "*Baissez-moi.*"

The award honored a curious resumé. Her finest performance in *Casino* would not be out in America for another month, months later in Europe. Her most artistic work was the ice-pick epic *Basic Instinct*. The knighthood becomes a bit more understandable when you learn of other honorees: Paul Newman, Jane Fonda, Clint Eastwood, Sylvester Stallone, and TV's Fonzie, Henry Winkler. The French still suffer from a terminal case of Jerry Lewis syndrome.

18

Last Tango, Last Chance?

HOW MUCH OF A CAREER STOPPER is it to be cursed with traffic-stopping good looks, branded a beauty by oversexed critics and panting fans alike? When the *Los Angeles Times*'s Sunday "Calendar" section ran a thoughtful think piece headlined "The Starlets Next Door," most of the starlets moved away and refused to participate. Sex goddesses are truly an endangered species among Hollywood fauna. Their brainless typecasting more often than not makes them the dodo bird of cinema. The June 9, 1996, *Times* article by Irene Lacher underlined this fatal beauty: "If feminism hasn't necessarily rewritten the scripts for female sex symbols in these days post-Marilyn [not to mention more recent casualties post-Kim and Geena], it has nevertheless had an impact: few actresses want to be identified as her successor. Accordingly, few agreed to be interviewed for this story."

A talent agent who found the same story so touchy he requested anonymity agreed. "A lot of smart actresses who have studied the career of sex symbols have noticed they are not careers of longevity. An actor wants to work forever and admitting you're a sex symbol may not be the way to do it. Now they want to say, 'I'm a serious actress and I do rep.'" We're still waiting for Stone to play all *Three Sisters* on a nightly rotation in an Equity-waiver production on Melrose Avenue.

By 1996 the *Times* had practically written the obituary for Stone's career. The usually circumspect newspaper said, "Actresses worried about being limited to bombshell roles need look only as far as their corner six-plex for ominous signs. Sharon Stone's attempts to break out in *Last Dance* and *Casino* snagged her an Oscar nomination for the latter, but the films performed far more poorly than the star."

Michael Medved, forgetting her services as the author of the introduction to his coffee-table effort *Golden Turkeys,* kicked Stone while she was down. The *New York Post*'s film critic said, "The public's response to *Last Dance* indicates that people like their female sex symbols to do glamorous stuff and not necessarily to be in hard-hitting, depressing dramas where they don't wear makeup. They had to subpoena people to see *Last Dance*— and Sharon Stone is a major star."

Being a sex goddess is a dirty job, and nobody wants to do it. Or as *Time* magazine's Richard Schickel put it, "It's a short-lived career being a sex goddess because people really can't stand the heat for very long." Survivors of sex-goddess syndrome, which the *Time* questionably labeled Madonna and Stone, try to put a spin on their sexuality. "Both are put-on artists," Schickel added. "They're playing in some ironic post modern way the role of sex goddess. They're almost sending up that kind of imagery."

Unfortunately, as the Broadway producer said, satire (*a.k.a.* send-up) is what closes on opening night. Send-ups of sex keep people out of movie theaters on Saturday night, too.

Stone's quirky choice to play a white-trash double murderer in *Last Dance* had critics comparing it to a similarly themed but superior work, *Dead Man Walking,* which allowed Susan Sarandon to beat Stone at the Oscars. Stone's effort was dismissed as "Dead Bimbo Walking." The punny possibilities were irresistible. Another writer labeled her film "Dying Sex Goddess Limping."

The actress's goal was laudable. She wanted to stretch rather than coast on her luscious laurels. How far can you go from *Basic Instinct*'s hundred-million-dollar heiress or *Sliver*'s tony book editor? Critics felt that the actress had gone off the deep end when she played a lumpy teenager on speed who slashes the throat of an ex-boyfriend and his girlfriend with a piece of broken glass in *Last Dance*. An ice pick is elegant. A sliver of glass is tacky, especially when the *coup de grâce* is filmed with all the sensitivity of Oliver Stone's *Natural Born Killers*.

Stone by this point seemed to be suffering from Eddie Murphy syndrome. During his reign as box-office king in the 1980s, Murphy described the yes-man mentality that studio executives exhibited toward a supernovaing star. "I could say, 'Hey, guys! I got a great idea for my next film. I'm going to throw shit at the screen!' and they'd say, 'Great idea. Here's thirty million dollars.'" (Remember, this was the early 1980s. After his sleeper hit *The Nutty Professor,* executives are probably saying, "Here's a hundred million, Eddie.") But between the disastrous *Beverly Hills Cop 3* and his *Professor,* the moneymen must have regretted their largesse.

For more than a decade, Murphy's career had taken the same turn as other superstars (like Liza Minelli), whose name attached to a project no longer guarantees automatic financing. (It's called being bankable.) It took a slew of flops before production executives stopped Murphy from throwing "shit at the screen." But to this day execs never seem to learn. The conventional wisdom says you're only as good as your last picture. Congenital stupidity proves you're only as good as your last five films.

The "shit at the screen" aesthetic kicked in for Sharon Stone as soon as *Basic Instinct* went ballistic. How else do you explain the green-lighting of such commercially iffy projects as *The Quick and the Dead* (Sharon Stone ugly *and* dirty) or *Last Dance* (the goddess as Charles Manson). Insanely, Stone didn't have an agent until September 1996. If she had, you could imagine him telling the studio, "My client wants to stretch."

Stretch is too restrictive a term for the reckless elasticity she demonstrated in a role that reeked of "for your Oscar consideration" as Academy voters were wooed with free tickets and T-shirts at screenings on the back lot before balloting day.

Last Dance proved again that Stone is a screen, not a glamour, queen. No makeup, brown hair by Supercuts, couture by South Carolina's Ridgeland state pen. Her dysmorphic body image, dating back to childhood, was also improving. Looking at her condemned con in the mirror, she said, "Not bad for thirty-seven."

Rob Morrow, the bleeding-heart lawyer who tries to save her from the business end of a syringe, felt Stone looked terrific even in prison chic and hair by Bubba. "I'm sure she even looks great when she rolls out of bed," he said on the set in Beaufort, South Carolina.

Last Dance may have appealed to the actress because it allowed her to shed her girl-toy image. No director or producer barged into the riverfront mansion she lived in during production to demand a camera strip. The only nude scene, she said more with relief than amusement, was the strip search, which ended up on the cutting-room floor, anyway. She told the bit actor who conducted the search, "Remember, whatever you find, you keep."

If the actress has her way, *Sliver* will be the last of Sharon unclad. She said in 1995, "I'd rather have more sex at home and keep my clothes on at work. I'm maturing." *Last Dance,* however, wasn't entirely a glamour-free zone. After a press screening, a librarian from the Academy of Motion Picture Arts and Sciences said to me, "I wonder how Rob Morrow got the eyebrow tweezers past the metal detector." *Entertainment Weekly* was even less kind, wondering, "Is hair gel really available on death row?" Her prison blues also didn't look like K-mart issue. Stone looks terrific in a white T-shirt and blue striped pants. The reason, it was rumored, was that an uncredited Valentino, her favorite designer, did the duds.

Despite her eventual disappointment, Stone wanted to do Death Row so much that she took a third of her usual salary, a measly $2 million. Besides the chance to stretch, the film put her in Triple A–list company, with director Bruce Beresford (*Driving Miss Daisy*), who managed to wrangle a Best Actress Oscar in 1989 for an octogenarian, Jessica Tandy, from an industry obsessed with youth. If the Australian director could get Oscar heat for an eighty-two-year-old, imagine the possibilities for the most beautiful woman in the world!

That fantasy was punctured by the final cut.

Stone had been so disappointed with the outcome of *Diabolique* that she refused to promote it and bad-mouthed the film in print. Her apparent distaste for *Last Dance* was so overwhelming, she tried to deny its existence, St. Peter–like. Jane Cantillon, a segment producer for TV's *Hard Copy,* told me that when she called Stone's publicity firm, PMK, and gently inquired about reports that preview audiences were howling at Stone's performance in *Last Dance,* PMK denied that Stone was in the film! This after both trades had announced its production start months earlier. Cantillon speculated that Stone wanted to spike bad word of mouth about *Last Dance* so that Academy and Golden Globe voters wouldn't change their minds about *Casino,* which was up for consideration at the time of *Last Dance*'s unfortunate release. At this point, Stone found herself performing triage on a comatose career.

Most critics felt that *Last Dance* shared Eddie Murphy's fecal aesthetic. *Newsweek* couldn't resist invidious comparisons to its superior competitor and headlined a review "Dead Gal Walking." Stone's interpretation was also found lacking. "At no point in this glum, synthetic film does Cindy Liggett [Stone] become flesh and blood, a woman with…an inner life. A Cracker accent isn't enough—Stone hasn't found any revealing behavioral tics to bring this cipher to life (she was more interesting in *The Specialist*!)." A perfect example of damning with faint praise.

Time said enough already with the Streeptease. "Occasionally, stars want to prove their seriousness. Art stirs in their breast like an edifying influenza, and they take on roles outside their expected range. Falling prey to the lure of sackcloth and Oscars, normally glammed-up female stars don drab frocks, sport the no-makeup make-up look, play a character who opts for the spiritual over the sexual, and if possible, speaks in an exotic accent. Hey, if it worked for Meryl…Sharon Stone is the latest entrant in the Streepstakes," a race *Time* felt the actress had already lost.

The *Los Angeles Times* lauded her for attempting a no-glamour turn but felt that the role still had "built-in glamour, and if anything, confirms Stone's position as a willing throwback to

Hollywood drama queens of yore." Even when she took a chance, she was accused of playing it safe. *Entertainment Weekly* engaged in a love-hate relationship with the actress. "Stone gives a heartfelt and subdued performance. If she never quite convinces us that she physically inhabits this woman...she certainly connects emotionally with her character."

The public reception proved once again that when stars stretch, the box office usually contracts. Opening weekend, the cell-block drama earned a penurious $2.7 million and suffered the ignominy of being beaten by another con-themed film, *Captives,* a low-budget art film from Miramax starring no-names Julia Ormond and Tim Roth. Within two weeks, the $30 million picture had fallen out of the Top Ten—to eighteen—with a total of only $5 million. The trades stopped tracking it by week three.

EPILOGUE

WHILE HER FILM CAREER stumbles in a blur of artistic missteps, Stone also seems to lack focus in her romantic life. Her liaisons are most notable for their brevity. Her taste in men is catholic. Her selections have breadth, but they lack depth and duration. No one can accuse the actress of being tied to one "type." She's been spotted nuzzling Michael Benasra, forty-four, CEO of Guess Jeans. The executive is short, fat, and French. Stone was photographed in Greenwich Village with her beau on what the tabs described as a "first-class shopping spree." At $7 million per picture, Stone can afford to do everything first-class. Still, the girl from Meadville, where $100 was a big family issue, knows the wisdom of Thornton Wilder's matchmaker that it's just as easy to love a rich man as a poor one. Or as one reporter said to me about Monsieur Benasra, "The thing she loves most about him is his wallet, which is apparently fatter than he is."

Even if the attraction was financial rather than physical, it wasn't strong enough to last through the summer. When the affair ended, Benasra said happily, "It was a glorious three months."

Although Benasra is six years her senior, Stone wasn't seeking a father figure. She has the real thing back in Pennsylvania. Another object of her desire was boy-toy Dweezil Zappa, twenty-six, son of Frank, brother of the most famous girl in the San Fernando Valley, Moon Unit Zappa. Stone and Zappa's relationship lasted a mere two weeks, according to a mutual friend.

A quickie with JFK Jr. was a total tabloid fantasy. While the son of the late President and Marilyn Monroe's avatar were allegedly getting it on, the two principals were separated by a continent.

An interviewer once commented on her catholic tastes. Or in the journalist's deathless prose, "Your boyfriends, there's like no pattern to them."

Stone begged to quibble. "They all have one thing in common. They're all smart and funny." She also volunteered, inaccurately as L'Affaire MacDonald showed, that she didn't "do married men," but if President Clinton suddenly became Hillaryless... "If he were single [I'd be on him] like white on rice."

Since *Basic Instinct,* her sole commercial triumph, Stone has basically been doing a medley of her greatest hit—bitch goddess. Even when she attempts weak or vulnerable roles, as in *Sliver* and *Intersection,* her steely *Überfräulein* keeps knifing the sympathetic viewer in the ribs. Most of the time, however, she has played to her strength, chewing up the scenery and spitting out men in epics of *machisma* like *The Quick and the Dead* and *Diabolique*. Even her most vulnerable character, *Last Dance*'s Cindy Liggett, was a double murderer. But her strength of characters has not translated into muscular box office, and Stone, pushing forty, remains a one-hit wonder.

In her Mediterranean palazzo amid the charmeuse and Degas, can Sharon Stone hear her biological bombshell clock ticking? Does it sound more like a bell tolling?

Unconfirmed press reports say she's mulling over a biopic on delusional heiress Doris Duke. Thematically, movies on dead millionairesses (See Farrah Fawcett as Barbara Hutton) end up on the small screen. The tortured Duke, who, it's rumored, adopted her lesbian lover, then cut her "daughter" out of her will, was allegedly done in by her butler, the beneficiary of a new will. A classic case of the butler did it. But will it be a classic for Stone or more derision from critics and indifference from dwindling fans? Another production story says that she's readying a project about a nurse-paramedic, which lends credence to Mrs. Rothenburg's story. Stone's production company recently purchased the rights to the 1958 supernatural romantic comedy *Bell, Book and Candle,* with Stone producing but not necessarily starring in the

Kim Novak role. To date, she has remained largely Hamlet-like on all projects as well as relationships—unable to commit.

The prognosis isn't encouraging. Other sex kittens, like Jane Fonda and Jeanne Moreau, tried to find rich roles as they matured. Fonda ended up retiring in the arms of a bipolar billionaire. Moreau became a director.

Stone's current obsession was disclosed by the actress in a December 1996 interview.

The old Hollywood adage claims that everybody in Los Angeles is writing a screenplay. Certainly every star has tried his or her hand at writing the perfect vehicle to display his or her talents. Very few have the clout to get their pet project off the ground because typically, although they're written by professional actors, the writing remains amateurish. An attorney who represents himself has a fool for a client, etc.

Superstars get anything they want. Demi, you want your Winnebago closer to the set than Jack Nicholson's, you got it, babe. Arnold, you only want fresh fruits and vegetables on the set's snack table? No sacher torte or strudel? *Ja wohl, mein Überstar.* And when a superstar trots out his 120-page baby, timorous studio heads are afraid to say no, especially if the little bundle of misery doesn't have the budget of *Waterworld.* Better to lose a mere $20 million on Tom Hanks's ode to bubblegum music, *That Thing You Do!* than really tick him off and lose his services on *Forrest Gump II.* (*Gump I* grossed $200 million in the United States and Canada alone.)

So it should come as no surprise that superstar see, superstar do, superstar write. And Sharon Stone is no exception. When I asked Stone to sit for an interview for this book, her publicist, Jennifer Allen, said that her client was too busy reading scripts. Actually, Allen was stonewalling in more ways than one. Stone was too busy writing a script to jabber to another writer, even one immortalizing her life story between hardcovers.

She did talk to the host of TV's *Politically Incorrect,* Bill Maher, for a really important interview in *Allure* magazine, the *New York Times* of low body fat culture. The subject matter she chose for her first writing effort also reflects her favorite reading matter, the magic realism of South American writers like Jorge Luis Borges and Gabriel García Marquez. In fact, on the South Carolina set of *Last Dance,* Stone learned that her fave Mexican poet, Octavio Paz, was just a mint julep's throw away in Atlanta for a literary award. She invited him to lunch and offered to pay his plane fare. Paz didn't know who this *loca muchacha* named Stone was until his wife told him. Then he still passed on the free lunch.

Undeterred, Stone has retained her fascination for magic realism and is writing a north-of-the-Suez-Canal version of, in her words, *One Hundred Years of Solitude* meets *Splash!* Her interviewer, Maher, commented that he didn't think of García Marquez's masterpiece and Ron Howard's fish story in the same category, but Stone explained, "Yeah, but it is all that same kind of thing. Where your fantasies actually happen. It rains rosebuds." The studio head who green-lighted her screenplay is hedging his bets that her next film after this will rain greenbacks. The executive's decision isn't quite the gamble it seems, since Stone has agreed to star in her screenplay, which at the very least will guarantee a strong opening weekend.

The odds for success have been further increased by the participation of Mexican director Alfonso Arau. His similar-themed *Like Water for Chocolate* was the highest-grossing foreign-language film of all time. Arau has already signed on to direct the actress's unfinished baby without so much as a taste of her salsa WASP writing.

Even while she's typing away on a script, Stone keeps an eye out for Oscar. In January 1996, the actress signed on for Miramax's *The Mighty,* playing the sympathetic mother of a handicapped child with a genius I.Q. It seems strange that the sexy star has voluntarily interred herself in the graveyard typically reserved for actresses of a certain age: sympathetic mother roles. Or as Goldie Hawn has said, there are only three roles for women as they age: babe, district attorney, and mother. On the other hand, the situation could be worse: her career may some day reach

Kelly McGillis (*Top Gun*) depths, and Stone could end up playing a mother in a Disease of the Week TV movie, career suicide for film actresses. If you have to be a mother, do it in 35 mm.

Stone's alliance with Miramax suggests that if she's crazy, she's crazy like a fox. Now owned by Disney, the mini-studio for the most part operates independently of the Magic Kingdom's lowest common denominator gestalt. Among actors, it has become famous as the little engine that could win you an Oscar. Miramax has earned a track record for backing little films that become big at Oscar time. While it's unusual for an actress with Stone's price tag to star in a low-budget film for a minor studio, Miramax's annual Oscar haul may have tempted her to cut her fee (as she did in *Casino*), and play an unglamorous mother, since another Oscar nomination might come along with the paycut and couture-free ensembles. And really, what's money to an actress who earns $21 million a year? Or as Jack Nicholson's private eye asks John Huston's greedy millionaire in *Chinatown*, "How many steaks can you eat? How many bottles of Scotch can you buy?" How many projection rooms can you furnish in charmeuse? No matter how rich you are, you can't buy an Oscar, unless you count the expense of taking out huge ads in the trades, plugging your performance with the copy: "For your Oscar consideration...ME!"

Stone clearly believes in art for art's sake, but sometimes the temptation to do art for big bucks is irresistible. While she's looking out for small, Oscar worthy productions like her magic realism script and *The Mighty,* she also has her eye on the bottom line. You can be sure she won't be taking a paycut to star with Dustin Hoffman in *Sphere,* a big-budget sci-fi adventure about a centuries-old spaceship at the bottom of the ocean. Based on the novel by *Jurassic Park*'s Michael Crichton, the film seems like a sure bet at the box office. Stone may not do any stretching to appear in a potboiler like *Sphere,* but its commercial success could give her the clout to be all the movie moms and magic realists she wants to be. Sometimes you have to play a crazy cop with a lethal weapon in order to play a crazy Scot in a kilt.

It's great that Stone has decided to branch out and enrich her professional life. Her track record on relationships doesn't suggest marriage as a career substitute. A man will never complete her. Maybe a scriptwriting credit will.

There is one last world to conquer in the all-gratifying universe of superstars who can have anything they want. The D word has already passed her lips, with Stone confessing, "What I'd really like to do is direct." She has the discipline and the determination to crack the whip on a movie set and impose her vision on chaos, which happens to be the name of her independent production company.

If she chooses a modestly budgeted film and agrees to star as well, her directorial debut will secure instant financing.

Sharon, the director's chair is in your corner. Let's see some "Action!"

SHARON STONE FILMOGRAPHY

A quick survey of Sharon Stone's sixteen years in film suggests she's a rarity, a gifted actress who can rise above the material. Admittedly, this is not much of a levitation act in howlers like *Cold Steel* and *Action Jackson*. But even when a great director in a great film like *Casino* straitjackets her into the role of a one-dimensional coke whore, Stone manages to flesh out the role without showing a big of skin. Unfortunately, in other films like *Basic Instinct* and *Sliver*, it seems there's a gynecologist rather than a psychologist behind the camera. But Stone perseveres, and unlike other superstars who keep playing variations on their greatest hits (Cruise, Gibson, Redford), she takes risks and pay cuts. The least narcissistic of screen goddesses, Stone will happily spend an entire film dressed in prison denim (*Last Dance*) or caked in mud (*The Quick and the Dead*). Or as she put it perfectly, "I'm not the Michael Bolton of acting." Herewith a list of her greatest hits and misses:

Stardust Memories, 1980
In her film debut, Woody Allen typecast Stone as an unobtainable fantasy goddess. In this labored salute to *8 1/2*, Allen doesn't get the girl. Stone doesn't get any dialogue.

Deadly Blessing, 1981
Stone's first starring role in a Wes Craven horror flick was described as Hitchcock meets *Green Acres*. Stone visits friends in a rural community plagued by possessed tractors and religious zealots. Her first scene includes a spider falling into her open mouth, an ominous sign for her career during this decade. Years later, superstar Stone dismissed *Deadly Blessing* as "*Charlie's Angels* on a bad hair day."

Les Uns et Les Autres, 1982
Claude Lelouch, director of the schmaltz classic *A Man and a Woman*, fell in love with Woody Allen's fantasy girl and gave her a two-minute scene in this romantic drama starring James Caan. Unfortunately,

her role was so small Stone didn't receive screen credit despite the box-office success of *Deadly Blessing*.

Irreconcilable Differences, 1984

A delectable roman à clef and a personal showcase for Stone about the real-life romance of director Peter Bogdanovich and Cybill Shepherd, with Stone perfectly inhabiting the skin of the latter. Her coked-out Scarlett O'Hara in a musical remake of *Gone With the Wind* is one of the funniest moments in film.

King Solomon's Mines, 1985
Allan Quatermain and the Lost City of Gold, 1987

Unrepentant ripoffs of the Indiana Jones films without their wit or sense of self-parody, this World War I African adventure and its sequel bombed at the box office and sent Stone's career into freefall for the rest of the decade. The local PLO and the Israeli security guards clashed on the set in Africa, while a restless NAACP picketed theaters for the film's less-than-anthropologically-correct depiction of the natives.

Police Academy 4: Citizens on Patrol, 1987

Question: What can Stone have been thinking when she signed on to this *Porky's* eye view of law enforcement? Answer: She needed to raise her mortgage payments. Trivia Note: Actor Bubba Smith got billing above Stone.

Cold Steel, 1988

Those pesky mortgage bills kept coming due. Brad Davis seeks revenge against the mob for the murder of his father. Stone, an employee of Murder Inc., picks Davis up in a bar and tries to kill him.

Above the Law, 1988

Chopsockey star Steven Seagal's film debut looked like Stone's swan song, as *Daily Variety* praised her role as his sympathetic wife but complained she only appeared on the screen for two minutes. Her billing nightmare continued. Cop Seagal's partner, Pam Grier, a relic from seventies blaxploitation films, had a bigger role and screen credit above Stone.

Action Jackson, 1988

Speaking of blaxploitation, the genre briefly came back from deserved internment in the Brady Decade with Stone as the wife of an evil auto tycoon (*Coach*'s Craig T. Nelson) battling Carl Weathers in a looney role as a Harvard Law grad who gives up a lucrative legal practice to work as a cop on Detroit's mean streets.

Personal Choice, 1989

A disease-of-the-week TV movie that somehow managed to escape to the big screen, it stars Martin Sheen as a burned-out astronaut who self-medicates with alcohol. Stone has a thankless role as the girlfriend of a minor character.

Blood and Sand, 1989

Stone is laughably miscast as a Spanish aristocrat (about as Hispanic as Goldie Hawn, one critic said). This heart of Stone gets her follies taunting a lovestruck matador who becomes bull-phobic. (We're not making this up.) Don't miss the scene where the torreador gets drunk and fights the bull in the nude.

Total Recall, 1990

Stone finally got her big break in this marvelously inventive fantasy about a Mars colony ruled by the *Fortune* 500. Stone plays a lethal twenty-first century housewife—Doris Day on steroids, who kicks the streudel out of her husband, Arnold Schwarzenegger. The actress took up kickboxing with such vigor for her *mano à mano*s with Arnold, she broke her hand punching the bag. Note to nasty film critics: the actress still practices Tae Kwon Do in her garage. Did we forget to mention how much we adore Sharon Stone and her films?

He Said, She Said, 1991

It was déjà vu all over again, with Stone typecast as the blond fantasy woman who shows up as a nice girl and a dominatrix in this twice-told tale of the breakup of a romance from the point of view of the man and the woman (Kevin Bacon and Elizabeth Perkins). After the box office success of *Total Recall*, it's inexplicable why Stone took what amounted to a cameo role.

Year of the Gun, 1991

Stone is a photojournalist who will do anything to get a scoop, including bedding *Weekend at Bernie's* Andrew McCarthy. Set in Italy during the Red Brigade's reign of terror in the seventies, the political thriller lacks the style its director, John Frankenhemier, showed in *The Manchurian Candidate* a decade earlier.

Diary of a Hitman, 1981

Stone did a cameo as star Sherilyn Fenn's tarty, obnoxious sister as a personal favor to her acting coach, Roy London, who made his directing debut with this story of a retiring hitman (Forest Whitaker) who agrees to make one more hit for a downpayment on a condo. One critic nicknamed it, "Yuppie's Honor."

Scissors, 1991

An art-house film vaguely based on a drama by Sartre, Stone plays against type as a twenty-six-year-old virgin trapped in an apartment by an unseen tormentor. Stone spends most of the film alone on screen and earned the best reviews of her career up to this time.

Where Sleeping Dogs Lie, 1991

Life imitates art, if that's the right word for it, with Stone as a mendacious superagent who ruins her client's career. In real life, Stone had recently left her talent agency in a huff because her rep was too busy ministering to another client, Tom Cruise.

Basic Instinct, 1992

The number one box office hit of the year, this deeply disturbed psychosexual drama turned Stone into an overnight sensation after twelve years of screen torture. Every name actress in Hollywood had turned down the role of the coke-snorting, bisexual serial murderess, and Stone got the job by default—after crashing the director's editing room. Michael Douglas is the coke-snorting, sex-addicted cop who, uh, reforms her.

Sliver, 1993

The much anticipated followup to *Basic Instinct* flamed out in the U.S., but ignited Europe with its steamy (literally) tale of bathtub autoeroticism and video voyeurism. Stone plays a frigid book editor who gets warmed by a charming neighbor, William Baldwin, who may or may not be a serial murderer. As they say, all the great guys are either gay or married or…perverted killers.

Intersection, 1994

Burned-out architect Richard Gere prefers his blowsy mistress (Lolita Davidovich) to his delectable wife (Stone). Who says they don't make good fantasy films anymore? With her newfound clout, Stone refused to play the obvious "other woman" role and stretched as the emotionally aloof wife.

The Specialist, 1994

As her box office clout waned, Stone needed a hit, so she teamed with Sylvester Stone, the Mount Rushmore of actors, in what he does best: beat up people and blow up buildings. This witless thriller casts Stallone as an ex-CIA agent hired by Stone to kill the drug kingpins who murdered her father when she was a child. The film tarnished her resume but burnished her bank account as its success raised her asking price to $7 million a film. Some thought taking a shower with Stallone was still too high a price to pay.

Casino, 1995

Stone does her best work to date with Martin Scorsese and Robert De Niro, two of the greatest cinematic talents of this or any other era. An Oscar nominee for her hooker-housewife from hell by way of Las Vegas, the actress bravely doesn't even bother to make her heartless character sympathetic or vulnerable.

The Quick and the Dead, 1995

In her new job as coproducer, Stone subverts the Spaghetti Westerns of Sergio Leone and does Clint Eastwood in drag. As an evil sheriff, Gene Hackman makes her day.

Diabolique, 1996

This remake of the 1954 classic about a wife and mistress who conspire to murder their abusive insignificant other is a cautionary tale about movie star clout run amok. The director wanted to make a respectful *hommage* to the original by France's Hitchcock, Henri-Georges Clouzot. Stone wanted to do Joan Crawford on a bad Chanel day. Both sides won, and two very different films uncomfortably inhabit the same screen.

Last Dance, 1996

It's hard to say if Stone is a good girl gone bad or a multiple murderer gone good in this vanity production that seems largely designed "for your Oscar consideration." (Oscar didn't.) Either way, Stone ends up on Death Row, where the love of a good man, her attorney (Rob Morrow), turns her into a tragic heroine with a rap sheet.

Stone, in January 1996, signed with Miramax, the mighty Oscar manufacturer, to play the mother of a gifted child in *The Mighty*. She is also writing a screenplay based on her favorite genre, the magic realism of South American writers Gabriel Garcia Marquez and Jorge Luis Borges. *Like Water for Chocolate*'s Alfonso Arau is set to direct. On the backburner to a remake of the 1958 cult classic, *Bell, Book and Candle*, with Stone reprising the Kim Novak role as a modern-day witch.

INDEX

ABOUT THE AUTHOR

FRANK SANELLO has been covering the entertainment industry for major news organizations for more than a quarter of a century. The New York Times Syndicate and United Press International have distributed his show-business articles worldwide. Sanello was also the film critic for the *Los Angeles Daily News* and a correspondent for *People* magazine and the *Chicago Tribune*.

His books include *Spielberg: The Man, the Movies, the Mythology; Cruise: The Unauthorized Biography;* and the upcoming *Saint Jim: The Life and Times of Jimmy Stewart; Will Smith: Safe for Stardom,* and *Eddie Murphy: Well Done*. Sanello is currently writing a book on child rearing with clinical psychologist Arnold Nerenberg and a biography of tort attorney Melvin Belli with the late attorney's son, Caesar Belli.

A native of Joliet, Illinois, Sanello graduated from the University of Chicago with honors and earned a master's degree from UCLA's film school.